Aboriginal Plant Use in Canada's Northwest Boreal Forest

Aboriginal Plant Use in Canada's Northwest Boreal Forest

Robin J. Marles, Christina Clavelle,
Leslie Monteleone,
Natalie Tays, and Donna Burns

Natural Resources
Canada

Ressources naturelles
Canada

ISBN 978-0-660-19868-2
Cat. no.: Fo134-7/1-2008E

Published by:
    Natural Resources Canada
    Canadian Forest Service
    Northern Forestry Centre
    5320–122 Street
    Edmonton, AB T6H 3S5
    780–435–7210

Library and Archives Canada Cataloguing in Publication

Aboriginal plant use in Canada's northwest boreal forest / Robin J. Marles ... [et al.].

Issued by: Canadian Forest Service.
Includes bibliographical references and index.
ISBN 978-0-660-19869-9 (pbk.).--ISBN 978-0-660-19868-2 (hbk.)
Cat. no.: Fo134-7/2-2008E (pbk.).--Cat. no.: Fo134-7/1-2008E (hbk.)

1. Ethnobotany--Prairie Provinces. 2. Native peoples--Ethnobotany--Prairie Provinces. 3. Plants, Useful--Prairie Provinces. 4. Taiga plants--Prairie Provinces. I. Marles, Robin James II. Canada. Natural Resources Canada III. Canadian Forest Service.

QK98.4.P7 A26 2008   581.6'3089970712   C2008-980382-5

Printed in Canada on acid-free paper   ∞

Contents

ℰ𝔞

A Note on the Text

ᛘᚹ

Disclaimer

The study on which this report is based was funded in part under the Canada-Alberta, Canada-Saskatchewan, and Canada-Manitoba partnership agreements in forestry.

The views, conclusions, and recommendations are those of the authors. The exclusion of certain manufactured products does not necessarily imply disapproval, nor does the mention of other products necessarily imply endorsement by the Canadian Forest Service, Alberta Land and Forest Services, Saskatchewan Environment and Resource Management, Manitoba Natural Resources, or UBC Press.

Medical Warning

This work describes traditional uses of plants as foods and medicines and for other purposes by Aboriginal peoples of Canada's northwestern boreal forest. We have included warnings about some of the most risky plants in the descriptions, but some plant foods can be toxic if the wrong plant part (such as fruit, leaves, stems, or roots) is harvested, or if it is not properly prepared, or if too much is eaten. Some toxic plants look similar to edible plants, and such mistakes can cause serious illness and even death. Never eat a plant if you are not certain of its identity. Learn the appropriate harvesting and preparation methods, and start with a small amount when trying a new plant food.

The fact that traditional medicines are "natural" does not mean that they are necessarily safe – after all, cyanide is natural and occurs in many plants as an effective but deadly protection against animals that want to eat them. Every medicine is a poison if used inappropriately or in the wrong dose.

Although we describe medicinal uses of many plants here, we could not encompass in one book all the knowledge of the Aboriginal elders who contributed information. In particular, at the request of the elders, we have deliberately omitted their recipes for the detailed preparation of the medicines, as that is their private knowledge that they must retain the right to control and share as they see fit. Thus, we are documenting and briefly describing traditionally used plants, not providing a manual on how to heal with plants. We encourage you to consult a health professional, such as a medical doctor, naturopath, herbalist with formal qualifications, or Aboriginal elder experienced in traditional healing, rather than to try these traditional remedies on yourself, your family, friends, or clients. Some of the plants described here could be fatal if used incorrectly.

Acknowledgments

༄

The people most important to this research project were the members of the First Nations and Métis communities who kindly agreed to share their traditional knowledge of plants. None of this work could have been done without their willingness to participate and provide information that they felt should be shared with all people interested in Canada's boreal forest. We also acknowledge the tremendous wealth of knowledge of plants held by the elders that is not reported here because it is either their intellectual property that they wish to protect or it is of a spiritual nature that they felt was not appropriate to record in writing. We have respected their decisions on which information to share and which to keep confidential. With sadness we note that some contributors to this study have already passed away, resulting in the loss to all of us of their warm personalities, great spirits, and traditional knowledge.

Special thanks are due to two Métis senior researchers: Donna Rea Paquette, Lakeland Schools Native Education Program, Bonnyville, Alberta, and Chad Rudiak, Métis community of Fort McMurray, Alberta, who made significant contributions during the first season of fieldwork.

We gratefully acknowledge the valuable research assistance of several other First Nations and Métis people, including Beulah Flett, Shoal Lake First Nation, Saskatchewan; Russell Willier, Sucker Creek First Nation, Alberta; Sandra Miles and Randy Burns, Opaskwayak First Nation, Manitoba; Gilbert Dumas, John François, and Raymond François, Nisichawayasihk First Nation, Nelson House, Manitoba; Ryan Castel, Pimichikamac First Nation, Cross Lake, Manitoba; Jesse Bruneau, Bonnyville, Alberta; and Catherine Methuen, Edmonton, Alberta. These people did much of the interviewing, plant collecting, and initial literature review, and were sometimes able to contribute their own firsthand knowledge to the project. We thank Kim Strutt, Barbara Gowan, Sandra Kurtz, and Val Habing, botany students at Brandon University, for working with the Manitoba First Nations students and helping to identify some of the plants. The language and cultural skills of the Aboriginal trainees, the scientific skills of the botany students, and the mutually beneficial exchange of skills that occurred between the students and trainees contributed greatly to the quality as well as quantity of the information they gathered. For the ethnobotanical work done in 1980-82, which is reported here with the recent field research, we remember with deep appreciation the assistance of Stan Bidou, of Stony Rapids, Saskatchewan, an expert interpreter, contributor, and friend.

We thank Edith Young of the Brighter Futures Program/Cree Nation Tribal Health Centre, The Pas, Manitoba, for her suggestions toward the development of a research proposal that would be acceptable to Aboriginal communities, and we thank the Band Councils of the participating communities for their permission to carry out the proposed research. We appreciate the assistance of Professors Sam Corrigan of Brandon University, Vernon Harms and David Meyer of the University of Saskatchewan, and Randy Bayer and Richard Price of the University of Alberta; they identified and in some cases helped supervise the students who assisted in this project. We also acknowledge Professor Norman R. Farnsworth and Mary Lou Quinn of the Program for Collaborative Research in the Pharmaceutical Sciences, Department of Medicinal Chemistry and Pharmacognosy, College of Pharmacy, University of Illinois at Chicago, for a grant and technical assistance to do extensive searching of the NAPRALERT computer database on natural products.

The authors wish to acknowledge the following staff at the Northern Forestry Centre, Canadian Forest Service in Edmonton: Joe De Franceschi for his vision, cooperation, and support during the initial stages of this project; Brenda Laishley for her editorial insights and her many contributions to the production and publication of this book; and Elaine Schiewe for designing the cover. We would also like to thank the editorial staff of UBC Press and the peer reviewers they employed – all did a fantastic job of checking everything in the book for accuracy and clarity. We thank and acknowledge the National Research Council of Canada, NRC Research Press, for permission to reprint the line drawing of *Claytonia tuberosa* Pall., which originally appeared in *Flora of the Yukon Territory* (1996) by William J. Cody. In addition, we acknowledge the contributions of the following individuals who provided photographs for this guide: Dale Vitt, Anna Roberts, Ken Baldwin, Derek Johnson, Rick Annas, Jim Pojar, and Don Cahoon.

Finally, we thank Natural Resources Canada, Canadian Forest Service, the Manitoba, Saskatchewan, and Alberta partnership agreements in forestry, and the Manitoba Model Forest for funding the project. Additional funds for student employment were generously provided by the Canadian Public Service Commission Native Employment Program and the Manitoba Education and Training CareerFocus and CareerStart Youth Career

Development Programs. The Saskatchewan Heritage Foundation is acknowledged for providing funding for some educational material preparation. The 1980-82 Chipewyan ethnobotany project was funded by the Canadian Ethnology Service (personal services contract no. 1630-0-133), grants from the Federal Northern Scientific Training Grants Program and the Institute for Northern Studies, Saskatoon, and scholarship support from the Institute for Northern Studies and the College of Graduate Studies and Research, University of Saskatchewan.

Introduction

❦

This work describes the traditional plant products of the Aboriginal people in Canada's northwest boreal forest. Products include plants used as foods, medicines, and materials for handicrafts and technology. The Aboriginal cultures included in this study are the Cree, Dene, and Métis people living in central to northern Manitoba, Saskatchewan, and Alberta, Canada. The northwest boreal forest region occupies more than 150 million hectares and represents more than half the land area of Canada's three prairie provinces. The science of ethnobotany can be defined as the study of the dynamic inter-relationship between people of a particular culture and their botanical environment. Thus, this ethnobotanical study attempts to do more than provide a list of useful plants. In addition to gathering botanical data, the original field research also gathered information on ritual uses of plants, the naming and classification of plants in the indigenous languages, beliefs regarding plants, and attitudes toward development of plant resources. The fieldwork is supplemented by information gleaned from a literature review of the ethnobotany of various boreal forest cultures across North America, the nutritive value of the wild plants eaten, the medicinal value of the wild herbal medicines, and a preliminary assessment of the ecological impact and economic potential of commercial development of these botanical resources.

The First Nations people of Canada's boreal forest region have been sustainably harvesting a wide variety of natural products from the forest for thousands of years. Their traditional environmental knowledge has never been a static body of facts, but rather is a dynamic process of learning from elders, observing from nature, and adapting that knowledge to enhance the quality of

A Cree elder with labrador tea (N. Tays)

1

life. Traditional knowledge has been preserved primarily by oral history passed from one generation to the next. Although oral traditions have been maintained or have even enjoyed a renaissance in some Aboriginal communities, much knowledge has been lost for a variety of reasons. Traditionally nomadic, these peoples made use of a variety of habitats, including the boreal forest proper, to the south the aspen parkland and northern edges of the prairie grasslands, and to the north the transition zone and southern edges of the tundra. Through settlement around trading centers, missions, and government administrative centers, their geographic range became restricted. Through displacement and relocation, some people were transplanted into unfamiliar ecosystems. The residential school system imposed a foreign education and values while actively suppressing the expression of traditional culture and customs. Social upheaval due to poverty and attendant malnutrition, substance abuse, and despair has further eroded the success of education, both traditional and modern.

A sense of self-worth and cultural pride is one important component of the complex solution needed to address the problems facing Aboriginal people today. One way to achieve this goal is by preserving, validating, and teaching the significance of traditional environmental knowledge. Such lessons become more relevant when learned from members of the community rather than from outsiders. Thus, an important objective of this study of traditional plant products has been to train First Nations and Métis residents to conduct scientifically sound yet culturally sensitive research within their own communities. Nine First Nations and five Métis trainees, assisted by five botany students and the principal investigator (Marles), learned how to collect voucher plant specimens and to record traditional knowledge of elders about plants used as foods and medicines and for handicrafts and technology during ethnobotanical fieldwork. We visited communities across

Cree high school students
learning from elders (N. Tays)

the boreal forest region of Manitoba, Saskatchewan, and Alberta (Figure 1, regions 1-8). By participating in the fieldwork and the literature research, the trainees produced a permanent record of traditional ecological knowledge and some educational materials. They also produced a summary of nontimber forest resources that could provide health benefits, forest industry diversification, and local business opportunities; the communities may choose to conserve or develop these resources according to their own requirements. The trainees have also become skilled resource people who can undertake natural resource assessment appropriate to their communities' needs. Several of the trainees involved in this project are now professional teachers in northern communities or are pursuing advanced university degrees.

Sustainable management of Canada's forest is an important objective of the Canadian Forest Service. The economic development of nontimber forest resources for diversification of the forest industry is one aspect of achieving this. It was the basis for the funding of this project under the partnership agreements in forestry. Although the northwest boreal forest constitutes 22% of Canada's forested land, the area harvested here represents only 9% of the national harvest. While 17% of Canada's population lives in the provinces of Manitoba, Saskatchewan, and Alberta, only 7% of Canadians employed directly or indirectly by the forest industry work in this region (see Table 1). There is, therefore, a significant potential for further development of the forest industry in the northwest region, but it is a resource that must be managed carefully to ensure both biological and economic sustainability.

Sustainability is a popular concept, but there is no consensus on precisely how to achieve it in any resource extraction industry. Close to 57% of Canada's forested land is considered commercial forest capable of producing both timber and nontimber products, but only about 50% of commercial forests (119 million hectares) are currently managed for timber production. The harvest rate of Canada's national forest (almost one million hectares each year or 0.4% of the commercial forest land base) is compounded by natural disturbances, such as fire and disease, that affects at least 0.6% of the commercial forest land base annually, and sometimes much more. For example, in 1995, forest fires affected 6.3 million hectares and insect defoliation and disease affected 11.6 million hectares. Over the last 15 years, 4.8 million hectares of previously harvested forest area was reseeded or replanted (36% of the area harvested), while the rest, including most of the areas affected by fire or defoliation, was left for natural regeneration. From 1979 to 1993, the net area not growing commercial species 10 years after harvest increased by 1.1 million hectares (Natural Resources Canada 1996).

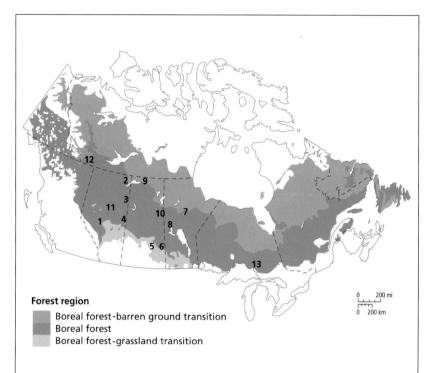

Forest region

Boreal forest-barren ground transition
Boreal forest
Boreal forest-grassland transition

Regions and participating communities for the current study
1. Northwestern Alberta: Enilda, Grimshaw, Grouard, High Prairie, Joussard, Kinuso
2. Western Lake Athabasca: Fort Chipewyan
3. Athabasca River: Anzac, Fort MacKay, Fort McMurray, Janvier
4. East-central Alberta: Bonnyville, Cold Lake, Elizabeth Métis Settlement, English Bay Reserve, Grand Centre, Kehewin (Long Lake) Reserve, LeGoff Reserve, Moose Lake, Saddle Lake, Wolf Lake
5. Central Saskatchewan: Chitek Lake, James Smith 100 Reserve
6. Eastern Saskatchewan: Shoal Lake
7. Northern Manitoba: Nelson House
8. Central Manitoba: Cross Lake, The Pas

Recent ethnobotanical studies from the literature
9. Northern Saskatchewan: Black Lake, Fond du Lac, Stony Rapids (Marles 1984)
10. East-central Saskatchewan: La Ronge, Pelican Narrows, Stanley Mission (Leighton 1985)
11. North-central Alberta: Wabasca/Desmarais (Siegfried 1994)
12. Western Northwest Territories: Fisherman Lake (Lamont 1977)
13. North-central Ontario: Garden River Reserve (Abou-Zaid 1996)

Figure 1   **Recent ethnobotanical study areas in the northwest boreal forest region of Canada**

Logging in the northern forest (R. Marles)

Table 1 **Provincial and national forest resources**

Region	Land area (million ha)	Forested land (million ha)	Harvested forest (million ha)	Population (millions)	Forestry jobs (direct and indirect)
Manitoba	54.8	26.3	0.013	1.139	13 000
Saskatchewan	57.1	28.8	0.024	1.018	9 000
Alberta	64.4	38.2	0.052	2.758	40 000
Canada	921.5	417.6	0.989	29.700	880 000

Source: Natural Resources Canada (1996).

A diverse economic base that will sustain a reasonable level of forestry employment and income in the area will require expanded opportunities for tree farming, increased local value-added processing of fine wood products, and development of a wide range of nontimber forest resources. A logical first step is to examine traditional uses of plants by the Aboriginal peoples who have sustained themselves from the boreal forests for millennia and to identify plants with potential for sustainable harvest or incorporation into silvicultural or agricultural programs. The connection with agriculture is important. Farm bankruptcies in the prairies have increased tenfold in the last 15 years, with almost three-quarters of all Canadian farm bankruptcies occurring in the Prairie provinces (Science Council of Canada

1992). Farm diversification is one way to achieve greater financial stability, and the feasibility of growing nontimber forest species in an agricultural setting has already been demonstrated by the tremendous success of American ginseng (*Panax quinquefolius* L., Araliaceae) cultivation in Ontario, British Columbia, and, lately, Manitoba.

Cree handicrafts of birch and spruce (N. Tays)

The best way to ensure that Aboriginal people will benefit from nontimber forest resource development is to train them to undertake original research and to be prepared to participate from the beginning in the development process. We hope that the results of the research reported here will lead to more detailed feasibility studies for particular plant products that we have identified, and that Aboriginal businesses will be at the forefront of the eventual production and marketing of these botanical resources.

We must note, however, that among the Aboriginal people who participated in this study there was no consensus on the desirability of economic development of plant products in general. Certain components of traditional knowledge, particularly the spiritual aspects of healing and rituals, are considered confidential by many elders. Consultation with Aboriginal advisors was a fundamental aspect of development and implementation of the research proposal, as described in the Research Methods section. Before interviewing started, we stressed to everyone involved that the information we were seeking was whatever the elders felt was important to be shared among

American ginseng under shaded cultivation (R. Marles)

A Cree family socializing
while on a berry-picking trip
(C. Clavelle)

the other communities of the north and with the general public. In this way information that was considered confidential or proprietary was deliberately excluded from this research. For example, although the elders agreed to describe uses of certain medicinal plants to provide verifiable examples of effective traditional remedies, the herbs described are generally used in mixtures, the composition of which was kept confidential to protect the intellectual property rights of the individual. There is a great deal of concern in Aboriginal communities that pharmaceutical companies might seek to profit from the development of medicines based on traditional remedies, without any recognition or financial compensation for the inventor of the remedy. Although the actual potential for economic development of herbal medicines will be discussed in detail for individual plants in the Traditional Uses section, we recognized the concern of the elders and always respected their decisions regarding confidentiality.

Even for food plants, Aboriginal people expressed concerns about commercialization. Berry picking is not just a food-gathering activity; it is a social activity that would be disrupted if berry picking was commercialized to produce value-added food products for export to large cities.

Whether plants are medicinal, nutritive, or useful in some other way, there is a strong belief among Aboriginal people that they are gifts from the Creator and that the spiritual connection will be broken by inappropriate use. Thus, local economic development decisions are best left to individual communities to work out according to the particular plants and uses involved and their own principles and needs.

Research Methods

The proposal for this research was developed in consultation with a First Nations professional community worker to provide a plan that would be acceptable to Aboriginal Councils and elders. The proposal was also reviewed and approved by the Brandon University Ethics Committee. Before any work was done in a community, the proposal was presented to the Band Council and elders by both English and Cree or Dene speakers, and work proceeded only after approval had been given.

Bilingual interviewing, mostly by the First Nations or Métis trainees, was done to minimize misunderstandings and make the oral-history recording more comfortable, since the elders could use their own language and talk to an interviewer who was already familiar with the language and customs. Since the interviewing was done by community members, the Councils were satisfied that elders would not feel duress and could easily set limits on the

DATE:	NUMBER:
LOCATION:	
PLANT LOCAL NAME:	
LANGUAGE/DIALECT:	
TRANSLATION:	
ENGLISH NAME:	
CONTRIBUTOR:	
USE NOTES:	
SCI. NAME:	
FAMILY:	
FLOWER/FRUIT CHAR.:	
HABITAT:	
HABIT:	HEIGHT:
SLOPE:	ASPECT:
ELEVATION:	SOIL:
COLLECTED BY:	DET. BY:

Figure 2 **Ethnobotany field notebook data entry form**

nature and extent of information provided. No formal questionnaires were used because previous experience has indicated that many elders are not comfortable with that style of interaction, and traditional environmental knowledge is mostly transmitted through stories and experiences shared while on walks in the forest, rather than as a listing of separate facts. However, each research team had data collection forms (Figure 2) that could gradually be completed as the information was gathered to ensure consistent final documentation.

The Aboriginal trainees ensured that local traditions were respected, such as gifts of tobacco and cloth for elders who preferred to follow that custom rather than a strict wage scale, and ritual burying of tobacco before plant harvest to show proper respect for the Spirits. The work also reinforced the trainees' own knowledge of their culture and respect for the depth of knowledge possessed by their elders. By working with the botany students, Aboriginal trainees learned the basics of plant voucher specimen collection, plant identification, and proper documentation techniques. In some cases the trainees became very skilled in these methods. The botany students gained an appreciation for Aboriginal culture and practices, and learned some of the language as well as the traditional environmental knowledge, so the experience was mutually beneficial.

For each plant discussed by an elder, a minimum of three voucher specimens of the whole plant were collected, pressed, dried, mounted, and labeled with the appropriate identification and a synopsis of the ethnobotanical information. Because common plant names vary from one location to another and are unreliable as a basis for storing and collating information, voucher specimens can be used to positively identify each plant described. The voucher specimens and their information could also be preserved in more than one location: the herbarium of the host institution (Brandon University, University of Saskatchewan, or University of Alberta) and in the host community. Toward this end, mounted specimens have been laminated in plastic and returned to the community to provide a teaching resource and permanent record for their own use. Ethnobotanical information was recorded in notebooks with data entry forms and space for sketches or

Tobacco buried at the four cardinal points around a medicinal plant (R. Marles)

9

freestyle notes. Plants were photographed with slide film or video camcorder. Interviews were tape-recorded to facilitate transcription. All this information will be incorporated in teaching materials as well as in scientific publications so that the results will be as widely accessible and useful as possible.

The names of the elders contributing the information have been substituted with a letter representing their cultural background (C = Cree, D = Dene/Chipewyan, or M = Métis) and a randomly assigned number for each individual. This was done to preserve confidentiality while still allowing quantitative ethnobotanical analysis of the results; identical information provided by several contributors from different communities or cultures would indicate a more widely accepted use that might take priority for follow-up investigation over a use reported only once. The codes and biographic data are provided in Appendix A.

Information was obtained from respondents in at least 25 communities. In north-central and northwestern Manitoba most of the information was obtained from the Nisichawayasihk First Nation of Nelson House, Indian Reservation (IR) 170, with a small amount provided by elders of the Opaskwayak First Nation (IR 21) of The Pas, both Cree communities. Some information was obtained secondhand (Diamant pers. comm.) regarding uses of plants by the Cree people of Cross Lake (Pimichikamac First Nation, IR 19). In central Saskatchewan, people from the Cree communities of James Smith 100 Reserve, northwest of Melfort, Shoal Lake (IR 28A), near the Pasquia Hills, and Chitek Lake (IR 191), northwest of Prince Albert, contributed. In east-central Alberta, some respondents were from the Chipewyan communities of LeGoff, which is south of Grand Centre, Cold Lake Reserve on the east end of the town of Cold Lake, and from English Bay on the west shore of Cold Lake (IR 149, 149A, and 149B). These three reserves comprise lands of the Cold Lake First Nation. At Kehewin (IR 123), south of Bonnyville, members of the Long Lake Cree Nation contributed. Information on useful plants was also obtained from the Saddle Lake (IR 125) Museum northeast of Edmonton, and plant-collecting trips with elders were made to traditional gathering and cabin sites at Long Lake, Moose Lake, Wolf Lake, Franchere Bay, and Frenchman's Bay. Cree-Métis people from the Elizabeth Métis Settlement east of Bonnyville on the Saskatchewan border also participated. A number of non-status Cree from private residences off the reserves in the surrounding rural and urban areas also contributed. In the Athabasca River region of northeastern Alberta, Chipewyan elders from the communities of Fort Chipewyan (IR 201, 217, 218, 219, 220) and Janvier (IR 194), which is south of Fort McMurray near the town of Chard, agreed to contribute information. Cree and Métis people from the communities of Fort

McMurray, Fort MacKay (IR 174), and Anzac (IR 176) were also generous with their knowledge. In the Lesser Slave Lake region of northwestern Alberta, Cree, Dene, and Métis contributors came from the communities of Grouard (IR 150B-D), Enilda, Joussard, and Kinuso, including the Driftpile (IR 150), Sucker Creek (IR 150A), and Swan River (150E-F) First Nations, while other contributors were from the communities of High Prairie and Grimshaw.

To provide more complete coverage of the boreal forest region, the 1994-95 work was supplemented with unpublished data collected earlier by the first author (Marles) using the same ethnobotanical techniques. In the summers of 1980 and 1981 and in January of 1982, 27 elders were interviewed (20 male and 7 female) from the Dene (Caribou-Eater Chipewyan) communities of Black Lake, Fond du Lac, Stony Rapids, and Stony Lake (only a few families remained in 1980; the rest had moved to Black Lake) in northern Saskatchewan. Thus, a total of 109 elders from 29 communities contributed information to this project.

Information gathered through the fieldwork has been supplemented by an in-depth literature review of boreal ethnobotany, the nutritive content of native food plants, the pharmacognosy (chemistry and pharmacology of natural products) of native medicinal plants, boreal forest ecology, and natural renewable resources. This literature review not only supplements the traditional knowledge, but also provides scientific validation and the information base necessary to make informed decisions about the potential benefits and risks of development of any of the nontimber forest resources described here.

Ecological Background

The boreal forest of Canada is a broad vegetation formation stretching from the northern Atlantic coast westward to the Rocky Mountains, across the southwestern Northwest Territories and Yukon, and into Alaska. The southern edge merges with the eastern hardwood forest, abuts the north shores of the Great Lakes, and in the west intergrades with the aspen parkland and prairie. The northern edge merges with the tundra. The following description of boreal forest ecology is drawn primarily from Scott (1995).

Portrayed as a broad swath of green on vegetation maps (e.g., Figure 1), the boreal forest is not really so homogeneous. Several classification schemes have been developed to try to more accurately describe its complexity. The Canadian Forest Service scheme classifies the boreal forest into three regions by vegetation type: a central band of Boreal Forest vegetation, with a northern Boreal Forest-barren ground transition zone, and a southern Boreal

Forest-grassland transition zone. Other schemes use typical plant associations as descriptors, such as the Black Spruce Mixedwood/Feather Moss association (Zoladeski et al. 1995).

Some hierarchical systems take into account climate and topography as well as vegetation. In the Ecoclimatic Province System, 10 ecoclimatic provinces are subdivided into ecoclimatic subprovinces, and then into 72 ecoclimatic regions. In the Ecoclimatic Province scheme, the boreal forest occurs within the Subarctic, Boreal, and Subarctic Cordilleran ecoclimatic provinces.

The Terrestrial Ecozone Classification System includes geology in the land classification; 15 ecozones are subdivided into ecoprovinces, ecoregions, ecodistricts, ecosections, ecosites, and ultimately ecoelements. In the Ecozone scheme, the boreal forest is described in terms of the Taiga Shield, Boreal Shield, Hudson Plains, Boreal Plains, Taiga Plains, and Boreal Cordillera ecozones (Scott 1995). The Ecoclimatic Province and Ecozone schemes have the advantage that they provide not only descriptions of the boreal forest, but also some of the reasons why the boreal forest occurs where it does.

The High Subarctic Ecoclimatic subprovince is characterized by a tundra-forest ecotone. The shrub zone is dominated by a lichen-heath-dwarf birch community on uplands and exposed sites, with a snow-trapping krummholz of black spruce (*Picea mariana* (P. Mill.) B.S.P.) in open areas, and spruce trees taller than 5 m only in protected basins. The forest subzone is dominated by coniferous forest that progresses from open- to closed-canopied

Caribou in the boreal-tundra ecotone (R. Marles)

toward the south, with lichen-heath-dwarf birch only in exposed areas. The northern and southern boundaries of this transition zone can be defined by the ratio of tree to tundra cover (1:1000 and 1000:1), but most vegetation maps use more subjective criteria, with resulting differences in where the lines are drawn. In northeastern Manitoba and toward the northwest, calcareous young soils create fens that favor the development of white spruce (*Picea glauca* (Moench) Voss) patches in sheltered, well-drained areas (such as eskers) near the tundra, while black spruce and tamarack (*Larix laricina* (Du Roi) K. Koch) are found in the acidic bogs. Farther west, white spruce is more abundant than black spruce, being more tolerant of the soil types and the greater summer heat and solar radiation. Fire plays a significant role in developing the mosaic characteristics of the boreal tundra ecotone. The summers are cool, the winters are cold, and precipitation is moderate (300 millimeters per year). Caribou, moose, and snowshoe hares are common herbivores (important for selective browse effects), wolves, foxes, and bears are common predators, and ravens are scavengers.

Proceeding south, one encounters an open lichen woodland that is self-perpetuating (in the absence of fire) because the lichen ground cover's thickness, water-holding capacity, and high albedo result in cooler soil temperatures. This forest type progresses to denser spruce forest as the crown closure becomes greater. Trees include jack pine (*Pinus banksiana* Lamb.) on drier sites and stands of aspen (*Populus tremuloides* Michx.) and birch (*Betula papyrifera* Marsh.), with alder (*Alnus incana* (L.) Moench), blueberry

Boreal open jack pine forest (R. Marles)

Boreal aspen stand (R. Marles)

(*Vaccinium uliginosum* L.), choke-cherry (*Prunus virginiana* L.), and high bush-cranberry (*Viburnum opulus* L.) shrubs in fire-cleared patches. Black spruce will eventually dominate if the succession reaches a climax. Balsam fir (*Abies balsamea* L.) is a component of the Mid-Boreal and Low Boreal Ecoclimatic Subprovince forests across the Prairie provinces, but becomes more widespread east of Hudson Bay in the Moist and Humid High Boreal and Mid-Boreal ecoclimatic regions. Low-lying areas may support sphagnum moss bogs or fens with a quite open tree cover of tamarack. Subarctic Cordilleran regions are typified by stunted white spruce in a matrix of willow (*Salix* spp.), dwarf birch (*Betula* spp.), and Labrador tea (*Ledum groenlandicum* Oeder), with a ground cover of mosses and lichens. Farther south, lodgepole pine (*Pinus contorta* Dougl. ex Loud.) on drier sites and alpine fir (*Abies lasiocarpa* (Hook.) Nutt.) at higher elevations form scattered associations with white spruce. Trembling aspen is again part of fire-induced seral stage vegetation, with balsam poplar (*Populus balsamifera* L.) in valleys.

Parkland: aspen-oak forest and mixed-grass prairie (R. Marles)

Alder and fireweed regeneration of a burned black spruce forest (R. Marles)

Boreal forest architecture is generally two-storied, with a dominant tree cover of spruce or pine and a ground cover of mosses (e.g., *Hylocomium splendens* (Hedw.) Schimp. in B.S.G.) and lichens (e.g., *Cetraria* spp.). Shrubs, such as Labrador tea and blueberries, occur abundantly only in more open sphagnum bogs or burn regeneration sites or at forest margins (e.g., high bush-cranberry around lakes). Gravel or cobble river beaches and flood plains support extensive shrub associations of willows, dwarf or bog birch (e.g., *Betula nana* L.), alder, grasses, and forbs (e.g., cinquefoil, *Potentilla* spp.).

In the Prairie provinces, the transition zone on the southern side of the Subhumid Low Boreal Ecoclimatic Region is dictated more by moisture stress than by improved growing-season temperatures. The boreal forest's four typical conifers – white spruce, black spruce, jack pine, and tamarack – occur less frequently together and become mixed with trembling aspen, balsam poplar, and white birch in a narrow transition zone called the Boreal Mixedwoods. Patches of aspen scattered throughout this region represent the successional stage of the first 50 years after fire, but eventually the conifers that were seeded at the same time as the aspen will overtop them and within 120 years the aspen will die out. The Boreal Mixedwoods zone gives way – over a band stretching from just west of Edmonton to just east of Winnipeg, in an area of moisture stress – to the aspen parkland. This aspen parkland is dominated by an open tree cover of clonal copses of aspen, balsam poplar, and, in the eastern area, bur oak (*Quercus macrocarpa* Michx.), over an understory of chokecherry, wolf-willow (*Elaeagnus commutata* Bernh. ex Rydb.), and fescue (*Festuca* spp.) grasslands.

The northern and southern transition areas of the boreal forest are not permanent fixtures of a particular region, but constantly shift with changing growing conditions. Thus in the south, the aspen parkland has been expanding into mixed-grass prairie regions because of changing climatic conditions combined with suppression of prairie fires during the historical period. The northern boreal-tundra ecotone has also fluctuated substantially in response to historical climatic changes.

Several factors affect the distribution of the boreal forest. The true boreal forest forms an almost continuous belt around the world (Alaska, Canada, Europe, and northern Asia, including northern Japan), covering almost 7 million square kilometers (30% of the world's forested land, 14% of world forest biomass). The boreal forest is characteristic of recently deglaciated lands, with a humid climate, low evaporation rate, low elevation, and many wetland areas. In Canada, the boreal forest band is V-shaped rather than latitudinal, because of the cool temperatures and high precipitation created by the Rocky Mountain topographic barrier, the Arctic Ocean extension into Hudson Bay, and the formation of the Polar Front – the contact zone between tropical air masses and polar air masses, with frontal systems moving southeast from Yukon to the Great Lakes, then northeast to the Maritimes. The boreal zone actually encompasses many ecoclimates, but in every case the climate favors the success of conifers over broadleaf deciduous or broadleaf evergreen species.

Fire is another important factor in boreal forest dynamics. Fire encourages regeneration and the release of nutrients stored in the biomass. Conifers, which are highly flammable but recover quickly, are able to outcompete less flammable, slower-recovering deciduous trees.

Boreal forest soils, which vary significantly due to differences in the acidity of the parent material, climate, drainage, and presence of permafrost, also influence the type of vegetation dominating particular locations. In the Low Boreal Ecoclimatic Subprovince of central Manitoba, Saskatchewan, and Alberta, positive moisture indices and high base saturations have encouraged the development of Gray Luvisols. In the Canadian Shield region of eastern Manitoba and northern Saskatchewan, extensive glaciation has left many parallel ridges of exposed bedrock. The extremely acid igneous and metamorphic rock parent material inhibits decomposition of leaf litter, leading to the formation between the ridges of shallow organic Folisols that support pine forests but dry out easily, leaving them very vulnerable to forest fires. To the northwest, alkaline calcareous glacial deposits are dominated by Eutric Brunisols in the cooler Mid- and High Boreal ecoclimatic subprovinces, except where permafrost has led to the formation of Cryosols.

Where drainage is only modest and there is a high water table, Humic Gleysols are found, while poorly drained lowlands are covered by poorly decomposed Fibrisol and Mesisol type organic soils. Particularly in the wetlands, soil profiles and their forest cover dominants constantly change as water table levels and peat accumulation rates vary with location and time (Scott 1995).

Nutrient cycling is slow, because of low temperatures and acidic inhibition of bacteria, and absorption of nutrients by the feather moss layer. Soil temperature is a limiting factor for growth, and permafrost affects soil microorganisms, root penetration, and drainage. Conifers, however, maximize their nutrient uptake from the soil with shallow fibrous root systems located close to the litter layer, further improved by ubiquitous mycorrhizae (symbiotic fungi growing on and in the roots), all of which prevent the extent of leaching one would anticipate from high-water-content, poorly developed soils.

Another factor is efficient photosynthesis. Conifers have many more leaves than broadleaf trees, and thus a greater leaf-area index, giving them an advantage for intercepting sunlight. Maximum photosynthetic rates (PSR) are low compared with those of broadleaf trees, but the PSR is greatest from 9°C to 23°C and light saturation for highest PSR is at 33% of full sunlight, so conifers are well adapted to cold and shade. Maintaining photosynthetically viable leaves for many years (the evergreen habit) reduces nutrient demands, and the leaves can conduct photosynthesis "out of season" whenever ambient temperatures are higher than the minimum level required for photosynthetic enzymes to function. The mean annual growing season in the boreal forest region is 130 days, resulting in a low average net primary productivity of 800 grams per square meter per year, but in ideal sites and conditions, productivity may be twice that rate. In addition, the extensive wetlands that occur throughout the boreal forest region often have much higher productivity than the surrounding woodland.

The composition, distribution, and ecology of the boreal forest are described here in some detail because an understanding of these factors will be important in assessing the environmental impact of any proposal to expand the economic development of boreal timber or nontimber plant species. The limited diversity and productivity of the boreal forest suggest that few if any native plant species could sustain large-scale commercial harvest from the wild. Economic and ecological sustainability will more likely succeed with small-scale harvest of a wide variety of materials coupled with silvicultural or agricultural production of those plant products in greater demand.

Cultural Background

The Canadian boreal forest region is home to many different culture groups whose members belong to either the Athapaskan language family (in the northwest) or the Algonkian (also spelled Algonquian) language family (in the south and east). The approximate distribution of these culture groups is shown in Figure 3, but in fact there are no sharp boundaries. The people of the boreal forest were nomadic hunter-gatherers and thus changed locations seasonally. Due to factors that include climatic, demographic, and socioeconomic changes and interactions with other cultures, they also changed locations over time. The names of the culture groups provided in Figure 3 are those commonly found in anthropology texts; we use them here to help with correlation of our information with other literature sources, but they are not necessarily the names preferred today by the First Nations communities. For example, most Athapaskan people use the term *Dene*, meaning "The People," with a modifier to refer to a local group, such as the *Etthën Eldeli Déné*, "The Caribou-Eater People" of northeastern Saskatchewan. Similarly, Cree people refer to the Cree culture group as the *Nehinawewak* and to other Cree as *Ininawak* or *Anisininawak* (in the "N" dialect of Cree). Ojibwa

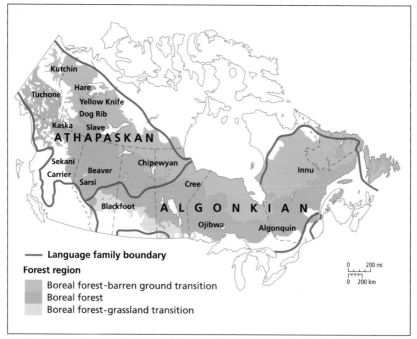

Figure 3 **Approximate distribution of culture groups in boreal Canada**

people generally refer to themselves as *Anishnabe*. Since there is a body of literature and general awareness of the Innu people of northern Quebec and Labrador, we have used that name rather than the outdated Montagnais-Naskapi terms.

By approximately 30 000 years ago, Paleolithic Siberian hunters of the caribou, mammoth, and other large animals that grazed on the Ice Age tundra had reached the northern Yukon. At that time much of North America was still under glaciers, except for a few ice-free corridors or refugia through which these early immigrants probably traveled, eventually making their way far to the south (McGhee 1978).

As the glaciers receded, the caribou herds followed the receding ice-edge tundra, and the caribou hunters followed the herds. Associations of human artifacts and caribou bones, dating from about 8500 BC, have been found in New York State (Gordon 1977). By about 6500 BC the central Canadian boreal region was free of glaciers, although colonization of eastern Manitoba was delayed by the gradual draining of glacial Lake Agassiz. Artifacts, possibly 7 000 years old, attributed to Paleo-Indians of the Northern Plano tradition, Agate Basin culture group, have been found in the Acasta Lake area of the Mackenzie District, Northwest Territories (Noble, cited in Nash 1975).

Over the last 6 000 years, the northwest boreal region appears to have been exploited by a variety of cultures, but cultural affiliations of the limited number of artifacts cannot be decided with certainty. With the onset of

Old tepee site in the tundra-boreal ecotone (R. Marles)

the Hypsithermal warming trend, which reached a maximum around 3500 BC, the boreal forest retreated northward and grasslands dramatically expanded in the southern regions of the Prairie provinces (Nicholson 1996). Shield Archaic hunters, who might have been descendants of the Northern Plano culture and the ancestors of modern Algonkians such as the Cree, hunted the caribou herds of the southern Keewatin District until about 1500 BC. After that date the climate deteriorated, resulting in the southward retreat of the tree line and its associated floral, faunal, and human ecosystems (Gordon 1981).

After the Shield Archaic hunters left the barren grounds, there was some marginal exploitation of the northern region by southeasterly advancing Pre-Dorset (Arctic Mongoloid) caribou hunters of the Arctic Small Tool tradition (McGhee 1978). The Pre-Dorset bands were the first example of a barrenland tradition associated with the predecessors of all four existing caribou populations within the four modern ranges. Their occupation spanned the period from 1500 BC to AD 700 (Gordon 1981). Incursions into the boreal forest as far south as Black Lake and Lake Athabasca, Saskatchewan, may have been isolated instances of pursuit of the Beverly caribou herd as it migrated south in winter (Minni 1976).

Tepee in the parkland (R. Marles)

The wetter post-Hypsithermal climate favored an expansion of the parklands and the southern edge of the boreal forest. This expanded forest and parkland created a territory suitable for larger populations of moose, bear, beaver, and the people who hunted them. The plains region formed the summer pasturage for the northern bison herds, but subsistence resources in the plains were available primarily during the growing season and were not sufficient to support year-round subsistence strategies by the prehistoric human populations. The resources of the boreal forest were thinly spread and accessible primarily along rivers and lakeshores. Migratory waterfowl and plant foods were markedly seasonal, and although fish, moose, woodland caribou, beaver, and bear were available throughout most seasons, procurement was difficult at times, especially during the fall freeze-up and spring thaw. In contrast, the parklands contained a wide range of resources, including moose, elk, bison, mule deer, bear, and aquatic rodents, supplemented by seasonally abundant waterfowl, fish, and vegetable foods. Feasible subsistence strategies could be based on exploitation of the parkland, the ecotones with the grasslands and boreal forest, and riparian habitats, with frequent shifting of base camps as local resources were depleted (Nicholson 1996).

From 200 BC to AD 1650 there is clear archaeological evidence for the diffusion of people and ideas from the eastern woodlands into the central and northern plains. During the Late Prehistoric Period, a heterogeneous but interrelated social and cultural configuration began to develop, spreading over the plains, parklands, and southern boreal forest. It was characterized by a set of artifacts that included small side-notched points, unnotched triangular points, and fabric-impressed ceramics. There is also evidence for a late diffusion of technological traits from the Middle Missouri area into the northern plains as woodland cultures encountered plains-oriented cultures. The resulting adaptive schemes were diverse, including bison pounding in the south and forest and freshwater animal hunting in the north, with a limited amount of horticultural activity, including corn cultivation, occurring more than 500 years ago in the prairie-parkland transition area of Manitoba (Nicholson 1996).

Although it is difficult to assign cultural identities to cultures known only from archaeological remains, there is evidence to suggest that the horticultural sites may have been occupied by people ancestral to the Hidatsa. Early historic evidence suggests that before AD 1700, the southern boreal forest region of the Prairie provinces was occupied by a Siouxan-speaking people, the Assiniboine, who gradually moved southward into the parklands and the margins of the plains on a seasonal basis. By the mid-1800s the Assiniboine

◀ Cree elder and
D. Burns in the boreal-
prairie ecotone
(C. Clavelle)

▼ Chipewyan elder with
his tambourine drum
(R. Marles)

had migrated southwest into southern Saskatchewan and Montana, adopting a plains lifestyle, and were replaced in the southern boreal forest by Cree and Ojibwa. In the mid-1600s, Algonkian-speaking Cree lived throughout the boreal forest from the southern shore of Hudson Bay westward along the Nelson, the Hayes, and lower part of the Saskatchewan rivers, and southward to Lake Nipigon and Rainy Lake, where they came into friendly contact with the Assiniboine. They gradually spread southward to the forks of the Red and Assiniboine rivers and westward through the southern boreal forest and into parklands as middlemen in the fur trade. In the early 1800s the Woodland Cree, who retained the original boreal forest subsistence strategy, became differentiated from the Plains Cree, who adopted a plains subsistence strategy learned from the Assiniboine.

The Algonkian-speaking Ojibwa were first reported in the historical literature of the 1600s living in the boreal forest of northern Ontario. In the early 1700s, under pressure from European colonization and participation in the fur trade, they expanded westward and northward into southern Manitoba – where they were also known as the Saulteaux – eventually inhabiting much of the parklands of southern Manitoba and the northern edge of the parklands in Saskatchewan as far west as the forks of the North and South Saskatchewan Rivers. The Saulteaux maintained a subsistence strategy of southern boreal forest hunting and gathering, harvesting wild rice, and cultivating small fields of corn and squash (Nicholson 1996).

The ancestors of the Athapaskans were probably the last people to enter North America by the shrinking Bering land bridge (McGhee 1978). Alexander Mackenzie (1801) recorded a legend of the Chipewyan that tells of the people fleeing from enemies by crossing a great shallow lake full of islands. It was a land of permanent winter with much ice and snow, and the people suffered greatly. In a slightly different version recorded by Father Gamache (1970) in Fond du Lac, Saskatchewan, an ancestral woman and her children waded across a shallow sea in two days of continuous walking; a wolf showed her the way. After she crossed, she saw a herd of caribou cross and killed one for food.

The history of the Chipewyan is uncertain due to scanty archaeological research, but artifacts of the Taltheilei Shale Tradition dating from 2600 years ago have been found near Dubawnt River in the Mackenzie District, Northwest Territories (Gordon 1977). This tradition is associated with the Athapaskan culture, and appeared with the beginning of a warm trend following the cold Pre-Dorset occupation. There is much evidence for a southwestern origin of the Taltheilei tradition, possibly in northeastern British Columbia (Gordon 1981). The expansion of the Athapaskans into the northwestern boreal forest appears to have been rapid. Artifacts found as far east as Tha-anne River in the Keewatin District, south at South Indian Lake, Manitoba, and north at Coppermine on the Arctic Ocean coast are only about 400 years more recent than those found at Dubawnt River (Gordon 1977). These areas were not continuously occupied, but probably represent extremes in the seasonal range of the caribou and forays against the Inuit (Eskimo). There has been continuous seasonal occupation of some parts of the barrenlands by the Chipewyan for 2500 years (Gordon 1977). The Black Lake, Saskatchewan, area has been occupied on a seasonal basis by the Chipewyan for at least 2000 years, with an occupation late in prehistory by Woodland Cree of the Clearwater Lake complex. This may represent both a spatial and temporal overlap of ranges. The Chipewyan have continued to occupy Black Lake throughout the historic period (Minni 1976).

The decimation of the Chipewyan in the 1780s smallpox epidemic and the southward move of many to participate in the fur trade created an empty niche on the barren grounds. This niche was filled by the Caribou Eskimo, descendants of the Thule who entered the Canadian Arctic in skin boats from Alaska after AD 1000 (McGhee 1978). Introduction of the fur trade economy and technology among the Eskimo, combined with the reduction in the numbers of the Chipewyan in the barrens, made the move inland safe and profitable. The Caribou Eskimo, therefore, have exploited the inland subarctic for only the last 300 years.

Thus there were several stable, successful subsistence strategies employed by a variety of cultures and based on the resources of the boreal forest and parkland. However, the opportunities offered by the fur trade and the excesses that it encouraged led to rapid depletion of animal resources. The introduction of the fur trade, new technology, and alcoholic beverages led to major shifts in adaptive strategies accompanied by serious social dislocations within indigenous society, culminating in the reserve system fixed by treaties with the Canadian government (Nicholson 1996).

Simple Chipewyan birch bark basket
(R. Marles)

Related Literature on Boreal Plant Uses

One objective of this research was to provide an information base for investigating the possibility of developing nontimber forest resources. To avoid "reinventing the wheel" it is necessary to become familiar with the literature on boreal ethnobotany and plants that are edible, medicinal, or otherwise useful. A review of relevant literature is provided here for readers who want more information than can be provided in a single report. Many different culture groups are described; the approximate geographic ranges are shown in the culture maps of Jenness (1963) and Driver (1969). See Figure 3 for a simplified version of these maps.

Almost every article written on the life-style of boreal Aboriginal people mentions birch bark canoes and containers, snowshoes, and other obvious items of technology. There are also references to food and medicinal plants (e.g., in Jenness 1963), but a recurring problem is the lack of adequate documentation, such as accurately determined botanical identities or preservation of voucher specimens. In many cases, the common names of plants mentioned are too ambiguous for the information to be of much use. Another problem (with historical roots) is that little of the information was recorded by researchers with a solid understanding of the language, culture, and customs of the people described. The result is that much information is presented out of the cultural context essential for understanding the dynamic interrelationship between traditional cultures and their botanical environment.

The following review of ethnobotanical literature is grouped by topic; general and ethnobotanical bibliographies are followed by literature referring to particular cultures, arranged geographically. Full publication information is provided in the References section.

General Bibliographies on Aboriginal Peoples

Jenness (1963) is the classic general reference on Canada's Aboriginal peoples. There are also several published bibliographies that focus on Aboriginal people and their material culture. Helm (1976), *The Indians of the Subarctic: A Critical Bibliography,* contains an opening essay on information sources for each named group under headings that include Basic Reference Works, Major Ethnographies, Prehistory, Histories and Historical Materials, Traditional Indian Culture and Society, and Language, followed by a bibliography of 272 references. Although this book lacks a topical index, it is an excellent starting place for literature studies on boreal people. Helm (1973), *Subarctic Athapaskan Bibliography,* provides 1 400 references in alphabetical order with brief coded annotations, followed by listings under topical, geographic, and cultural headings. Hippler and Wood (1974), *The Subarctic Athabascans: A Selected Annotated Bibliography,* list 645 references in alphabetical, cultural, and time-line order. Some unpublished and foreign language works are also cited.

An exhaustive listing of articles on Canadian Aboriginal people published within a 10-year period is provided by Abler et al. (1974), *A Canadian Indian Bibliography 1960-1970.* This book contains 3 038 citations under culture, regional, and topical headings, and is completely cross-indexed. The references deal primarily with cultural material and a case law digest. A more recent annotated bibliography is that by Annis (1985), *Abstracts of Native Studies,* which organizes an extensive literature review under topical headings, such as Economic Activities and Native Culture and Material.

Some bibliographies are available on individual cultures, such as that by Poppe (1971), *Kutchin Bibliography: An Annotated Bibliography of Northern Yukon Kutchin Indians,* which has relevant sections on ethnography and natural sciences. Tanner's (1976) *The Ojibwas: A Critical Bibliography,* although focused on people south of the boreal area, contains much useful information. Murdock (1960), *Ethnographic Bibliography of North America,* contains approximately 1 750 references organized by culture and geographic region.

Ethnobotanical Bibliographies

Lynas (1972), *Medicinal and Food Plants of the North American Indians: A Bibliography*, lists 350 references in alphabetical order, with some boreal ethnobotanical references, but is not annotated, subdivided, or indexed. The Alberta Provincial Museum has an unpublished, unannotated bibliography, *Ethnobotany in North America* (Hrapko 1978). Ford's (1986) *An Ethnobiology Source Book: The Use of Plants and Animals by American Indians* is an excellent source for older literature.

General Ethnobotanical Works

Moerman's (1998) *Native American Ethnobotany* is one of the most useful ethnobotanical compilations. It is a revised and expanded version of his previous two-volume work, *Medicinal Plants of Native America* (Moerman 1986), which is very comprehensive for early ethnopharmacological references and has been analyzed for particular trends (Moerman 1979). This is a valuable source for comparative information. Ford (1981) discusses a phytogeographic perspective on North American ethnobotany, and French (1981) reviews some of the "neglected" aspects of North American ethnobotany. Winterhalder and Smith (1981) discuss some of the theoretical aspects of ethnobotany with regard to hunter-gatherer foraging strategies. Cowen (1984) reviews the impact of North American native peoples' medicines on modern professional practice. Ford (1985) provides a series of papers on prehistoric food production in North America, which, along with nutritional information, could prove useful for indigenous food plant development. Vogel (1970) discusses some of the herbal medicines of one boreal culture, the Ojibwa, as well as other North American native peoples. Freeman and Carbyn (1988) present papers on traditional knowledge and renewable resource management in northern regions. Their focus is primarily on wildlife management, but they also include some plant and land-use information. Kuhnlein and Turner (1991) take a nutritional approach to traditional foods, covering the food plants of all Canadian indigenous peoples. Turner (1981) and Turner and Szczawinski (1978, 1979) provide thoroughly documented information on Canadian native food plants, and Turner and Szczawinski (1991), in *Common Poisonous Plants and Mushrooms of North America*, provide cautionary and therapeutic information useful for ethnobotanical research.

Boreal Alaskan Ethnobotanies

Heller and Scott (1967) provide valuable preliminary work on the nutritional aspect of Koyukon ethnobotany and modern diet, but further research on ethnobotany is required. Ingalik ethnobotany has been fairly thoroughly studied (Osgood 1940), but more details are needed on plant-material preparation and methods of use. Tanaina food and medicinal plants were not adequately studied by Osgood (1937), and some plant identities already recorded need to be verified. A more detailed ethnobotany of the Tanaina was published by Kari (1995). The ethnobotany of the Upper Tanana people has been studied to some extent by McKennan (1959) but needs more indepth research. Eyak traditional plant knowledge is covered by Birket-Smith and de Laguna (1938), but their work needs to be extended. Some ethnobotanical information on the Han is covered in Osgood (1971). Some Kutchin ethnobotanical information is incorporated into publications by Gibbs (1867), Jones (1867), Osgood (1936), Leechman (1954), McKennan (1965), Savoie (1970), Nelson (1973), and VanStone (1974). No ethnobotanically useful information could be found for the Ahtena people. Viereck (1987) has compiled ethnobotanical information from a variety of Alaskan sources, with a focus on medicinal plants, but she also provides some culinary and technological uses.

Inuit Ethnobotanies

Although marginal to the boreal forest, the Inuit practiced some seasonal forest exploitation in river valleys. Inuit ethnobotany is described by Mathiassen (1928), Anderson (1939), Porsild (1953), Oswalt (1957, 1967), Lantis (1959), Young and Hall (1969), Nickerson et al. (1973), Smith (1973), Hoffman (1976), Draper (1977), Indian and Northern Affairs (1978a, b), Wilson (1978), Ager and Ager (1980), Overfield et al. (1980), and Jones (1983).

Boreal British Columbia Ethnobotanies

In north-central British Columbia, Tahltan ethnobotany received a brief treatment by Emmons (1911), and the literature on food plants and technological uses of plants has been compiled by Turner (1978, 1979, 1981), but further fieldwork is definitely required. The ethnobotany of the Carrier was first studied by Harlan I. Smith (1920-1923a-g, 1928); the 1920-1923 manuscripts have been compiled and edited by Brian Compton (unpublished). A general Carrier ethnobotanical work was published by the Carrier Linguistic Committee (1973). Ethnobotanical research has also been published on a related Athapaskan group, the Wet'suwet'en or Witsuwit'en (Johnson-Gottesfeld 1992a, 1993, 1994a, b, 1995; Johnson-Gottesfeld and Hargus 1998). Between 1925 and 1927, Smith also prepared a manuscript on the ethnobotany of the Gitksan people, which has recently been edited and published (Compton et al. 1997). Food plants of the Gitksan have been described by the People of 'Ksan (1980), and further work on the ethnobotany of the Gitksan has been published by Johnson-Gottesfeld and Anderson (1988), Turner et al. (1992), Johnson-Gottesfeld (1992a, b, 1994a), and Johnson (1997).

Northwest Boreal Ethnobotanies

The northwest boreal region is located in northern Manitoba, Saskatchewan, Alberta, and adjacent areas of the Northwest Territories and Yukon Territory. Five very thorough studies have been completed on the ethnobotany of specific groups in this region, including the Slave of Fisherman Lake, Northwest Territories (Lamont 1977), the Wabasca/Desmarais Cree of northern Alberta (Siegfried 1994), the Woods Cree of east-central Saskatchewan (Leighton 1982, 1985), the southern boreal forest Cree of Saskatchewan (Clavelle 1997), and the Chipewyan of northern Saskatchewan (Marles 1984).

Ethnobotanical information on the Hare primarily deals with food plants (Brown 1965; Savishinsky 1974; Hara 1980). Some ethnobotanical information for the Great Bear Lake people has been compiled by Morris (1972), but more original fieldwork is necessary. For the Tutchone, Tagish, Atlin, Teslin, Kaska, Mountain, Yellowknife, and Beaver groups of the Dene Nation, not much ethnobotanical research has been published (e.g., Mason 1913; Harper 1931; Osgood 1933). The Dogrib subsistence economy has been studied by Helm and Lurie (1961), but plants were not the focus of the research. Honigmann (1946) presents a general ethnography of the Slave, but with little ethnobotany. Birket-Smith (1930) provides some information on Chipewyan ethnobotany, Bompas (1890, 1894) worked with the Chipewyan in the Northwest Territories, Lowie (1909, 1912) writes about the Chipewyan of Lake Athabasca, and Duchaussois (1928) writes about the Athapaskan and Inuit people in his memoirs. Blanchet made a number of studies of the Chipewyan in the 1920s (Blanchet 1925, 1928, 1946), but many were never published. D.M. Smith (1973) reviews some of the ritual practices of the Chipewyan. Shay (1980) describes native food plants of Manitoba. Heffley (1981) describes the relationship between northern Athapaskan settlement patterns and natural resource distribution. Clark (1974) provides an overview of northern Athapaskan culture. Brandson (1981) published a resource manual for information on the Chipewyan. Brumbach et al. (1982) use an ethnoarcheological approach to learn more about Chipewyan adaptations. Johnson (1992) also covers the subject of traditional environmental knowledge, particularly among the northern Dene people.

Anderson (1980, 1982) provides a general report of Alberta Cree ethnobotany. Flexon (1898), Strath (1903), Beardsley (1942), and Leach (1973) provide some information on Cree medicinal plants. Young et al. (1989)

describe some of the traditional healing practices of a Cree healer who was also a contributor to this project. Wein et al. (1991) describe some uses of food plants by the Cree, Chipewyan, and Métis of northern Alberta. Lewis (1977) discusses the use of fire by the Cree and Dene of northern Alberta to modify the botanical environment for human benefit. Kerik (1985) summarizes much of the available information on Alberta ethnobotany. Two studies of the ethnobotany of the Blackfoot (Hellson and Gadd 1974; Johnston 1987) give good coverage for this group just to the south of the boreal forest. Further work is being done in northern Alberta by the Grand Council of Treaty 8 First Nations (1993) with the support of the Western Canadian Wilderness Committee. Information on the Sarsi and Northern Assiniboine, presented by Curtis (1928), is very scanty. Some ethnobotanical information on the Attawapiskat Cree is given by Honigmann (1948), but this is very brief and the plants are poorly identified.

Central and Eastern Boreal Ethnobotanies
A useful compilation for the central and eastern boreal forests of Ontario, Quebec, Labrador, and the Maritimes is by Arnason et al. (1981), who summarize much of the ethnobotanical information for eastern Canada, including some of the more obscure references. Recently, a preliminary ethnobotanical study on medicinal plants was done with the Ojibway Garden River First Nation near Sault Ste. Marie, Ont. (Abou-Zaid 1996). The modern diet of the eastern James Bay Cree has been studied by Berkes and Farkas (1978). The ethnobotany of the Chippewa has been described in detail by Densmore (1928). Ethnobotanical coverage for the Mistassini Cree and eastern Ojibwa is limited (e.g., Rogers and Rogers 1959; Rogers 1967). Black (1980) studied Algonquin ethnobotany in southwestern Quebec. Black (1978) has also described some plants whose dispersal in the Canadian subarctic appears to have been facilitated by Aboriginal peoples who found the plants useful, a subject also investigated by Gilmore (1931) and Moseley (1931). Clément (1990) has done an ethnobotanical study of the Montagnais of Mingan. For other Innu or Montagnais-Naskapi, a few economically important plants are described by McGhee (1961) and Henriksen (1973), and some of their ideology associated with plants is recorded by Speck (1935). Recently, Inkpen (pers. comm.) has been working with the Innu of eastern Labrador to record some of their ethnobotanical and traditional ecological knowledge. Since the Beothuk of Newfoundland were all killed, only historical and archaeological research will add to the few ethnobotanical items described by Oswalt (1966). Chandler and Hooper (1979), Chandler et al. (1979), and Hooper and Chandler (1981) studied some medicinal plants of

the Micmac, but more information is needed to supplement Wallis's (1959) description of their food and technological uses of plants. Duke (1986) reviews the medicinal plants of the native peoples of the American northeast, and Erichsen-Brown (1979) provides a thorough historical review of northeastern ethnobotany.

Popular and Technical Books on Useful Boreal Plants

A number of popular books on edible and medicinal plants cover the boreal forest region geographically. Willard (1992) provides good coverage of edible and medicinal plants of the Rocky Mountains and neighboring Territories, but sometimes does not specify the culture (they are referred to as "Indians" or "Amerindians"), and most of the therapeutic claims made for the herbs are not supported by citations of scientific evidence. Even more general in their descriptions of uses are Millspaugh (1892), Weiner (1972), Hutchens et al. (1973), Veninga and Zaricor (1976), Angier (1978), Coon (1979), Foster and Duke (1990), and Foster (1995) in their books on American medicinal plants.

Some more general sources of supplementary information will assist in the development of plant resources, particularly for medicinal plants. These include (in alphabetical order by author): Bisset and Wichtl (1994), *Herbal Drugs and Phytopharmaceuticals*; Blumenthal et al. (1998), *The Complete German Commission E Monographs: Therapeutic Guide to Herbal Medicines*; Bradley (1992), *British Herbal Compendium*, Volume 1; Castleman (1991), *The Healing Herbs*; Colegate and Molyneux (1993), *Bioactive Natural Products*; Dobelis (1986), *Magic and Medicine of Plants*; Duke (1985), *CRC Handbook of Medicinal Herbs*; Duke (1992a), *Handbook of Biologically Active Phytochemicals and Their Activities*; Duke (1992b), *Handbook of Phytochemical Constituents of GRAS Herbs and Other Economic Plants*; Duke (1997), *The Green Pharmacy*; Foster (1993), *Herbal Renaissance*; Foster and Tyler (1999), *Tyler's Honest Herbal*; Gruenwald et al. (1998), *PDR for Herbal Medicines*; Harborne and Baxter (1993), *Phytochemical Dictionary*; Leung and Foster (1996), *Encyclopedia of Common Natural Ingredients Used in Food, Drugs, and Cosmetics*; List and Schmidt (1989), *Phytopharmaceutical Technology*; Newall et al. (1996), *Herbal Medicines: A Guide for Health-care Professionals*; Nigg and Seigler (1992), *Phytochemical Resources for Medicine and Agriculture*; Robbers and Tyler (1999), *Tyler's Herbs of Choice*; Schulz et al. (1998), *Rational Phytotherapy: A Physicians' Guide to Herbal Medicine*; Wijesekera (1991), *The Medicinal Plant Industry*; Williamson et al. (1996), *Selection, Preparation and Pharmacological Evaluation of Plant Material*; and World Health Organization (1991), *Guidelines for the Assessment of Herbal Medicines*. The recent dates of these publications indicate the tremendous resurgence of interest in the economic and pharmaceutical potential of traditional plant products.

Internet-based searchable databases provide essential supportive information for ethnobotanical research. A particularly useful database, NAPRALERT (Farnsworth 1999), is available on the Internet by subscription and may soon be available on CD-ROM. This large database, prepared by the Program for Collaborative Research in the Pharmaceutical Sciences, University of Illinois at Chicago, provides worldwide coverage of medicinal plants – their ethnobotany, clinically or experimentally proven biological activities, toxicity, and chemical constituents. The US Agricultural Research Service (1999) sponsors James Duke's searchable Internet-based database on phytochemistry and ethnobotany. Moerman (1999) provides a searchable Internet-based Native American ethnobotany database.

A number of research journals regularly contain ethnobotanical information, including: *Economic Botany; Fitoterapia; Journal of Ethnobiology; Journal of Ethnopharmacology; Journal of Herbs, Spices, and Medicinal Plants; Journal of Natural Products; The Lawrence Review of Natural Products; Pharmaceutical Biology; Phytomedicine, Phytotherapy Research; Planta Medica;* and, occasionally, the *Canadian Journal of Botany.*

Economic and Sustainable Development

For economic development of boreal forest species, several publications will be useful. Mater Engineering (1993) produced a special forest products market analysis for Weyerhaeuser Canada. Barl et al. (1996), *Saskatchewan Herb Database*, provides information on 26 species of useful herbs of Saskatchewan, including each plant's scientific and common names, description, distribution, traditional and current uses, chemistry, pharmacology, toxicology, nutritional value, products currently available, cultivation, plant or seed sources, quality evaluation, market information, and regulatory status. The authors anticipate providing periodic updates. Hetherington and Steck (1997), *Natural Chemicals from Northern Prairie Plants,* provides information on the phytochemical constituents of 1000 North American plant species. Mazza (1998), *Functional Foods: Biochemical and Processing Aspects,* provides recent information on economic development of food plants that promote good health.

Sustainable development is another area of significant concern. Sustainable development should take into consideration ecological, economic, and cultural sustainability, and thus encompasses issues of biodiversity, prospecting, conservation, patenting, and the intellectual property rights of Aboriginal peoples. Some significant recent publications in these areas include

Akerele et al. (1991), *The Conservation of Medicinal Plants;* Bodeker et al. (1997), *Medicinal Plants for Forest Conservation and Health Care;* The Crucible Group (1994), *People, Plants, and Patents: The Impact of Intellectual Property on Biodiversity, Conservation, Trade, and Rural Society;* Cunningham (1996), *Ethics, Biodiversity, and New Natural Products Development;* Pan American Health Organization (1996), *Biodiversity, Biotechnology, and Sustainable Development in Health and Agriculture: Emerging Connections;* Posey and Dutfield (1996), *Beyond Intellectual Property: Toward Traditional Resource Rights for Indigenous Peoples and Local Communities;* Reid et al. (1993), *Biodiversity Prospecting: Using Genetic Resources for Sustainable Development;* Wood Sheldon et al. (1997), *Medicinal Plants: Can Utilization and Conservation Coexist?;* and World Health Organization et al. (1993), *Guidelines on the Conservation of Medicinal Plants.*

The information found in this literature review will serve as a strong foundation for ethnobotanical field research, but it is no substitute for new work – ethnobotany is not static. The literature provides information from a particular time or even tries to extrapolate back to some Aboriginal period before contact with European cultures, but plant usage is dynamic – constantly changing and adapting – and modern Aboriginal people have experiences and needs different from their ancestors, despite the importance of tradition. Modern needs can only be served by identifying which plants are useful today and by trying to provide sufficient supportive information for Aboriginal people to make informed decisions about which plants might meet future nutritive, health, spiritual, and economic needs.

Traditional Uses of
Boreal Forest Plants

୫ର

This section provides information on the traditional uses of plants by the Aboriginal peoples of the boreal forest. Information provided includes the common English name and other common names (in Chipewyan, Cree, English, French, and Slave); the scientific name (genus, specific epithet, authority, and family); voucher specimen numbers; a brief description of the plant and its habitat; its uses for food, medicine, technology, and ritual; properties of the plant that may be relevant to its traditional and potential future uses; and a preliminary evaluation of its potential for economic development.

Many plants have adverse or toxic effects if not properly used or identified. Please read the Medical Warning at the beginning of the book regarding the use of the food and medicinal plants described.

Common and Other Names

Common and other names have been obtained from contributors to this study and the floras mentioned below. The students who recorded the Cree and Chipewyan plant names had taken university courses in the Cree and Chipewyan languages and therefore had some formal training with the orthographies (methods of writing the language), but they could not be expected to be as proficient as professional linguists. Bilingual English/Cree or English/Chipewyan speakers were always present to help verify transcriptions. Most interviews were tape-recorded to assist note-taking and transcription. When obtained from the literature, Cree, Chipewyan, and Slave names were recorded as published, but some letters were converted from the very accurate International Phonetic Alphabet (IPA) transcriptions of Siegfried (1994) to a less accurate but more generally accessible standard Cree orthography. French common names are mainly from Boivin (1967-1981), Marie-Victorin and Rouleau (1964), and Scoggan (1978-1979).

In both Cree and Dene, some words are pronounced differently by young people and their elders. One Cree researcher for this project referred to the difference between her speech and that of her grandfather as Low Cree versus High Cree. In Chipewyan, one example is the word for *water*, said by young people as *tu* and by the elders as *tux* (the "x" is pronounced like the "ch" in the Scottish "loch"). All languages change and evolve with time, as we can hear in the difference between Shakespearean and modern English.

Cree

Several dialects of Cree are spoken by the people who contributed to this research and, as the transcriptions were not made by trained linguists, there are often several variants of one name, as well as different common names for the same plant. An example of Cree dialectal differences is shown by the personal pronoun "I" (Clavelle 1997):

Plains Cree	*niya*
Athabasca Cree	*nira*
Woods Cree	*nitha*
Swampy Cree	*nina*
Saulteaux/Ojibwa	*nin*
Labrador Algonquin	*nila*

The pronunciation of Cree words can be derived from this chart:

Cree orthography

Consonants	
p	"p" or "b"*
t	"t" or "d"*
k	"k" or "g"*
h	never initial, often before a stop, e.g., *askihk* = earth
s	as in English or "sh"
c	"ts" as "cats"
m	as in English
n	as in English

Semivowels	
w	like "cow" or "coward"
y	like "boy" or "boyish"

Vowels	
a	like "about"
ā	like "car"
ē	like "reign"
i	like "bit"
ī	like "machine"
o	like "book"
ō	like "stone"

* Voiceless or voiced depending on word position and environment.

Chipewyan

The standard orthography for Dene languages, such as Chipewyan or Slave, is difficult for people who do not speak these languages; several sounds do not occur in English, so an English alphabet transcription can only be approximate. For example, the Chipewyan for *birch tree* is *k'i*, in which the glottalized consonant "k'" is a "k" sound made into a click. The Chipewyan for *grass* is *tlh'ogh*, in which the glottalized voiceless lateral fricative "tlh'" is a click made at the side of the tongue when the tongue tip is pressed to the roof of the mouth. The "gh" is a voiced velar fricative made at the back of the throat (the Scottish "loch" sound, except vibrating like the "th" vibrates when you say "there"). Chipewyan is also a tonal language with two tones that change the meaning of a word completely. For example, *k'á* with the voice rising on the "a" as if asking a question means *arrow*, but *k'a* with the voice not rising means *fat*. There are exact ways of writing the sounds of any language in the International Phonetic Alphabet, but it requires a special font to print the text and training in the meaning of the special symbols. The standard Dene orthography used here for Chipewyan words is shown in this chart:

Chipewyan orthography

Consonants	
b, d, g, h, j, k, l, m, n, r, s, t, v, w, x, y, z	as in English
ch, sh, th	as in English
dl, dz, kw, ts	as in English but initial
dh	like "th" in "there" (đ)
ddh, tlh, tth	combined dđ, tł, tθ
k', t', ts', ch', tlh', tth'	glottalized consonants*
lh	voiceless lateral fricative (ł)*
xh, gh	voiceless and voiced velar fricatives (x, ɡ)*
zh	like "azure" (ž)
'	glottal stop like before "it" said strongly (ʔ)

Vowels	
a, i, o, u	like "cat," "bit," "tote," "jute" (low tone which is unmarked)
e, ë	like "bet," "but" (ə or ɛ)
á, é, í, ó, ú	phonetically distinct high tone (voice rises)*
aⁿ, eⁿ, iⁿ, oⁿ, uⁿ	nasal vowels*

* No English equivalent.

Scientific Name and Voucher Specimens

Scientific names for the plants were determined by reference to the major floras of the region (Scoggan 1957, 1978-1979; Boivin 1967-1981; Porsild and Cody 1980; Budd et al. 1987; Vitt et al. 1988; Moss and Packer 1994; Johnson et al. 1995) and to verified herbarium specimens. Sometimes the floras disagreed on the correct scientific name, so all were checked for correctness and synonymy with several World Wide Web databases (International Organization for Plant Information 1999; Missouri Botanical Garden 1999; Royal Botanic Gardens 1999; United States Department of Agriculture 1999). Classification of the

Voucher specimen of ostrich fern (R. Marles)

fungi is based on *Ainsworth and Bisby's Dictionary of the Fungi*, 8th edition (Hawksworth et al. 1995).

Voucher specimen numbers (listed in Appendix B) refer to plant specimens collected during the field research as proof of the identity of the plant under discussion. A complete set of voucher specimens is on deposit in the herbarium of Brandon University, Brandon, Manitoba; regional subsets were deposited in the herbaria of the University of Alberta, Edmonton; and the University of Saskatchewan, Saskatoon; and mounted and plastic-laminated color photocopies of specimens of the more important plants, with their ethnobotanical information, were donated to participating communities as an educational resource.

Description and Habitat

The descriptions of the plants, their habitats, and distributions are from *Flora of the Prairie Provinces* (Boivin 1967-1981), *The Flora of Canada* (Scoggan 1978-1979), *Vascular Plants of Continental Northwest Territories, Canada* (Porsild and Cody 1980), *Budd's Flora of the Canadian Prairie Provinces* (Budd et al. 1987), *Mosses, Lichens and Ferns of Northwest North America* (Vitt et al. 1988), *Flora of Alberta* (Moss and Packer 1994), and *Plants of the Western Boreal Forest and*

Aspen Parkland (Johnson et al. 1995). Current distribution maps for the United States were checked using the *PLANTS National Database* (US Department of Agriculture 1999).

The descriptions of the fungi and their distributions are from *The Polyporaceae of the European USSR and Caucasia* (Bondartsev 1953), *The Polyporaceae of the United States, Alaska, and Canada* (Overholts 1967), *The Fungi: An Advanced Treatise* (Ainsworth et al. 1973), *Edible and Poisonous Mushrooms of Canada* (Groves 1979), and *Common Poisonous Plants and Mushrooms of North America* (Turner and Szczawinski 1991).

Food Uses

The descriptions of food uses are based on interviews with elders in various communities (see Research Methods), supplemented by relevant information from the literature. We deliberately avoided using statements such as "the Cree used it...," "the Chipewyan used it...," or "the Slave used it...." Such statements, although common in the literature, suggest a generality of use that in many cases is not supported by our experience. Although some plants are very widely used, many usages are unique to an individual or small group. The cultural affiliation of the contributor is indicated by a code (C = Cree, D = Dene/Chipewyan, M = Métis), and each person is identified

Chipewyan elders cooking berries and bannock (R. Marles)

by a number. As described in the Research Methods and listed in Appendix A, this system was developed to protect the contributors' confidentiality. For information on food use derived from the literature, the most significant sources are Birket-Smith (1930), *Contributions to Chipewyan Ethnology;* Lamont (1977), *The Fisherman Lake Slave and Their Environment: A Story of Floral and Faunal Resources;* Leighton (1985), *Wild Plant Use by the Woods Cree (Nihīthawak) of East-Central Saskatchewan;* and Siegfried (1994), *Ethnobotany of the Northern Cree of Wabasca/Desmarais.* For the cultural focus of other references cited, please see the References section.

The Aboriginal peoples of northern Canada have a long tradition of hunting and gathering, with wild game being the main food source. Bush foods are still an important component of the diet in many communities. Consumption patterns differ from southern Canadian society. For example, meat is often consumed dried but not cooked, which retains a higher vitamin content, and organ meats are eaten more often.

A wide variety of wild fruits are available both in season and preserved by drying, freezing, or canning. They include chokecherries, pincherries, saskatoons, rosehips, strawberries, raspberries, cloudberries, currants, gooseberries, crowberries, buffalo berries, high-bush cranberries, mountain cranberries, bog cranberries, blueberries, and hazelnuts.

Wild vegetables were never a major part of the traditional northern diet but do have significant health benefits. Traditional vegetables include wild onions; the inner bark of birch, aspen, and pine; young shoots of bulrushes, reeds, and cattails; young flower spikes of cattails and their starchy rhizomes; and the young inner stems, leaves, and flowers of fireweed.

Although plain water was the most common traditional beverage, several plants continue to be used in beverages, including Labrador tea, wild mint, and concentrated saps of birch and Manitoba maple. In many Aboriginal languages the word for "tea" is borrowed from French or English, as there is no indigenous distinction between a herbal tea taken for pleasure and one taken for health benefits.

An explicit connection is made by elders between declining levels of "bush food" consumption among young people and their multitude of health problems. Plant foods have played a significant if somewhat seasonal role in the traditional diet as sources of vitamins, minerals, carbohydrates, and a wealth of health-promoting phytochemicals. Health Canada (1997) defines a functional food as one that is similar in appearance to conventional foods and is consumed as part of a usual diet, but has been demonstrated to have physiological benefits beyond basic nutritional functions or in reducing the risk of chronic disease.

What makes traditional bush foods "functional" rather than "ordinary" foods? When dealing with any minimally processed fruits and vegetables, there may not be a valid distinction. However, health-promoting natural compounds may be present in higher amounts in some wild plants, such as fireweed leaves (*Epilobium angustifolium* L., Onagraceae), than in cultivated species, such as lettuce, which is bred for mild flavor and pale color. To distinguish a food as "functional" we may look for the presence of particular types of naturally occurring chemical compounds with known health benefits, which may be referred to as "nutraceuticals." A nutraceutical product, as defined by Health Canada (1997), has the following distinguishing characteristics: it is produced from a food but sold in pills, powders, or other medicinal forms, and it has demonstrated physiological benefits beyond basic nutritional functions or reduces the risk of chronic disease. Nutraceutical constituents present in northern food plants may include: monoterpenes, diterpenes, and triterpenes; limonoids, phytosterols, and carotenoids; flavonoids, phenylpropanoids, and lignans; polyphenols (catechins, gallotannins, ellagitannins, and proanthocyanidins); sulfur compounds (allylic, aromatic, and isothiocyanate); and complex carbohydrates, lipids, and indoles.

Even simple sugars can play a nutraceutical role. Consumption of cranberries or their juice has been clinically proven effective in treating and reducing the recurrence of urinary tract infections, due to the content of fructose and special tannins that inhibit the ability of pathogenic bacteria to adhere to the lining of the urinary tract. In addition to nutritious vitamins and minerals, wild fruits contain abundant phenolics, including proanthocyanidins, catechins, and other flavonoids with potent antioxidant activity. Hazelnuts have heart-friendly monounsaturated fatty acids. Fruit-gathering is also an outdoor social activity, providing further health benefits.

In addition to containing nutrients such as vitamins A and C, wild vegetables are particularly important as dietary sources for complex carbohydrates, including starches and fiber. Fiber is well known to promote smooth functioning of the digestive tract and to reduce the risk of colon cancer. Complex carbohydrates are particularly important for people with diabetes because they are more slowly absorbed from the digestive tract and thus have less tendency to cause an after-meal spike in the blood glucose level. At one time, carbohydrates were important to help correct metabolic problems caused by the restricted diet of lean meat typical of northern hunter-gatherers in the late winter and early springtime.

Volatile oils and tannins are major bioactive compounds of Labrador tea and mint tea, with known beneficial effects on the digestive system when consumed in moderation. Birch and maple sap are further sources of carbo-hydrates (sugars) in early springtime, and were considered to be health drinks as well as treats.

Minerals from traditionally used plants may also have special health benefits. Mineral salts extracted from red samphire (*Salicornia rubra* A. Nels., Chenopodiaceae) by boiling and evaporation were used by the Cree of Shoal Lake, Saskatchewan, to season food. This crude salt would provide trace minerals that act as enzyme cofactors critical for the maintenance of good health. Consumption of small amounts of chromium, manganese, and magnesium salts has been shown to be beneficial in the treatment of non-insulin-dependent diabetes.

Traditional plant foods could play an important role in alleviating some modern health problems, such as obesity, high blood pressure, maturity-onset diabetes, and vitamin and mineral deficiencies caused by reliance on the worst aspects of a typical urban Canadian diet (highly processed, fatty, salty, or sweet foods) combined with a more sedentary lifestyle.

The habits of smoking and chewing plant materials for nonmedicinal purposes were not part of precontact Cree or Chipewyan culture (D9; Morice 1909). However, after its introduction, tobacco came to be considered a necessity for which considerable quantities of provisions and a few skins would be traded (Macdonell 1760; Simpson 1821). Because of the high cost and short supply of tobacco, many local plants were tried as extenders, substitutes, and aromatics. The current easy access to stores has made the use of tobacco extenders and substitutes unnecessary most of the time, but many elders remember their use. A number of plants described in the next section have been used as smoking materials.

Medicinal Uses

Traditional medicine among the Aboriginal peoples of the boreal forest is based on oral traditions and spiritual power. The spiritual and psychological aspects of healing rituals are probably at least as important as the plants used – some would say much more important. Their traditional medicine is therefore a cultural phenomenon, dynamic and adaptive like language and other cultural practices.

Although plants play a significant role as materials for remedies, there is no fixed pharmacopoeia, nor can it be assumed that a scientific analysis of a given plant will always provide a complete explanation for its traditional use. Elders of every culture have a repertoire of home remedies, some of which may be widely known and some of which may be unique. A particular use may have been learned from another member of the same culture, or

Cree elders
stripping balsam fir
bark for medicine
(C. Clavelle)

a member of a different culture, or it may be a discovery of the individual. Methods of discovery of traditional remedies are quite varied and are not just trial and error. They include observation of animal behavior: what plants the animals eat and how it affects them. There may be an association of a particular smell, taste, color, or shape of a plant with a curative action. This may involve the "Doctrine of Signatures" concept common to many cultures, where the appearance of a plant is believed to be a divine sign of how it is to be used. For example, a blood-red leaf might be for treating problems related to bleeding, or a kidney-shaped leaf for treating kidney problems. Communication with the spirit world through dreams, visions, and, in some cases (especially among South American cultures), with the aid of psychoactive plants, may also be an important way of learning about plants with medicinal properties.

There are several important consequences of the cultural nature of traditional medicine. It would not be correct to say "the Chipewyan or the Cree use plant x to treat condition y" because that suggests a uniform base of knowledge that does not really exist. In contrast, Chinese traditional medicine is based on widely disseminated writings going back perhaps 4 000 years. The composition is more fixed, and more generalizations can be made. The traditional medicine of the boreal Aboriginal people is an oral tradition that is much less uniform and much more subject to individual experience and interpretation. Different people may have similar uses for particular medicinal plants, reflecting shared knowledge or independent discovery, but many plant uses are unique to one individual or family.

Health Canada (1995a, b) has established a separate category of nonprescription drugs for marketing products previously sold as dietary supplements, but for which there are references supporting therapeutic use. Key aspects of the definition of a "Traditional Herbal Medicine" include: they are finished drug products, intended for self-medication for minor self-limiting ailments that are suitable for self-treatment; the active ingredients are herbal; and there may be limited scientific documentation, but well-documented traditional use. One traditionally used boreal plant in this category is bearberry (*Arctostaphylos uva-ursi* (L.) Spreng., Ericaceae), the leaves of which are now sold encapsulated as a registered non-prescription Traditional Herbal Medicine-class diuretic drug.

Chipewyan elder shaping snowshoe frames with a draw-knife (R. Marles)

Technological Uses

The practical uses of plants were a very important part of everyday life in the boreal forest. Although some of these uses still persist (e.g., the manufacturing of birch bark baskets and snowshoes), many of the traditional skills are being lost as young people fail to take the opportunity to learn the old ways from their elders. These skills are useful in many ways – they are practical and deeply rooted in tradition, and they may be applied to marketable handicrafts, such as toy canoes, snowshoes, and dream catchers that sell for high prices in gift shops in Canadian cities.

Ritual Uses

Although perhaps not of great economic importance, ritually used plants have been and continue to be important to the spiritual well-being of Canada's Aboriginal peoples. No description of useful plants would be complete without reference to sweet-grass and tinder fungus, which serve many roles in traditional culture and religion.

Chipewyan elder gathering tinder fungus for ritual use (R. Marles)

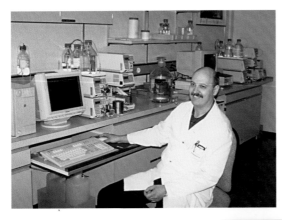

◄ Plant extracts being tested chemically (R. Marles)

▼ Commercial Uva Ursi leaf diuretic drug (R. Marles)

Properties

The plant property descriptions are derived from a review of the literature. For nutrient content, the main source was Kuhnlein and Turner (1991). For the chemistry and pharmacology of the medicinal plants, the main sources were Duke (1985), Dobelis (1986), Bradley (1992), Bisset and Wichtl (1994), Hetherington and

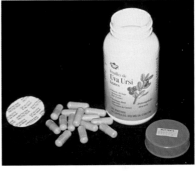

Steck (1997), and the NAPRALERT computer database (Farnsworth 1999). The preliminary evaluation of each plant as a nontimber forest resource is based on how widespread and significant the uses are, how well they are supported by the literature, and the ecological status of the species.

To provide the context for understanding the significance of particular levels of nutrients, Table 2 lists the recommended daily nutrient intake for young Canadians, derived from Hawkins (1983).

Potential

This section provides a brief statement of, in our opinion, the potential of the plant for economic development. It is important to keep in mind that almost all the species described here, even the common ones, are probably not abundant enough to withstand long-term commercial-scale harvesting from the wild. When a market is established for the plant or some products derived from it, the agronomics of sustainable production will be an essential area of research.

Table 2 **Recommended daily nutrient intakes for Canadians, ages 19-24**

Nutrient	Male (71 kg)	Female (58 kg)
Protein (g/day)	57	41
Energy (kcal/day)	3 000	2 100
Vitamin A (retinol equivalents, RE/day)	1 000	800
Thiamin (vitamin B_1, µg/day)	800	800
Riboflavin (vitamin B_2, mg/day)	1.5	1.05
Niacin (vitamin B_3, niacin equivalents, NE/day)	14.4	14.4
Pantothenic acid (vitamin B_5, mg/day)	5	5
Pyridoxine (vitamin B_6, µg/day)	900	600
Cyanocobalamin (vitamin B_{12}, µg/day)	2	2
Ascorbic acid (vitamin C, mg/day)	60	45
Calciferol (vitamin D, µg/day)	2.5	2.5
Tocopherol (vitamin E, mg/day)	10	7
Folacin (µg/day)	210	165
Biotin (µg/day)	106.5	87
Phylloquinone (K_1) or menaquinone (K_2) (µg/day)	30	30
Sodium (Na, mg/day)	2 485	2 030
Potassium (K, mg/day)	4 970	4 060
Chloride (Cl, mg/day)	3 550	2 900
Calcium (Ca, mg/day)	800	700
Phosphorus (P, mg/day)	800	700
Magnesium (Mg, mg/day)	240	190
Iron (Fe, mg/day)	8	14
Zinc (Zn, mg/day)	9	8
Manganese (Mn, mg/day, estimate)	2.5	2.5
Copper (Cu, mg/day, estimate)	1	1
Molybdenum (Mo, µg/day, estimate)	120	120
Iodine (I, µg/day)	160	160

The listing of useful plants that follows contains many technical terms in order to provide specific and accurate information on the plants' appearance, uses, and properties. While jargon has been avoided or explained wherever possible, a short glossary is provided at the back of the book to assist readers with some of the more frequently used terms with which they might not be familiar.

Listing of Useful Plants

❦

The plants used by the Aboriginal people of Canada's northwest boreal forest are grouped in this section according to their genetic relationships. They are first divided into fungi, lichens, nonvascular plants, vascular spore-producers, gymnosperms, and angiosperms. Each category begins with a brief introductory description. Within these broad categories, the plants are arranged alphabetically by the family's scientific name, and within each family by the species' scientific name. In this way, information about similar plants can be found close together, making it easy to compare uses and properties. To quickly find the plant you want by the common or the scientific name, use the index at the back of the book.

Medical Warning
The traditional and therapeutic uses and modern medicinal values of the plants described here are given for information purposes only. Medicinal use of plants should be carried out under the care of a qualified, well-informed health professional. Please note that some plants included in this book are poisonous, and others may cause adverse reactions in some individuals.

Fungi

From a biologist's point of view, fungi are not plants at all but members of a separate kingdom of life. Recent genetic studies suggest that fungi may be more closely related to the animal kingdom than to the plant kingdom. Nevertheless, mushrooms and other types of fungi are commonly used in a manner similar to plants, and are therefore included in this study. There are four main groups, or phyla, of fungi, the Chytridiomycota (microscopic parasites), the Zygomycota (conjugation fungi including black bread mold), the Ascomycota (sac fungi including *Myriosclerotinia* listed below, powdery mildews, morels and truffles, and cup fungi), and the Basidiomycota (club fungi including the common mushrooms, puffballs, and bracket fungi listed below).

BASIDIOMYCOTA (CLUB FUNGI)

AMANITACEAE
(Amanita Mushroom Family)

Fly Agaric

Other Names: Chipewyan: *dlíé eba^{n}dzaghé* ("squirrel's apple" = mushroom in general, i.e., squirrels store fruiting bodies of large edible mushrooms in trees for later use); French: *agaric-à-la-mouche*.

Scientific Name: *Amanita muscaria* Fr.

(R. Marles)

Description: A large mushroom with a warty cap that is usually pale yellow to orange in the northwest boreal forest, although it is often red on the west coast. Other distinctive features are the gills that just reach the stipe, a loose veil (annulus) around the stipe, a rounded base (volva) adhering to the stipe in irregular rings, and a white spore deposit.

Habitat: Fairly common and widely distributed in both coniferous and deciduous open woods across the northern hemisphere.

Medicinal Uses: This poisonous mushroom is never taken internally, but is boiled with other plants to make eye-drops for sore eyes (D9, D23).

Properties: Fly agaric is poisonous because of its content of ibotenic acid, muscimol, and variable but usually insignificant amounts of muscarine. In use as eye-drops the ratio of mushroom constituents is important because muscarine will stimulate the formation of tears and contract the pupil, but ibotenic acid and muscimol will have the opposite effects of dilating the pupil and drying the eyes (Gilman et al. 1980; Turner and Szczawinski 1991).

Potential: Although this drug will definitely affect the eyes, there is no market for poisonous mushrooms.

CORIOLACEAE
(POLYPORACEAE, Pore Fungus Family)

Tinder Fungus

Other Names: Chipewyan: *basketl'a-to nok*; Cree: *wehkimasikun, wikemasikun, waskatamow, wāsāsukwītwī, wāsaskwītoy, posākan.*

(N. Tays)

Scientific Name: *Fomes fomentarius* (L. ex Fries) J. Kickx f.

Description: A conk type of fungus growing from the trunk of a tree. The fruiting body is stalkless, hoof-shaped (20 × 15 × 15 cm), with the upper surface distinctly banded with gray and brown, the lower spore-releasing surface flat and light brown or gray, and the soft, corky inner tissue dark tan to brown.

Habitat: It is commonly found on the trunk of dead or wounded birch, aspen, or other trees throughout the northern hemisphere (and in Africa).

Medicinal Uses: The fruiting body can be burned in tepees or homes to get rid of mosquitoes and flies (M6, M9). The Woods Cree burn pieces on the skin as a counterirritant to treat arthritis (Leighton 1985).

Technological Uses: The fruiting body can be crumbled and a small amount placed in a pipe with plug tobacco and red willow bark to keep the smoking materials burning (M6; Leighton 1985). Chipewyan children used to play ball with the almost round fruiting bodies (M6). It can also be carved into jewelry (C53). Pictures can be drawn on the flat spore-releasing surface (C23, C27). The Woods Cree use it as tinder for starting a fire (Leighton 1985).

Ritual Uses: Pieces of the dry fruiting body can be burned for smudging instead of sweet-grass (M9).

Properties: The corky nature of the fruiting body makes it effective as tinder.

Potential: There is not much demand for tinder now, although as a smudge against mosquitoes it might be useful. The main economic potential lies in its use in dried flower arrangements and artistic items.

Bracket Fungus

Other Names: None known.

Scientific Name: *Fomitopsis pinicola* (Swartz ex Fries) Karst., common synonym: *Fomes pinicola* (Swartz ex Fries) Cooke.

Description: A bracket fungus growing from the trunk of a tree, with a stalkless fruiting body varying in shape from horizontally flattened to convex or even

Bracket fungus artwork (L. Monteleone)

hoof-shaped at maturity, up to 40 cm wide, projecting 30 cm from the tree and from 2.5 to 22 cm thick. The upper surface is often at least partly covered by a reddish, brown, or black resinous crust (especially when growing on conifers), shows distinct annual bands of light yellow, orange-yellow, rusty, chestnut, gray and eventually black, and has a rounded margin. The pore surface underneath may be white, yellow, or yellowish brown, and the hard corky or woody inside tissue may be lemon yellow in young specimens, but turns pale brown in mature specimens.

Habitat: Very common on dead trees, stumps, or logs, either deciduous (most commonly birch or maple) or coniferous (including spruce, pine, fir, and tamarack). Distributed across North America (except the south), Eurasia, and Australia.

Medicinal Uses: The fungus can be cut into small pieces, mixed with tobacco, and smoked in a pipe to treat a headache (Lamont 1977).

Technological Uses: The fungus can be burned as a smudge to chase mosquitoes away (Lamont 1977).

Properties: The flat shape of the fruiting body and its corky texture establish its value.

Potential: There is not much demand for tinder now, although as a smudge against mosquitoes it might be useful. The main economic potential lies in its use in dried flower arrangements and artistic items. Bracket fungi make popular "canvases" for nature-theme miniature paintings.

Bracket Fungus

Other Names: None known.

Scientific Name: *Ischnoderma resinosum* (Fr.) Karst., common synonym: *Polyporus resinosus* Schrad. ex Fries.

Description: A bracket fungus up to 25 cm wide, projecting up to 15 cm from the tree, but only 4 cm thick. The corky fruiting body (sporophore) is flat on top, dark brown to blackish brown, often with blackish-blue metallic-colored zones and a white band around the outer edge. The texture is velvety when young but becoming smoother at maturity, often with furrows, creases, and wrinkles on the surface, and usually thin margined. The white pore surface underneath is only shallowly sloped to the tree. Inside, the tissue

(R. Marles)

is straw colored or slightly darker next to the spore tubes.

Habitat: Found on old logs and near the base of stumps of conifers such as fir, tamarack, and spruce and deciduous trees such as maple, birch, poplar, aspen, oak, and willow. Distributed across North America and Eurasia.

Medicinal Uses: The fungus can be boiled for 30 minutes and the decoction drunk to treat a cough (Lamont 1977).

Properties: Other species of *Polyporus* have been shown to have experimental anticancer, antibiotic, and anti-inflammatory activities. Bioactive compounds isolated from *Polyporus* species include sesquiterpenes, triterpenes, steroids, one alkaloid, and complex polysaccharides (Farnsworth 1999).

Potential: Not enough information is available on this species to make a judgment, although there is clear medicinal potential in related fungi.

Diamond Willow Fungus

Other Names: Chipewyan: *k'ái tlh'elht'áré* ("willow tinder"); Cree: *wiy(h)kimāsiygan.*

Scientific Name: *Trametes suaveolens* (L. ex Fries) Fries.

Description: An annual bracket fungus with a convex fruiting body that has a grayish, creamy white, or pale yellow upper surface

(R. Marles)

that is velvety when young but later becomes smooth, a porous undersurface from which the spores are released, spore-releasing tubes of unequal lengths, corky white flesh, and a distinctive, pleasant aniseed scent.

Habitat: Growing on diseased or dead willow (e.g., *Salix discolor* Muhl., Salicaceae) stems (occasionally birch, aspen, or poplar) around sloughs, lakes, riverbanks, swamps, or moist woods from Alberta east to the Maritimes, in northern USA east of the Rockies, and in northern Eurasia.

Medicinal Uses: The fruiting body can be burned and the smoke inhaled to treat a headache, or crumbled into an ear to treat earaches (D26). It can be one component of a complex love potion, which also requires a hair of the intended victim (D3, D29). It can also be used, dried and powdered, in other compound medicines (D11).

Technological Uses: The dried fungus can be used for tinder to start a fire and to carry fire as a hot ember over long distances (Siegfried 1994).

Ritual Uses: The dried fungus is burned as an incense used during prayers, giving thanks and offerings to the Creator, and the smoke is wafted over the head as a spiritual bath (Siegfried 1994).

Properties: The corky texture and pleasant anise-like fragrance are the desirable properties of this fungus.

Potential: There is a very limited demand among Aboriginal people who use it as an incense in rituals.

HYMENOCHAETACEAE
(Wood-infecting Fungus Family)

Tinder Fungus

Other Names: Chipewyan: *ch'áⁿlhtthi, ts'áⁿtthi*; Cree: *pōsākan, Wīsakīchak omīkī, Wīsakecak omikīh* ("Wisakeichak's [a Cree legendary figure] scab").

Scientific Name: *Inonotus obliquus* (Ach. ex Pers.) Pil., common synonym: *Poria obliqua* (Pers. ex Fries) Karst.

Tinder fungus on a birch log (R. Marles)

Description: A fungus that colonizes birch (to some extent also maple, elm, mountain ash, and beech). It develops under the bark and into the wood, spreading extensively and eventually pushing off the bark. It can be seen as a large crusty black growth on the trunk of the birch, with a dense, slightly spongy orange central mass.

Habitat: Found throughout the circumboreal forest and also in Australia and Sri Lanka.

Food Uses: The fungus can be boiled to make a beverage (C23, C27, C34, C37; Leighton 1985). It can be mixed with tobacco (Siegfried 1994).

Medicinal Uses: A decoction of the fungus (alone or mixed with other plants) can be drunk to treat heart conditions (C23, C27) or mixed with other plants in a medicinal tea for high blood pressure (C38). The fungus can be soaked in water overnight and then given to an underweight child to help the child gain weight: "it's like a vitamin" (C35, C36). The Woods Cree burn pieces on the skin to produce a counter-irritation to treat arthritis (Leighton 1985).

Technological Uses: The orange center of the fungus is dried and used as tinder (Chipewyan: *tlh'elh t'áré*) to catch the sparks from a flint and steel (traditionally probably flint and pyrites) (C27, C32, C34, D3, D9, D11, D24; Ebner pers. comm.; Hearne 1795; Morice 1907, 1909; David Thompson, cited in Hopwood 1971; Lamont 1977; Leighton 1985). The ignited fungus could be carried from one location to another to start a new campfire without going out (C23, C27).

Ritual Uses: Finely crumbled tinder fungus is used in a divination ritual called *etsën dek'on,* meaning "it smells when it's burning." Two long piles of tinder, said to represent two events (e.g., hunters returning versus caribou coming) can be arranged end to end and ignited at their far ends. Whichever pile burns through to the middle first signifies which of the two events will happen first (D11, D18, D24, D29, D32). Tinder fungus can be burned as a smudge or incense (Siegfried 1994), a practice adopted for Catholic ritual in some remote northern communities long ago when the usual church incense was not available. One priest mixed it with spruce pitch (D3, D6, D32).

Properties: The fruiting body contains ergosterol derivatives, a number of triterpenes including lanostane derivatives, lignans, and phenylpropanoids (Farnsworth 1999). After consumption, ergosterol derivatives can be converted by ultraviolet light from the sun shining on the skin into vitamin D_2 (ergocalciferol) (Harborne and Baxter 1993). The corky texture of the fruiting body makes it a good tinder material.

Potential: Although there is not much demand for tinder, there is some demand for this fungus as an incense in Aboriginal religious practices.

LYCOPERDACEAE
(Puffball Fungus Family)

Puffball Fungus

Other Names: Chipewyan: *datsáⁿtsíé*; Cree: *bībōgīthā-min, bīpōgīthamin, pesohkan, pissoskum, kōkōsīwathaman, kāpwīpocīpathisit, kāpi-kiy(h)tiypayta* ("ones that smoke"), *wathaman*; French: *vesse-de-loup*.

Scientific Name: *Lycoperdon perlatum* Pers. Also *L. pyri-forme* Pers., *L. gemmatum* Batsch., *L. umbrinum* Pers., *Bovista pila* B. & C., *Geastrum* sp.

Lycoperdon pyriforme Pers. (R. Marles)

Description: A small spherical fungal fruiting body that, when mature, releases spores through an apical opening when crushed.

Habitat: Common on many soil types, depending on the species, around the world.

Medicinal Uses: To stop bleeding from a cut, the mature puffball can be torn open and the inside surface of the skin (peridium), with its adhering cottony mass (spores and capillitium), applied to the wound. The spores may also be squirted from the puffball onto the cut (C34, D9, D23, D24, D28, D29, D32, D33, M6; Lamont 1977; Leighton 1985). Some elders said the spores could be squirted into the nose to stop a nosebleed (C44, D24, D32, M6; Leighton 1985; Siegfried 1994) but others thought that might be dangerous (D6, D33). The spores can also be used as a baby powder to prevent chafing (D9).

Properties: The texture of the spores and capillitium aid blood coagulation.

Potential: Immature puffballs are considered delicious to eat. No other economic development opportunities seem likely.

ASCOMYCOTA (SAC FUNGI)

SCLEROTINIACEAE
(Sclerotinia Fungus Family)

Sedge Sclerotium

Other Names: Cree: *mwākōkot.*

Scientific Name: *Myriosclerotinia caricis-ampullacea* (Nyberg) Buchw.

Description: A fungal parasite of *Carex aquatilis* Wahl. (Cyperaceae) and other sedges. The sclerotia (hard resting bodies) are found in the sedge seed head and are up to 2 cm long, thin, conical, black on the outside, and pale on the inside.

Habitat: Rarely described but perhaps not uncommon on sedges in marshes across Canada.

Medicinal Uses: A small piece of the sclerotium can be eaten or ground up and taken in water by a woman giving birth to speed up a difficult labor. It may also be taken with other herbs in an infusion or decoction to aid in the expulsion of the afterbirth or to treat menstrual irregularity (Leighton 1985).

Properties: The sclerotium might have ergot-type alkaloids that would provide a smooth-muscle contracting effect, explaining the traditional use. No information has been found yet.

Potential: There is probably no reason to develop this fungus.

Fungal sclerotium on sedge seed head (R. Marles)

Lichens

Lichens are fungi (mostly from the phylum Ascomycota) that have formed a mutually beneficial (symbiotic) partnership with a green alga. The fungus provides structural support, nutrients absorbed from the substrate, and a protected environment for the algae to grow and produce carbohydrates from carbon dioxide and water using the energy of sunlight (photosynthesis). In some cases, such as on rocks and in wet bogs where there is a shortage of nitrogen as a nutrient source, the lichen may also have a cyanobacterial partner. The cyanobacterium can convert nitrogen gas from the air into ammonia. Thus a lichen is two or three organisms living as one, but classification is based on the fungal host, which in most cases provides the shape of the lichen.

CLADONIACEAE
(Reindeer Lichen Family)

Reindeer Lichen

Other Names: Chipewyan: *tsanjú*; Cree: *wāpiskastaskamihk, atikōmīciwin.*

Scientific Name: *Cladina stellaris* (Opiz) Brodo, common synonym: *C. alpestris* (L.) Nyl.

Description: A yellow-green, much-branched fruticose lichen forming rounded clumps on the ground. The branches have no central stem and terminate in a star-shaped whorl of branchlets.

Habitat: Widespread on soils under open northern coniferous forests, often in areas of late snow.

Food Uses: Reindeer lichens and other herbs partially digested by natural bacterial fermentation in the caribou's rumen have been a traditional part of the diet of northern peoples including the Montagnais (Provencher and La Rocque 1976) and Chipewyan. The contents of the caribou rumen (Chipewyan: *ebúrti*) were boiled using heated rocks in the cut-out rumen or large intestine, with added bits of meat, fat, and blood (Chipewyan: *ebíe hechélh,* "bowel soup") (D3, D24, D28; Hearne 1795; Birket-Smith 1930; Leechman 1948; Hopwood 1971; Smith 1976), or they could be further fermented to improve digestibility (Hearne 1795). Depending on season

Reindeer lichen with mountain cranberry flower (R. Marles)

and locality, these stomach contents consist of the natural rumen micro-organisms and possibly partially digested *Cladonia*, *Cladina*, and *Cetraria* ground lichens, some tree lichens, various mushrooms, horsetails, shoots of sedges, cottongrasses, grasses, young leaves of glandular birch, blueberry and other shrubs, berries, and herbs such as lupines and avens (Kelsall 1968). Hearne (1795) states that this food was preferred in winter when the caribou have been feeding on fine white "moss" (i.e., *Cladina*) rather than the coarser summer feed.

Medicinal Uses: A decoction or the dried and powdered lichen suspended in water can be taken to cause the expulsion of intestinal worms (Leighton 1985).

Properties: There are a number of lichen acids present, including usnic and barbatic acids, plus quinoids, benzenoids, and the triterpene ursolic acid. Antitumor activity has been demonstrated (Farnsworth 1999). Lichen acids are known to irritate the gastrointestinal tract and so could cause purgation (Kuhnlein and Turner 1991).

Potential: There is a strong demand and immediate market potential in the floral and craft trade for *Cladina* or *Cladonia* and *Peltigera* lichens (Mater Engineering 1993). However, due to their slow growth and ecological importance as ground cover and food for caribou, ecologically sustainable development seems doubtful.

PARMELIACEAE
(Parmelia Lichen Family)

Iceland Moss

Other Names: French: *lichen d'Islande.*

Scientific Name: *Cetraria islandica* (L.) Ach.

Description: Not a moss at all but a fruticose (branched) lichen with olive brown to dark brown lobes up to 10 cm long that are channeled towards the tips (edges rolled inward) and broader toward the reddish bases. The lobe edges are lined with tiny thornlike spines and the undersurface is lighter in color with tiny scattered white patches. The fruiting bodies, rarely seen, are reddish brown and located at the tips of the lobes.

Habitat: Found in clumps on the ground in tundra and open northern or subalpine forests, and occasionally on old wood or lower twigs of spruce trees that are covered by snow in winter. A circumpolar species that is quite common across most of Canada and in the mountains south into western USA.

Medicinal Uses: The decoction can be drunk three times daily to treat tuberculosis (Lamont 1977).

Properties: Historically this lichen was used in the manufacture of antibiotics to inhibit the growth of the microorganisms causing tuberculosis, athlete's foot, and ringworm (Vitt et al. 1988) and was widely used in northern Canada,

(A. Roberts)

Iceland, and northern Europe as a food thickener and digestive bitter (Johnson et al. 1995). It contains hot-water-soluble polysaccharides ("lichenin," approximately 50% of the plant's weight) that gel when the water cools, plus bitter lichen acids, such as the depsidones cetraric acid and fumaroprotocetraric acid. The decoction is used in modern European herbal medicine as a demulcent (soothing effect of the polysaccharides) and expectorant for alleviating irritation of the throat in coughs, where the antibiotic and bacterial-growth-inhibiting effects of the lichen acids may also be beneficial (Bisset and Wichtl 1994). The bitterness of the lichen acids has resulted in use of the lichen to stimulate the appetite, which may also prove useful in convalescence (Dobelis 1986).

Potential: The traditional use is clearly substantiated by scientific evidence, but the low biological productivity of lichens suggests little market potential.

Waxpaper Lichen

Other Names: English: powdered shield lichen.

Scientific Name: *Parmelia sulcata* Taylor.

Description: This lichen has a leaflike body (foliose thallus) which is gray-green on the upper surface, with a network of ridges and margins that produce granules for asexual reproduction (soredia). The undersurface is brown at the edges and black in the middle and has short projections (rhizines) that anchor it to its host tree's bark.

Habitat: Commonly found growing on the bark of coniferous and deciduous trees and shrubs throughout the northern hemisphere.

Medicinal Uses: The lichen can be rubbed on the gums of teething babies to relieve discomfort (M9).

Properties: There is antiseptic activity from the lichen acids (Farnsworth 1999).

Potential: There is not likely to be much economic potential for this lichen.

Lichens on a spruce branch (N. Tays)

UMBILICARIACEAE
(Rock Tripe Family)

Rock Tripe

Other Names: Chipewyan: *tthe tsî^n* ("rock dirt"); Cree: *asinīwāhkona, wakoonak, asinīwākon*; French: *tripe de roche.*

Scientific Name: *Actinogyra muhlenbergii* (Ach.) Schol. Also *Umbilicaria vellea* (L.) Ach. and related species.

Description: A flaky black leafy lichen that is rounded in outline, attached centrally by a single holdfast, with fruiting bodies bearing concentric or radial ridges.

Habitat: Common on acidic rocks (e.g., granite) in open areas of the circumpolar boreal forest and tundra.

Food Uses: The flakes can be cleaned of grit and boiled in soups as a thickener (C38, C44, D6, D9, D24, D30; Hearne 1795; Mackenzie 1801; Franklin 1823; Dodge 1871; Curtis 1928; Birket-Smith 1930; Leighton 1985). It gives a sour, mushroom flavor and will make the soup gel when it cools. The soup made with it can also be given to dogs to fatten them up (C38). The lichen should be leached to remove toxic lichen acids by first soaking it in boiling water and discarding the water before adding it to the soup (Leighton 1985).

Actinogyra muhlenbergii (Ach.) Schol. (R. Marles)

Although not a common food source today, rock tripe has been important in the past particularly when there was little other food available (Franklin 1823).

Medicinal Uses: The lichen can be either chewed or fried, ground, and then boiled to make a syrup which can be swallowed to rid the body of tapeworm (D9, D29). The decoction can be given to someone with a stomachache to "clean out the stomach" (C38, C44).

Properties: Lichens are difficult to digest because of their complex polysaccharides and bitter acids (e.g., usnic, vulpinic) which are irritating to the digestive tract or even toxic. Lichen polysaccharides are broken down into simple sugars by the action of digestive tract bacteria. Herbivores that frequently eat lichens, such as caribou, have a well-developed intestinal microflora in their rumen for this purpose, but humans must eat only a little at a time to avoid a stomachache. It is recommended that traditional methods of preparation be followed, for example, washing the lichens with water and ashes and then boiling with at least one change of water to leach out and neutralize the acids (Kuhnlein and Turner 1991). Using rock tripe as a food has reportedly caused severe purgation (Provencher and La Rocque 1976). Lichen acids can also be leached and/or neutralized with baking soda to make rock tripe more digestible (Szczawinski and Turner 1980; see also Llano 1951).

Potential: Probably its only potential will be to remain a useful emergency food.

USNEACEAE
(Old Man's Beard Lichen Family)

Northern Perfume Lichen

Other Names: Chipewyan: *k'i tsaⁿjú* ("birch lichen"); English: spruce moss; French: *lichen d'épinette.*

Scientific Name: *Evernia mesomorpha* Nyl.

Description: A semierect or hanging shrub lichen with yellowish green, wrinkled branches.

Habitat: Commonly found growing on the bark and twigs of conifers and (to a lesser extent) deciduous trees across the boreal forest.

Medicinal Uses: A cooled decoction of the lichen harvested from birch trees can be used as eye drops to treat snow blindness (D7, D9, D29).

Properties: Several species of *Evernia* have been studied and found to contain usnic acid, depsides, ergosterol, benzenoids, phenylpropanoids, monoterpenes, sesquiterpenes, and triterpenes. Extracts have shown antibacterial activity against several different species of bacteria (Farnsworth 1999).

Potential: The traditional use is validated by science. In Europe, oak moss (*E. prunastri* (L.) Ach.) has been used for centuries to fix the fragrance of perfumes so they will last for hours instead of minutes, and as a source of dye (Johnson et al. 1995).

(R. Marles)

Old Man's Beard Lichen

Other Names: Cree: *miyapakwan, mithapakonuk.*

Scientific Name: *Usnea hirta* (L.) F.H. Wigg. and related species.

Description: A yellowish green branched (fruticose) lichen growing in thick tufts (like a beard) on the lower branches of trees. It has a central cord inside each branch, abundant short pointed projections (papillae) near the base of the main branches, and clumps of granules (soralia) for asexual reproduction near the tips.

Habitat: Old man's beard lichens are commonly found on the lower branches of conifers (e.g., white spruce, black spruce, and tamarack) throughout the circumboreal forest.

Medicinal Uses: It can be used to pack a nostril to stop a nosebleed (D19; Leighton 1985). A decoction can be used to wash sore or infected eyes (Siegfried 1994).

Technological Uses: Dry branches covered with lichens (voucher specimen Paquette D-44-94 had lichens of the genera *Usnea, Evernia, Bryoria, Ramalina, Parmelia*, etc., Spence 65 had *Hypogymnia* instead of *Parmelia*) are commonly used as kindling to start a fire (C38, D3, D6, D19, D22; Goddard 1912; Leighton 1985).

Properties: There is antiseptic activity due to the content of usnic acid and other lichen acids (Johnson et al. 1995).

Potential: There is a strong demand and immediate market potential for old man's beard lichens in the floral and craft trades (Mater Engineering 1993).

(R. Marles)

Nonvascular Plants

Mosses (division Bryophyta), liverworts (division Hepatophyta), and hornworts (division Anthocerotophyta) are referred to as nonvascular plants because they are not complex enough to require veins supported by lignin to carry water and nutrients throughout their bodies. Mosses and liverworts are common in Canada's boreal forest and wetlands, but the hornworts are not found here.

BRYOPHYTA (MOSSES)

DICRANACEAE
(Hummock Moss Family)

Cushion Moss

Other Names: Chipewyan: *nódhulé.*

Scientific Name: *Dicranum groenlandicum* Brid. and related species.

Description: A moss that grows tightly packed in hummocks. It has very long (up to 30 cm) erect stems and leaves that curve to one side.

Habitat: Common, forming fairly dry hummocks that rise above the muskeg in the subarctic tundra.

Technological Uses: Long narrow clumps can be cut out of hummocks, soaked in melted caribou fat, allowed to harden, and lit to make crude candles (D6, D9, D29, D33).

Properties: The usefulness of this moss depends on its growth habit as a very deep cushion moss with long parallel stems that absorb grease and make a good wick.

(R. Marles)

Potential: A number of mosses are in demand in the floral and craft industries for ornamental purposes and in nurseries for production of hanging baskets. Depending upon the requirements of individual buyers, fresh, air dried, or glycerin-treated mosses may be needed (Mater Engineering 1993). Mater Engineering (1993) identified a list of potential buyers for Canadian material.

HYLOCOMIACEAE, HYPNACEAE, BRACHYTHECIACEAE
(Feather Moss Families)

Feather Mosses

Other Names: Cree: *astās-kamik.*

Scientific Name: *Pleurozium schreberi* (Willd. ex Brid.) Mitt., Hylocomiaceae; *Ptilium crista-castrensis* (Hedw.) De Not., Hypnaceae; *Tomentypnum nitens* (Hedw.) Loeske, Brachytheciaceae.

Description: Mosses with feather-shaped branches and spore capsules that arise on

Hylocomium splendens (K. Baldwin)

stalks from the middle of the stem. They form extensive mats covering the ground under the boreal forest. Red-stemmed feather moss (*Pleurozium*) can be distinguished by its red stems and irregularly once-pinnate branches. Knight's plume feather moss (*Ptilium*) has beautifully regular triangular pinnate branches on green stems. Golden feather moss (*Tomentypnum*, also spelled *Tomenthypnum*) is golden green and has sharply pointed, folded leaves. Commonly found with these is stair-step feather moss (*Hylocomium splendens* (Hedw.) Schimp. in B.S.G., Hylocomiaceae), which is distinguished by its two (or more) feathery branches occurring one on top of the other to form a stairlike arrangement.

Habitat: Feather mosses can form a continuous ground cover in the boreal forest. *Pleurozium* occurs on hummock tops, *Hylocomium* below it or on smaller hummocks, *Ptilium* in the moist depressions between the hummocks, and *Tomentypnum* in hummocks in wet fen areas, often next to peat mosses.

Technological Uses: Moss can be used as a dish scrubber (D9), as stuffing for leather balls (Hall pers. comm.), and for chinking the cracks in log cabins (D6, D9, M4; Leighton 1985), and was draped over scarecrowlike arrangements of sticks placed on the barren grounds in two converging rows to funnel caribou into a pound (surround), where they could be tangled in snares and speared (Hearne 1795). For cooking, food (e.g., eggs) can be placed

Tomentypnum nitens (Hedw.) (D. Vitt)

between two thick layers (30 × 30 × 15 cm) of soaking-wet moss, and then a fire is built on top. Eggs will be cooked in 10 to 20 minutes this way (C60). Meat can be stored for several days during the summer in a "bush fridge" made by digging a pit, say, 90 × 60 cm and approximately 100 cm deep, through the moss down to the permafrost layer, putting the meat on the frozen ground, placing supporting sticks across the hole 20 to 30 cm down from the opening, and then covering them with a lid of the moss (C60, M11).

Properties: The uses described depend on the physical characteristics of the moss and are not necessarily specific taxonomically.

Potential: See previous species.

SPHAGNACEAE
(Peat Moss Family)

Peat Moss

Other Names: Chipewyan: *tthal*; Cree: *uske, muskak, askīyāh, mīkaskwahkawow, āsāskumkwa, eskiya*; French: *tourbe*.

Scientific Name: *Sphagnum fuscum* (Schimp.) Klinggr., *S. nemoreum* Scop., and other species.

Description: An upright moss growing in thick mats that has dense tufts of branches at the top, whorls around the stem, and other branches that hang down and twist around the stem. The dark spore capsules are on short stalks sprouting from the apex of the green branches, and their lids pop off on warm, dry days to release the spores.

Habitat: Common in damp woods, muskeg, and bogs throughout the circumboreal forest and parklands.

Food Uses: Moss was sometimes mixed with tobacco as an extender (C35, C36).

Medicinal Uses: Red peat moss can be applied directly to cuts or skin infections and the affected area is then bandaged (C24, C25). Green peat moss diapers can be used to treat diaper rash (Leighton 1985).

Technological Uses: Green peat moss can be cleaned of twigs, dried, and used as "environmentally friendly" disposable diapers (Chipewyan: *tth'al*

(R. Marles)

Peat moss being harvested for use in traditional diapers
(N. Tays)

dhéth) (C20, C35, C36, C44, D3, D6, D9, D28, M7, M9; Hearne 1795; Curtis 1928; Birket-Smith 1930; Munsterhjelm 1953; Oswalt 1967; Lamont 1977; Leighton 1985; Siegfried 1994). Babies in peat moss diapers never get diaper rash (D6; Siegfried 1994). Red peat moss is never used for diapers because it is believed to irritate the skin (D6, D24; Leighton 1985). Peat moss can also be used for toilet paper (M9; Siegfried 1994), sanitary napkins (M9), paper towels and baby wipes, including cleaning babies at birth (Leighton 1985), and floor scrubbers, and can be mixed with mud for chinking between the logs of a cabin (Siegfried 1994). Peat moss can be put on fires to create smoke for preserving leather or meat (D6, D9, D24).

Properties: Sphagnum moss has a long history of use as an absorbent material. It was used during both World Wars in field dressings because it absorbs 3 to 4 times as much moisture as cotton, retains and distributes this moisture better (due to its entrapment in special hollow hyaline cells), is faster to make, cooler, softer, less irritating, and has natural antiseptic properties. Sphagnol, extracted from peat moss, has been used to soothe and heal hemorrhoids and a variety of skin problems including eczema, psoriasis, and acne (Johnson et al. 1995).

Potential: Sphagnum is in great demand in the floral trade for making potting mixes and modifying soil texture (Mater Engineering 1993). It is also being used in small amounts in feminine hygiene products (Willard 1992). Mater Engineering (1993) identified a list of potential buyers for Canadian material.

Vascular Spore-Producing Plants

Vascular spore-producers include several different divisions of plants: the whisk ferns (Psilotophyta); the horsetails (Equisetophyta); the clubmosses, spikemosses, and quillworts (Lycopodiophyta); and the ferns (Polypodiophyta). Although not closely related to each other, these plants all have lignified veins and are distinguished from more complex plants by the fact that they reproduce from single-celled spores rather than seeds. Horsetails, clubmosses, spikemosses, and ferns are common in the boreal forest, and quillworts are found occasionally in ponds or lake margins. Whisk ferns are not found here.

EQUISETOPHYTA (HORSETAILS)

EQUISETACEAE
(Horsetail Family)

Horsetail

Other Names: Cree: *mistatimosoy* ("horse's tail"), *okotāwask, enskowusk* ("segmented plant"), *kiychiwiykusk* ("squeaky plant"); French: *queue de renard, prêle*; Slave: *ha^hdo^n* ("geese eat").

Scientific Name: *Equisetum arvense* L. Also *E. sylvaticum* L., *E. pratense* Ehrh.

Description: The common or field horsetail (*E. arvense*) is a perennial herb growing up to 30 cm tall from deep rhizomes, with a ridged, tough stem, each conspicuous joint (node) surrounded by an encircling leaf sheath with large brown teeth and pierced by a whorl of slender, simple green branches, and a separate unbranched fertile shoot at the top

Equisetum sylvaticum L. (R. Marles)

of which there is a spore-producing cone. The woodland horsetail (*E. sylvaticum*) differs in having reddish brown teeth on the leaf sheath and branches on both the vegetative and fertile shoots, which are themselves often further branched. The meadow horsetail (*E. pratense*) is similar to the field horsetail but is an annual-stemmed species in which the sterile stem first internode (stem between the nodes) is very short, branch leaf sheaths have only three teeth, and the fertile stems (infrequently seen) have branching toward the top at maturity.

Habitat: Fairly common in moist open woodlands. The common horsetail is found throughout the northern hemisphere, while the woodland horsetail and meadow horsetail are circumboreal (i.e., a more northerly distribution across Canada, northern USA, and Eurasia).

Medicinal Uses: Above-ground fertile horsetail shoots can be boiled and the decoction drunk as a diuretic for kidney trouble alone (C20, C47, C57; Siegfried 1994) or mixed with other plants (C10). The stems and leaves of *E. arvense* can be burned and the ashes placed on running sores (M6). The rhizomes of *E. sylvaticum* can be mixed with other plants and boiled to make a wash for skin diseases (D29). The root can be heated and placed against aching teeth to treat the pain (M6). The rhizome decoction can be drunk as a diuretic or as part of a stomachache medicine (Lamont 1977).

Technological Uses: The stems may be used as a pot scrubber (C60; Siegfried 1994).

Properties: Common horsetail greens (100 g fresh weight, 90% moisture) contain: food energy (20 kcal), protein (1.0 g), fat (0.2 g), total carbohydrate (4.4 g), crude fiber (1.1 g), riboflavin (0.07 mg), niacin (5.6 mg), vitamin C (50 mg), vitamin A (18 RE), and minerals (ash: 0.7 g), including Ca (120 mg), P (54 mg), K (116 mg), Mg (101 mg), Cu (0.1 mg), Zn (0.5 mg), Fe (2.9 mg), Mn (0.6 mg), Mo (<0.1 mg), and Cl (56.8 mg) (Kuhnlein and Turner 1991). **NOTE:** Mature horsetails are known to be toxic to livestock. They contain thiaminase, an enzyme that destroys thiamine, leading to a thiamine deficiency condition. Deposits of silica in the outer layer of the stems, which make the "scouring rushes" so effective for scrubbing pots, also make mature horsetails tough to eat and irritating to the digestive tract. Although they are a traditional food of some Canadian Aboriginal peoples, only small quantities and only young horsetails should be consumed (Kuhnlein and Turner 1991). For their use described here as a medicinal decoction, boiling probably inactivates the thiaminase. The constituents of *E. arvense* stems include water-soluble derivatives of silica, flavonoids (apigenin, luteolin, quercetin derivatives), polyunsaturated and other long-chain organic acids, and traces of alkaloids (nicotine and spermidine types). The infusion is useful as a diuretic for treatment of edema (posttraumatic and static but not from impaired heart or kidney function), bacterial and inflammatory disorders of the urinary tract, and renal gravel, without altering the electrolyte balance when used appropriately (Bisset and Wichtl 1994). There is evidence that *E. arvense* also has antibiotic properties (Dobelis 1986). Correct identification of the horsetails is important because *E. palustre* L. is toxic due to a higher content of the alkaloid palustrine (Bradley 1992), which is also present in *E. arvense* and *E. sylvaticum* (Harborne and Baxter 1993).

Potential: Some of the traditional uses (mainly its diuretic effect) are substantiated by scientific evidence. It propagates readily from the rhizomes, so it has potential for agricultural production if a market can be secured, but given the toxicity of horsetails, especially if used improperly or misidentified, it is likely the market will remain restricted to experienced herbalists. The essential oil is in demand for aromatherapy (Rogers 1997). The market demand for horsetail is not just as a medicinal, however, but as a decorative plant for the fresh and dried floral markets. Mater Engineering (1993) categorizes horsetail as a Priority Level 3 product for further development and describes the market in some detail. Barl et al. (1996) provide some information on horsetail products currently available in Canada.

LYCOPODIOPHYTA
(CLUBMOSSES, SPIKEMOSSES, QUILLWORTS)

LYCOPODIACEAE
(Clubmoss Family)

Clubmoss

Other Names: English: ground pine; French: *petits pins*; Slave: *mbedzīti*[h] ("caribou horns").

Scientific Name: *Lycopodium annotinum* L. (stiff clubmoss). Also *L. obscurum* L. (ground pine).

Description: A perennial trailing herb with roots coming from the underside of the creeping stems, erect stems forking once or twice, tiny narrowly triangular leaves that are short, stiff, sharply pointed, single-veined, and tightly overlapping, and a narrowly cylindrical pale brown cone at the end of the branch producing yellow spores from little sacks in the axils of the modified leaves. Ground pine differs from stiff clubmoss by having creeping stems underground and erect stems much more branched.

Habitat: Found occasionally in moist woods, often among mosses, which the leafy stems superficially resemble (true mosses do not have roots or cones), with a circumboreal distribution including most of Canada and, in the USA, Alaska, the western mountains, and the northern and eastern states.

Lycopodium obscurum L. (R. Marles)

76

Technological Uses: Raw fish eggs can be separated from the membranes by wringing the egg mass in a handful of clubmoss (Leighton 1985). When no wood is available, clubmoss can be used to make a fire, as can mountain heather (*Cassiope tetragona* (L.) D. Don, Ericaceae) (Lamont 1977).

Properties: The traditional uses described depend on physical properties of the moss. In fire-making, the oil-rich spores are extremely flammable and were once used as flash powder for photography and theatrical special effects (Dobelis 1986).

Lycopodium annotinum L. (R. Marles)

Potential: Although used in European folk medicine as a diuretic, its alkaloid content makes clubmoss toxic (Bisset and Wichtl 1994). There is some potential for growing ground pine as an ornamental. In the floral trade, there is a strong demand and immediate market potential for ground pine, clubmoss, and ground cedar (*L. complanatum* L.), which can be specially processed and dyed, then used to produce value-added products such as wreaths. Mater Engineering (1993) identified a list of potential buyers for Canadian material for these decorative purposes, and mentions the possibility of there being a pharmaceutical market (unspecified).

POLYPODIOPHYTA (FERNS)

DRYOPTERIDACEAE
(Shield Fern Family)

Spiny Wood Fern

Other Names: Chipewyan: *ts'ëli dhér, niteli ts'u choghé* ("muskeg white spruce"); Cree: *ku(h)kuguwpuk* ("raven's beak"); English: spinulose shield fern; Slave: *eya ha dala*.

Scientific Name: *Dryopteris carthusiana* (Vill.) H.P. Fuchs, common synonyms: *D. spinulosa* (O.F. Muell.) Watt, *D. austriaca* (Jacq.) Woynar ex Schinz & Thellung var. *spinulosa* (O.F. Muell.) Fisch. Also *D. expansa* (K. Presl) Fraser-Jenkins & Jermy, common synonyms: *D. assimilis* S. Walker, *D. s.* var. *dilatata* (Hoffm.) A. Gray.

Dryopteris carthusiana (Vill.) H.P. Fuchs
(R. Marles)

Description: A fern growing from a thick rhizome, with fronds divided pinnately three or more times and ending in pointy segments. The spore capsule clusters (sori) are located on the underside of the fronds and are covered by a kidney-shaped tissue (indusium) when young. The narrow spiny wood fern (*D. carthusiana*) has narrower lance-shaped and bipinnate-pinnatifid (divided three times) fronds, while the broad spiny wood fern (*D. expansa*) has triangular fronds up to 40 cm wide with finer divisions (tripinnate-pinnatifid).

Habitat: Common in moist woods, thickets, and swamps, with a circumboreal distribution including all of Canada and northern and eastern USA. The broad spiny wood fern extends farther south into California and not as far into eastern USA.

Food Uses: The fiddleheads (curled shoots) are part of a compound decoction that can be taken as an appetite stimulant (Siegfried 1994).

Medicinal Uses: The frond stipe bases can be boiled with other plants to make a decoction drunk for pain in the kidneys (D3, D22), in a different mix as a wash for skin diseases (D29), or as part of a treatment for cancer (Siegfried 1994), and can be smoked with other plants to treat "insanity" (D23).

Properties: *Dryopteris* rhizome infusions contain an oleoresin that paralyzes intestinal worms, which can then be expelled from the body by using a saline laxative (Dobelis 1986). The oleoresin's bioactivity is due mainly to its phloroglucinols including albaspidin, filixic acids, aspidin, filmarone (the most active agent against intestinal worms), and numerous other components; tannins are also present. In excessive doses it will act as an irritant poison affecting the gastrointestinal tract, muscles, and eyes, and could even cause convulsions and cardiac or respiratory failure (Duke 1985).

Potential: There are a number of interesting pharmacologically active compounds in this attractive fern. It should be investigated further.

Ostrich Fern

Other Names: Chipewyan: *nítéli ts'u choghé* ("dry muskeg white spruce"); English: fiddlehead fern; French: *fougère-à-l'autruche*; Slave: *eya ha dala*.

Scientific Name: *Matteuccia struthiopteris* (L.) Todaro.

Description: A large fern with deeply lobed once-pinnate sterile green fronds and spore-producing brown fronds that are distinctly different, with simple pinnate divisions whose edges are rolled over the clusters of spore capsules.

Habitat: Fairly common in damp woods and river margins across Canada, northern USA, and Eurasia.

Medicinal Uses: The base of the green fern frond can be boiled with other herbs to make a decoction

(R. Marles)

drunk four times a day or chewed with other plants every 2 hours to slow a pounding heart. It can also be used to treat stomach pain (D22, D23) or back pain, and to speed expulsion of the afterbirth (Leighton 1985). The stipe buds on the rhizome can be used in a medicine for treating cancer and to help the patient gain weight (M9).

Properties: Ostrich fern contains a complex mixture of flavonoids, some phenylpropanoids, and the stilbene pinosylvin. The rhizome has been shown to have blood-sugar-lowering and anti-polio-virus activities (Farnsworth 1999). Pinosylvin has antibacterial and antifungal activities (Harborne and Baxter 1993).

Potential: The fiddleheads are available as a frozen vegetable in grocery stores. The medicinal properties of the stipe base and rhizome might be worth further investigation.

POLYPODIACEAE
(Polypody Fern Family)

Rock Polypody Fern

Other Names: Cree: *kākā-kīwīkoc, kāthīthīkipakākī, kinī-pikōtīthanīwīpak*; English: rock tripe fern; French: *fougère tripe-de-roche*.

Scientific Name: *Polypodium virginianum* L., common synonym: *P. vulgare* L. var. *virginianum* (L.) D.C. Eaton.

Description: A fern growing from stout rhizomes that are covered with fibrous scales,

(R. Marles)

with fronds up to 35 cm long, having a stipe of 5-15 cm and a blade that is oblong with up to 20 pairs of divisions (pinnae) that are alternate to almost opposite, the clefts not quite reaching the middle of the frond, and on the undersurface near the edges, tiny round clusters (sori) of spore capsules (sporangia) that are not covered by a protective flap of tissue (indusium) but do have some microscopic sterile filaments (paraphyses) among the spore capsules.

Habitat: Common on moist rock outcrops in open forests, usually of pine, from northern British Columbia and western Yukon to the Maritimes, and south through eastern USA, and in eastern Asia.

Medicinal Uses: The leaf decoction can be drunk to treat tuberculosis (Leighton 1985).

Properties: The rhizome infusion has been proven to relieve coughs (Dobelis 1986).

Potential: Other species of polypody fern are grown as ornamentals. The medicinal potential is probably not very significant.

Gymnosperms

Gymnosperms include our common conifer trees and shrubs (division Pinophyta), the ginkgo tree (division Ginkgophyta), cycads (division Cycadophyta), and ephedra (division Gnetophyta). In northern Canada we have only the Pinophyta. Gymnosperms do not have flowers or fruit, but produce their seeds on specially modified leaves that are usually clustered together into cones (e.g., the typical pine cone).

PINOPHYTA (CONIFERS)

CUPRESSACEAE
(Cypress Family)

Common Juniper

Other Names: Chipe-wyan: *datsánjíé*; Cree: *kahkakew-mina, kahka-kewatik* ("raven tree"), *ahaseminanatik, kaka-kīmīniatik* ("crow berry tree"), *kākākīmīnātik, kākākīwīmināhtik, mā-sakiys*; English: low or ground juniper; French: *genève, buis*; Slave: *mbethiⁿ zīele, mbethiⁿ dzhī* ("owl berries").

(R. Marles)

Scientific Name: *Juniperus communis* L.

Description: A shrub up to 1.5 m high with stiff, narrow, awl-shaped leaves that are deeply grooved and white on the upper surface, dark green below, with bluish berrylike cones borne along the branches at the base of the leaves.

Habitat: Common on light rocky or sandy soil in open woods and on hillsides across central and northern North America, Greenland, Iceland, and Eurasia.

Food Uses: The blue berrylike cones can be eaten or used to flavor home brew (Lamont 1977).

Medicinal Uses: The berrylike cones, when still green, can be boiled to make a diuretic remedy for kidney trouble (M6; Strath 1903; Welsh, cited in Leighton 1985), but mature ones must not be eaten or they will cause severe indigestion (M6). They can be smoked in a pipe to treat asthma (M6; Welsh, cited in Leighton 1985). One berrylike cone can be eaten as a cure-all medicine (D29, D33). The inner bark can be softened in water and used to poultice wounds, and the debarked stems can be used to make a tea to treat diarrhea (M6; Leighton 1985) or a sore chest associated with a lung infection

(Leighton 1985). The bark can be mixed with another plant and soaked in warm water but not boiled, then the infusion can be drunk lukewarm to treat aches and pains (C23, C27). The branches are part of a compound decoction for "women's troubles," postpartum sickness, infants' teething sickness, fevers, or coughs (Leighton 1985). The roots can be boiled with other plants to make a decoction drunk to treat menstrual cramps (D23), kidney stones, or inflammation of the kidneys or bladder (Strath 1903). The dried, powdered leaves can be used to treat psoriasis and eczema (Strath 1903). It is part of a confidential compound medicine for treating cancer (Siegfried 1994).

Technological Uses: The berrylike cones can be used to make a brown dye (M6).

Properties: Juniper leaves contain a number of nutrients, including (per 100 g fresh weight): protein (12.8 g), vitamin C (167 mg), Ca (500 mg), P (260 mg), K (1150 mg), Mg (180 mg), Cu (2.4), Fe (22 mg), and Mn (5.2 mg). The shoots of *J. virginiana* L. contain (per 100 g fresh weight, 90% moisture): protein (0.9 g), fat (1.5 g), total carbohydrate (7.3 g), crude fiber (3.0 g), and minerals (ash: 0.3 g), including Ca (147 mg), P (23 mg), Na (5 mg), K (75 mg), Mg (24.5 mg), Cu (0.1 mg), Zn (3.1 mg), Fe (2.9 mg), and Mn (5.0 mg) (Kuhnlein and Turner 1991). Juniper "berry" essential oil has more than 70 known constituents, primarily monoterpenes. Catechol tannins and flavonoids including leucoanthocyanidins are also present. The decoction's action as a diuretic is due primarily to its content of terpinen-4-ol (Duke 1985). It also has urinary antiseptic properties, but some of the terpenes irritate the kidneys, so this use is not considered safe, particularly where there are inflammatory kidney disorders or during pregnancy due to the possibility of stimulating uterine contractions. Avoiding these contraindications, and when used in low doses in combination with other herbs, it may be helpful in treating kidney and bladder problems. The wood of juniper contains diterpenes, gallocatechin tannins, and lignans, and so will have some astringency, but there is no professional use (Bisset and Wichtl 1994).

Potential: The proven diuretic and smooth-muscle-contracting effects of juniper "berry" extracts substantiate some of the traditional uses, but the risk of kidney damage and danger to pregnant women suggests this is not a herb to be used casually, but only by experts. Juniper "berries" are also famous as a flavoring for gin and other foods and as a fragrance component of many cosmetics (Duke 1985). The essential oil is in demand for aromatherapy (Rogers 1997).

Creeping Juniper

Other Names: Cree: *ahaseminanatik, napakasehtak, masekesk, masikeskatik;* French: *savanier.*

Scientific Name: *Juniperus horizontalis* Moench.

Description: A prostrate shrub with long, twisted stems up to 5 m long, mature branches bearing short, scalelike, overlapping leaves on narrow branchlets, although some young branches may have awl-shaped leaves. The dark blue berrylike cones are found at the ends of the branches.

Habitat: Very common on dry banks or prairie and rocky or sandy hillsides where it forms large mats. It is distributed from Alaska and central British Columbia east across Canada and south across northern USA.

Medicinal Uses: The leafy stems can be boiled with other herbs to make a tea for treating colds and teething babies, and for use as a general "system cleanser" (C13). The leaves can be burned and the smoke inhaled to clear sinuses plugged by a head cold. The leaves can also be burned as an incense in the home and as a smudge with sweet-grass (*Hierochloe odorata* (L.) Beauv., Poaceae) during ceremonies (M6).

Properties: See *Juniperus communis* for details.

Potential: This shrub is a very effective and attractive ground cover. It is not likely to have economic medicinal uses.

(R. Marles)

White Cedar

Other Names: Cree: *mascakēs, masīkīsk, māsikīskāsiht*; English: arborvitae; French: *cèdre, balai.*

Scientific Name: *Thuja occidentalis* L.

Description: A tree up to 20 m tall, with widely spreading branches whose branchlets form a flattened spray. The leaves are scalelike, tight to the surface of the branchlet, with a keel along their length and a yellow aromatic resin gland near the tip, and the woody egg-shaped seed cones are about 10 mm long.

Habitat: Found in moist woods, swamps, and calcareous rocky banks of the southeastern coniferous forest, distributed from Manitoba (recently extending into Saskatchewan) to the Maritimes and northeastern USA.

Medicinal Uses: The crushed leaves can be mixed with other herbs and boiled to make a decoction used as a wash and drink to treat a "twisted face" caused by a stroke (C10), or drunk to treat a sore bladder, urine retention problems, or pneumonia (Leighton 1985). The powdered leaves can be mixed with other ground plants and water to make a paste used as a poultice to treat a "twisted face" caused by "bad medicine" (similar in appearance to the effects of a stroke but not involving paralysis of the tongue and

(R. Marles)

not treatable by modern medicine) for which it can be applied to the unaffected side of the face to "draw the face back to normal" (C20, C33). It can also be part of a compound medicinal poultice for treating pain (C54).

Properties: White cedar volatile oil contains the monoterpenes: alpha-thujone (39-56%), fenchone (6-15%), beta-thujone (7-11%), sabinene (2-9%), and smaller amounts of beyerene, bornyl acetate, camphor, borneol, and more than 30 other related compounds (Hetherington and Steck 1997; Farnsworth 1999). There are also at least 14 different sesquiterpenes and at least 10 diterpenes. The leaves also contain several lignans and flavonoids. The volatile oil has demonstrated activity against amoebas and other parasites, bacteria, fungi, and viruses, and laboratory results suggest possible anticancer activity (Farnsworth 1999). Thujone is known to be toxic, although its poor water solubility means there would be relatively little in traditional preparations (Bisset and Wichtl 1994). The leaves contain vitamin C (Kuhnlein and Turner 1991).

Potential: There is an excellent market for cedar volatile oil, and its constituents may have medicinal uses; but care should be taken to minimize the content of thujone in products intended for consumption. The white cedar's range is being extended westward from its original distribution due to cultivation as an ornamental (Harms pers. comm.).

PINACEAE
(Pine Family)

Balsam Fir

Other Names: Chipewyan: *ts'u reki*; Cree: *pikew-ahtik, nupukasik, pīkowāhtik* ("gum tree"), *napakāsīt* ("flat branch"), *nāpukasītuk, nāpukasī*; French: *sapin baumier*; Slave: *tsutsi*.

Scientific Name: *Abies balsamea* (L.) P. Mill. Also *A. lasiocarpa* (Hook.) Nutt. (alpine fir).

Description: Balsam fir is a tall conifer with smooth gray bark covered with pitch blisters. The branches appear flat because the flat, slightly notched needles, which are shiny green above and whitish beneath, appear to grow in two rows. The large, cylindrical, erect, dark purple cones do not drop off the tree whole, but the scales fall off leaving the core attached to the tree. Alpine fir

Abies balsamea (L.) P. Mill.
(R. Marles)

differs in having thicker bark that fissures with age rather than being scaly as in balsam fir, the needles on the lower branches are not flatly two-ranked but are turned forward and upward, the pollen cones are blue-violet rather than yellow-red, and on the seed cones the scales are much wider (2.5 cm versus 1.5 cm) and about three times longer than the long-pointed bracts.

Habitat: Balsam fir is common in moist woods, often mixed with white spruce and poplar, throughout the boreal forest from Alberta east to Newfoundland and south to central USA. Alpine fir hybridizes with balsam fir in the northwestern boreal forest, but is common at low altitudes in Alaska, Yukon, southwestern Northwest Territories, and northern British Columbia, and at higher altitudes in the subalpine forests of British Columbia and western USA.

Medicinal Uses: Balsam fir inner bark may be boiled and drunk as a general tonic for the treatment of colds, influenza, etc. (C6, C8, C13, C60, D14, D24, D26, M1). The sap may be collected and boiled to make a cure-all drink (D14) or the steam can be inhaled to treat asthma (C13). Dried bark with pitch blisters can be ground and mixed with lard to make a poultice for infected wounds, such as an ingrown toenail (C57, C58), or for arthritis (C47,

C57). Dried bark with pitch blisters may also be grated with other plants and the resulting powder mixed with water to make a paste applied to infections with surrounding tender swelling, including boils (C1, C2, C3, C54). The bark can also be part of a compound medicine applied topically for pain relief (C54), and in another compound preparation drunk after childbirth (C58). The root decoction can be good for chest colds (C23, C27), aches and pains (C42), and backaches (C39), and as an emetic (C35, C36, C39, C42). To treat tuberculosis the roots can be dried and boiled with another plant to make 4-5 cups of decoction, which can be stored in the refrigerator, roots and all. A person taking this medicine for the first time will throw up and the color will be black if the person is really sick. The decoction can be drunk for 4 days, during which time no caffeinated beverages or other medicines should be taken as they would interfere with the effectiveness of this medicine. After 4 days the patient should stop taking it for 7 days, and only then resume taking it. To successfully treat TB the person must continue taking the medicine for 3 months (C39). The Woods Cree of Saskatchewan also drink the bark infusion to treat tuberculosis and coughs due to colds, and they use the pitch in a remedy for menstrual irregularity and with grease as an ointment for cuts, scabies, boils, and other skin problems (Leighton 1985; Welsh, cited in Leighton 1985). Alpine fir resin can be used as a poultice to treat a sore back or applied to the stomach to treat internal bleeding from an injury (Lamont 1977).

Technological Uses: The wood can be used for canoe frames (Birket-Smith 1930) and canoe paddles. It dries easily (C42; Leighton 1985). The boughs can be used to make temporary shelters (Leighton 1985). The needles can be used to get a fire going quickly (Lamont 1977).

Properties: The essential oil contains beta-pinene, bornyl acetate, 3-carene, limonene, and a number of other terpenoids; other parts contain lasiocarpenone and the insect juvenile hormone analogues juvabiol, juvabione, and derivatives (Hetherington and Steck 1997). It has been used as an antiseptic (Foster and Duke 1990).

Potential: Although there is no current therapeutic use, there is a strong demand for balsam fir boughs, wood, resin, and bark for essential oil extraction. It is used to produce an "absolute" for perfumes and is an aromatic and antiseptic ingredient in soaps, cosmetics, flavorings, floor polishes, and disinfectants (Mater Engineering 1993). Balsam fir wood is too soft and perishable to make good lumber, so its primary use is for pulp. The resin has been used as a source of turpentine and as an adhesive for microscope slides and optical lenses (Canada balsam) (Dobelis 1986). Balsam firs are also grown as Christmas trees (Johnson et al. 1995).

Tamarack

Other Names: Chipewyan: *nídhe, nithe*; Cree: *wakinakum, wakinakun, wakinākin* ("bends easily"), *wāginagun*; English: larch; French: *épinette rouge*; Slave: *nduthe.*

Scientific Name: *Larix laricina* (Du Roi) K. Koch.

Description: A slender conifer with flaky reddish brown bark and clusters of 10-20 thin, pale green needle-shaped leaves on short spurs on the main branches. This is our only deciduous conifer: the leaves turn golden in autumn and then drop off.

Habitat: Common in bogs, muskeg, and marshy woods across Canada, Alaska, and northeastern USA.

Medicinal Uses: The inner bark is a common poultice for burns (D9, D28, D32), boils (D6), frostbite (C29; Leighton 1985), hemorrhoids, infected wounds (C29, C62, M9; Welsh, cited in Leighton 1985), or cuts (C44; Leighton 1985). An inner-bark tea can be used as an eyewash or for ear irrigation (C29) or as a wash for wounds (Leighton 1985), or drunk to treat depression (C29) or with another plant to treat heart ailments (Siegfried 1994). The gum can be chewed to relieve indigestion (C29). The outer bark and roots can be

(R. Marles)

boiled twice (boiled until concentrated, then more water is added and it is boiled again) with another plant and then the decoction can be drunk daily to treat arthritis, aches and pains, or colds (C23, C27, C44). The fresh root decoction can be used on cuts to aid healing (Lamont 1977).

Technological Uses: The wood is commonly used to make toboggans (Chipewyan: *beth chëné* = "load stick") (C29, D6, D32; Hearne 1795; Mackenzie 1801; Ross 1862; Morice 1910; Birket-Smith 1930; Leighton 1985). It may also be used as a substitute for birch wood in the construction of snowshoe frames (Birket-Smith 1930), drum frames (D13) and canoe paddles (D3). The roots can be peeled, split, and used to stitch birch bark canoes although spruce roots are more commonly used for this purpose (Birket-Smith 1930; Adney and Chapelle 1964). Larch twigs or roots could be sewn onto a birch bark bottom to make a coiled type of basket (Birket-Smith 1930). The rotted wood can be burned to smoke fish (D3, D6) and hides (Irimoto 1981; Leighton 1985). The bark may also be burned to smoke hides (C29).

Properties: Hetherington and Steck (1997) summarize much of the work on volatile oils of tamarack. Bornyl acetate is an expectorant and other terpenoids have antiseptic activity (Harborne and Baxter 1993).

Potential: There is some interest in looking at tamarack as a source for an essential oil. The cones are also in demand as decorative items (Mater Engineering 1993).

White Spruce

Other Names: Chipewyan: *ts'u chogh* ("big spruce"); Cree: *wapiskimnahik, eyinatik, minuhik, mīnahik, sī(h)ta*; French: *épinette blanche*; Slave: *tsu*.

Scientific Name: *Picea glauca* (Moench) Voss.

Description: White spruce is a large, shapely conifer with stiff sharp needles, pale smooth young twigs, and pale brown cylindrical seed cones 5 cm long with smooth-edged scales.

Habitat: A common tree of dry, rich soils in the coniferous forests of Canada and northern USA.

(R. Marles)

Food Uses: Spruce pitch (Chipewyan: *dzé*; Cree: *mīnahikopikēw*) is occasionally chewed as a confection (C1, C2, C3, C4, C6, C8, C13, C20, D24, D26, M6; Ross 1862; Lamont 1977; Jarvenpa 1979; Leighton 1985; Siegfried 1994). Spruce cambium can be scraped off the tree and eaten as an emergency food (D26). The wood may be burned to smoke meat (M8).

Medicinal Uses: The inner bark can be used as a poultice or boiled to make a wash for decayed teeth, skin sores, and burns (sometimes mixed with caribou grease) (D6). The pitch alone or most commonly mixed with rendered fat from a bear, otter, or beaver, or lard or petroleum jelly, can be applied as a salve for skin infections, cuts, rashes, burns, persistent sores, and chapped or cracked skin (C1, C2, C3, C4, C6, C13, C20, D3, D6, D9, D14, D26, D29, D32, D33, M6; Jarvenpa pers. comm.; Smith GW 1973; Leighton 1985). The pitch may be wrapped in a cloth and used as a compress to draw the infection out of sores (Siegfried 1994). The pitch may be chewed and the juice swallowed to treat a sore throat (M6). A decoction of the small branches together with the pitch can be drunk to treat colds or influenza (Siegfried 1994). Rotted spruce wood can be ground to make baby powder and a treatment for rashes, and the inner bark was part of a compound decoction for treating arthritis (Leighton 1985).

Technological Uses: White spruce wood is commonly used for canoe (Chipewyan: *ts'i*) frames and paddles (C17, D3, D5, D6, D9, D29, M6; Ross 1862; Adney and Chapelle 1964; Oswalt 1966; Lamont 1977; Leighton 1985;

Siegfried 1994), arrow (Chipewyan: *k'á*) shafts (Curtis 1928), fish net floats (Chipewyan: *et'áídzéré*) (C17, M6; Leighton 1985), basket (Chipewyan: *t'íli*) frames (Leighton 1985), snowshoe (Chipewyan: *ay*) frames (M6; Petitot 1868; Lamont 1977; Siegfried 1994), and bowls (Chipewyan: *tth'áí tsóghaze*) (Leighton 1985). The branches can be used to make lean-to shelters (Chipewyan: *darétthel*), caribou-hide tepee (Chipewyan: *nibáli*) poles, wind-breaks (Chipewyan: *ónuré^{n}tthel*), tent-base wind barriers (Chipewyan: *tthí'ali elé*), carpets (Chipewyan: *elnídela*), caches, meat drying racks (Chipewyan: *dzi^{n}lhtí^{n}*) (C8, C51, D3, D6, D9, D11, D26, D33, M3, M4, M11; Goddard 1912; Curtis 1928), and hide stretchers (Chipewyan: *edhé dechëné*) (C51, M6; Leighton 1985).

The fresh roots can be peeled, split, soaked in water if not fresh, and used to stitch birch bark canoes (C60, D5, D6, D29, M6; Ross 1862; Waugh 1919; Breynat 1948; Adney and Chapelle 1964; Li 1964; Lamont 1977; Leighton 1985; Siegfried 1994) and for both the stitching and reinforcement of seams and edges of birch bark baskets (C60, D17, M6; Mason 1913; Lamont 1977; Leighton 1985; Siegfried 1994). The roots can also be used to make coiled sewing baskets (Chipewyan: *ha^{n}i^{n} teli*) (D29; Hall pers. comm.; Mason 1913; Curtis 1928; Idiens 1979).

Melted spruce pitch is used to seal the joints in birch bark canoes (D5, D11, D24, D29, M6; Ross 1862; Li 1964; Lamont 1977; Leighton 1985; Siegfried 1994) and baskets (D17), to stick together the strands of willow bark twine, and to waterproof rawhide ropes and twine (D23). The boiled pitch was mixed with lard or moose fat to make a less brittle sealant (Siegfried 1994).

Spruce bark is also used to make canoes (Ross 1862; Curtis 1928; Adney and Chapelle 1964; Lamont 1977), mats or tent flooring (Lamont 1977; Leighton 1985; Siegfried 1994), and shingles (Ross 1862; Blanchet 1928; Leighton 1985; Siegfried 1994). See also the technological uses of black spruce.

Properties: Norway spruce needles (*P. abies* (L.) Karst., 100 g fresh weight, 58% moisture) contain: protein (4.7 g), vitamin C (174 mg), and minerals (ash: 1.8 g), including Ca (289 mg), P (85 mg), K (313 mg), and Fe (10.8 mg) (Kuhnlein and Turner 1991).

Potential: There is some demand, with potential for expansion, for white spruce boughs, wood, resin, and bark for essential oil extraction. It can be used to produce an "absolute" for perfumes and as an aromatic and anti-septic ingredient in soaps, cosmetics, flavorings, floor polishes, and dis-infectants. The cones are also in demand as decorative items (Mater Engineering 1993).

Black Spruce

Other Names: Chipewyan: *el* ("branch"); Cree: *ithinā(h)tik, minahik, setakwunatik, pekewatik, mīthawapakōnuk, mistikōpikī* ("spruce gum"); French: *épinette noire*; Slave: *tsua^h*.

Scientific Name: *Picea mariana* (P. Mill.) B.S.P.

Description: Black spruce characteristically is more slender than white spruce, with a top tuft of branches, stiff but more blunt needles from darker, finely hairy twigs, and purplish to gray-brown egg-shaped seed cones 2-3 cm long with rough-edged scales.

Habitat: Common on acidic muskeg and water-saturated soils, and on drier sites at higher latitudes or altitudes, in the coniferous forests of Canada, Alaska, and northeastern USA.

Food Uses: Black spruce pitch is chewed as a confection (C39, C44, C52, D24; Ross 1862; Jarvenpa 1979; Leighton 1985). See also white spruce.

(R. Marles)

Medicinal Uses: The pitch is used like white spruce pitch. Spruce gum can be chewed for endurance while running; one will not get short of breath and it can be good for the heart (C23, C27). When the spruce gum is white it can be used to treat infected wounds or prevent cuts from becoming infected. The gum can be scraped off the tree, cleaned, chewed to soften it, soaked in hot water, then applied to infected wounds (C23, C27, C35, C36, C39, C42, C52). Chewed spruce gum can be applied to a sore ear to draw out the infection (C35, C36). A warm spruce gum decoction may also be drunk to clean out the stomach (C39, C52) or to treat a stomachache (C52). Spruce gum can be boiled, sometimes with spruce cones, together with water and lard, until the mixture turns pink, then cooled to make an ointment (Cree: *pīkīmin*) used to draw the infection out of cysts (C38) or to treat infected wounds (C44), rashes (C23, C27, C35, C36, C44), scabs on the head (C35, C36), or chicken pox (C23, C27). The tip or bud of the young spruce branch (Cree: *wanuskōgunasask, wanuskōgūnaskōsk, wanuskohgunus, wānusōgōnusōsuk*) can be peeled and eaten so one will not get short of breath while running (C23, C27) or held in the mouth to treat heart problems (C24, C25, C44) or high blood pressure (C44). For treating someone with heart problems and shortness of breath it can also be boiled and then eaten (C38). The branches can be boiled with another plant and the decoction can be used as eye drops to treat sore eyes (C24, C25). Spruce boughs (Chipewyan: *el tthú*, Cree: *sītuk*) can be burned outside the home to chase away mosquitoes (C38). To clean an infection, soak the area in water, then sharpen a spruce branch like a needle (Cree: *wasgōnatīgon, waskunatīkwān*) and use it to lance the infection, draw out the infection, and then apply spruce gum to the wound and bandage it (C23, C27). The young cones (Chipewyan: *najuli, na*ⁿ*júlé*) can be boiled to make a mouth wash for mouth infections, toothache or sore throat, or to clear phlegm from the throat (D6, D29, M6; Jarvenpa pers. comm.; Leighton 1985), or the decoction can be drunk to treat diarrhea (M6; Leighton 1985), "sore heart" (heartburn? Lamont 1977), or as part of a remedy for venereal disease (Leighton 1985), or the cones may be chewed to treat a toothache or sore mouth (Leighton 1985). Dried rotted spruce wood (Chipewyan: *echi*ⁿ*jëré*; Cree: *thoskichitakwah*) can be ground finely and used as a soothing and deodorant baby powder (D6, D9, D29, D30). Charcoal could also be used as a baby powder (D9, D29, D30).

Technological Uses: Spruce is used in many ways by trappers. Logs are used to make sampson-post type deadfall traps (Chipewyan: *dachét'a*ⁿ) for mink, marten, or wolverine (D25; Cooper 1938). Spruce saplings are often bent to make a spring-pole snare (Chipewyan: *xuíé*), placed in the fork of

Cree elder gathering spruce pitch (N. Tays)

another tree as a lever for a toss-pole snare (Chipewyan: *dalhá^{n}t'a^n*), or tied to a noose set in a fence across an animal trail as a dragging-pole snare (Chipewyan: *bí^{n}lh*) for porcupines, hares, beaver, or lynx (D3, D25; Mackenzie 1801). Squirrel poles are made by cutting a spruce log 180 cm long and attaching a noose every 10-30 cm along it, then leaning this pole against a tree frequented by squirrels (M3, M4, M11). Beaver poles with snares are cut longer and stuck through the ice on a beaver pond into a beaver run or near the entrance to a lodge (M3, M4, M11). The pitch can be rubbed on rawhide (French: *babiche*) snare nooses to preserve them (D23). The branches are also boiled and the water used to wash the scent of humans from steel traps (Chipewyan: *i^{n}lhdzúsé*) (D6, D9; Munsterhjelm 1953). Spruce wood can be used to make hide cleaning and stretching frames and boards (Chipewyan: *dhédh chëné*) (D33; Hall pers. comm.). Rotted wood can be burned to smoke hides (C24, C25, C57, M6, M8; Goddard 1912; Leighton 1985) and dye hides (Leighton 1985). The young cones can be boiled to make a reddish dye for fishnets (D6; Lamont 1977; Siegfried 1994, referring to white spruce cones) or quills (Lamont 1977). Spruce saplings are stuck in the snow in the middle of clearings or frozen ponds and then traps are hidden around them to catch wolves that come to urinate on the "trees" as territorial markers or other animals that come to them in search of shelter or food (D6).

Black spruce saplings have been used for the frame and ribs of spruce bark canoes (Lamont 1977). Logs and boughs are used to build shelters such as tent or tepee frames and lean-tos (D9, D23; Lamont 1977; Leighton 1985). Meat drying racks are made from four green (so they will not burn) spruce poles tied into a pyramid that supports crossbars of dry (so they will not taint the meat) spruce poles (D3, D6, D33, M6; Mackenzie 1801). Snowshoe frames may be made of black spruce wood (M6). Spruce boughs are used to make carpets (D3; Lamont 1977; Leighton 1985). Part of a spruce tree (Cree: *piskowōhkskrut*) was used long ago to make dolls for little girls. A face was painted on the round part (C34). The roots (Cree: *watubīah*) were used to make baskets for storing berries or dried meat (C24, C25). Fishnets have been made of spruce roots (Hrapko pers. comm.). Other uses of the branches, wood, roots, and pitch may be the same as for white spruce.

Black spruce killed by forest fires but still standing are one of the main sources of firewood for many northern communities (D24; Irimoto 1981). The small dead branches at the base of the tree (Chipewyan: *detthî*[n]), covered with lichens, are an important source of kindling for fire-making (D3, D6, D19, D22; Goddard 1912). Charcoal was used for tattooing (Isham 1743; Graham 1775).

Properties: Black spruce needles (100 g fresh weight, 49% moisture) contain: protein (2.5 g), total carbohydrate (11.8 g), and vitamin C (120 mg) (Kuhnlein and Turner 1991). Spruce needles, buds, bark, and resin, which are generally waste products of the lumber industry, are excellent sources of volatile oils having antibacterial (especially antimycobacterial), antifungal, and antiviral activities. Major constituents include the monoterpenes: alpha-pinene, betapinene, limonene, myrcene, camphor, camphene, 3-carene, cadinene, borneol, bornyl acetate, 1,8-cineole, beta-phellandrene, sabinene, santene, alphaterpineol, terpinen-4-ol, terpinolene, and tricyclene (Duke 1992b; Hetherington and Steck 1997; Farnsworth 1999). White spruce and black spruce volatile oils differ primarily in the relative amounts of the monoterpenes; there are no major qualitative differences. Several alkaloids are also found in the leaves of both species, including ethanolamine, dihydroepipinidine, and pinidinol (Farnsworth 1999).

Potential: There is some demand, with potential for expansion, for black spruce boughs, wood, resin, and bark for essential oil extraction. The oil can be used to produce an "absolute" for perfumes and as an aromatic and antiseptic ingredient in soaps, cosmetics, flavorings, floor polishes, and disinfectants. The cones are also in demand as decorative items (Mater Engineering 1993). The essential oil is in demand for aromatherapy (Rogers 1997). The strong activity of spruce volatile oil against the mycobacterium that causes tuberculosis suggests a potential for new drug and antiseptic product development.

Jack Pine

Other Names: Chipewyan: *gane, gani*; Cree: *ōskāhtak, oskatik*; French: *pin gris*; Slave: *koheʰ*.

Scientific Name: *Pinus banksiana* Lamb. Also *P. contorta* Dougl. ex Loud. var. *latifolia* Engelm. (lodgepole pine).

Description: Jack pine is a coniferous tree with thin reddish brown bark, needles 2-5 cm long in bundles of two but twisting and spreading. The seed cones are generally in pairs, curved and usually pointing toward the tip of the branch, with knobby but not prickly scales. Lodgepole pine intergrades with jack pine in the northwest boreal forest where their ranges overlap (e.g., central Alberta), but normally can

Pinus banksiana Lamb. (R. Marles)

be distinguished by its longer needles (3-6 cm), not usually twisted and spreading, seed cones less curved and spreading at right angles to the branches or more commonly bending back and down, and cone scales with a small curved prickle.

Habitat: Jack pine is abundant on sandy or rocky soils throughout the boreal forest east of the Rocky Mountains, from Alaska across Canada and into northeastern USA. Lodgepole pine is distributed from Alaska south through British Columbia and the eastern slopes of the Rockies in Alberta into western USA, with a disjunct stand in the Cypress Hills of southeastern Alberta and southwestern Saskatchewan.

Food Uses: Pine cambium can be eaten fresh (M6; Morice 1907, 1910; Curtis 1928; Leighton 1985).

Medicinal Uses: Pine inner bark can be soaked in water, softened, and used as a poultice to help heal a deep wound (M6; Leighton 1985). Pine needles can be dried, powdered, and applied as a poultice to frostbite (Birket-Smith 1930). Pine gum can be chewed as a cold medicine (Siegfried 1994). Lodgepole pine root decoction can be used to clean wounds and promote healing (Lamont 1977).

Technological Uses: Dry pine cones can be used with rotten white spruce or tamarack wood to tan hides (C51, M6; Leighton 1985). Pine logs are used for making cabins and the smaller branches for windbreaks around tents (D3). Chipewyan toboggans are sometimes made from pine planks (Macdonell 1760; Ross 1862). Pine wood is also used for boat planking (D29) and fishnet floats and mesh measures (a tapered block used in net making) (D24; Ebner pers. comm.). Fish hooks can be made from a pine knot (Macdonell 1760). The pitch could be used like spruce pitch for caulking (Birket-Smith 1930) but tends to dry too quickly and so is not as popular (D24). The roots can be used for making coil-type baskets (Birket-Smith 1930). Pines are a common source of firewood (Irimoto 1981; Sharp 1973).

Properties: Ponderosa pine needles (*P. ponderosa* P. & C. Lawson, 100 g fresh weight, 52% moisture) contain: protein (3.1 g), fat (4.5 g), total carbohydrate (39.9 g), crude fiber (14.1 g), vitamin A (385 RE), and minerals (ash: 1.0 g), including Ca (166 mg), P (68 mg), Fe (6.8 mg), and Mn (1.6 mg). White pine (*P. strobus* L.) needles contain 31.5 mg/100 g fresh weight of vitamin C (Kuhnlein and Turner 1991). Pine leaf oil consists mainly of borneol, cadinene, camphene, and beta-pinene. The resin contains alpha-pinene and other monoterpenes, and diterpene resin acids of the abietic and pimaric types (Duke 1985). Pine oil continues to be used effectively as a disinfectant in commercial products (Dobelis 1986), such as pine cleaners; they turn white when added to water as the insoluble terpenes precipitate out.

Potential: There is a strong demand for jack pine and lodgepole pine boughs, wood, resin, and bark for essential oil extraction. The oil is used to produce an "intermediary" for perfumes and is an aromatic and antiseptic ingredient in soaps, cosmetics, flavorings, floor polishes, and disinfectants. Hollowed pine log sections have been made into candles, and cones are used in wreaths and potpourri (Mater Engineering 1993).

Angiosperms

Angiosperms are the flowering plants (division Magnoliophyta). They produce their seeds inside the pistil of the flower, which develops into the fruit. Flowering plants are the most complex of all the types of plants, both in their structure and in their chemistry, which makes them very interesting as sources of food, medicines, and other useful materials. There are two main classes of flowering plants. The Magnoliopsida, named after the magnolia tree, is the class whose members, for the most part, have two seed leaves or cotyledons in the embryo stage (hence the term "dicots"), net-veined leaves, and flower parts in fours, fives, or multiples thereof. The other class of flowering plants is the Liliopsida, named after the lily. Members of this class usually have just one cotyledon in the embryo ("monocots"), parallel-veined leaves, and flower parts in threes or multiples thereof.

MAGNOLIOPHYTA: MAGNOLIOPSIDA

ACERACEAE
(Maple Family)

Manitoba Maple

Other Names: Cree: *sōkawahtik* ("sugar tree"), *mistikosōkaw* ("tree sugar"); English: box elder; French: *érable à giguère*.

Scientific Name: *Acer negundo* L.

Description: A tree up to 12 m tall with rough grayish bark, widely spreading branches, and opposite leaves that are divided pinnately into three to five oval, coarsely toothed segments. The drooping clusters of flowers, male and female on separate trees, appear before the leaves in spring and lack petals to facilitate wind pollination. The fruit is a typical maple double-winged nutlet (samara).

(R. Marles)

Habitat: Found naturally along streams and in ravines and wooded valleys from the Northwest Territories to Nova Scotia and south to Florida. It is also widely planted.

Food Uses: The sap can be tapped in April and caught in birch bark bowls. It is then boiled down to make syrup or sugar (C1, C4, C23, C27).

Properties: Manitoba maple has a strong spring sap flow, but the sucrose content is only about 2% (Hetherington and Steck 1997) versus about 4% in sugar maple (*Acer saccharum* Marsh.). When concentrated into syrup with 35% water, in addition to the sugar (the primary source of its food energy of 348 kcal/100 g), maple syrup has 0.1% protein and the following nutrients (in mg/100 g): Ca (107), P (8.7), Na (7.7), K (163), Mg (17.5), Cu (90.1), Zn (2.9), Fe (4.2), and Cl (17.3) (Kuhnlein and Turner 1991). Although the role of maple sap and syrup in the traditional diet is primarily as a source of carbohydrate (often in short supply in early spring and thus nutritionally significant) and the pleasure of the sweet taste, the supply of minerals is clearly a bonus.

Potential: Manitoba maple has already been used as a commercial source of syrup (Kuhnlein and Turner 1991) and could continue to be, particularly in the Prairie provinces, where it is adapted to overwinter successfully, unlike the sugar maple.

APIACEAE
(Celery Family)

Wild Celery

Other Names: English: angelica; French: *angélique*; Slave: *noga etso[h] (the)* ("wolverine cow parsnip," "wolverine rhubarb").

Scientific Name: *Angelica lucida* L.

Description: A stout perennial growing up to 1 m tall from a stout taproot. The stem is smooth at the base but roughly fuzzy near the top. The inflated leaf stalks give rise to smooth leaves that are divided two or three times into three segments, each of which is toothed and three-lobed. The compound umbrella-shaped inflorescence generally loses the bracts at the base of the main umbel, but has several lance-shaped little bracts at the

(J.D. Johnson)

base of the umbelets and small white flowers that develop into pairs of cylindrical dry fruits (mericarps) bearing ribs with thick corky bases, narrow edges, and numerous oil tubes. The seeds are loose inside the fruit at maturity.

Habitat: Found rarely inland, in shrubby alpine tundra of Alaska, Yukon, and the Northwest Territories, but more commonly along the Pacific coast from Alaska to northern California, the Arctic/Hudson Bay/James Bay coast, the Atlantic coast south to New England, and the Siberian Pacific and Arctic coasts.

Food Uses: Nonflowering stems can be eaten (Lamont 1977).

Properties: Stems of *Angelica archangelica* L. have (per 100 g dry weight): protein (7.6 g), Ca (840 mg), P (260 mg), K (1320 mg), and Mg (210 mg) (Kuhnlein and Turner 1991). *Angelica archangelica* (used in Europe) and *A. atropurpurea* L. (used in North America) leaves have carminative and anti-inflammatory properties; the root is rich in essential oils (aromatic) and sesquiterpenes (bitter) and is used to stimulate appetite and treat gastrointestinal upset by stimulating gastric secretion, reducing intestinal spasms, and acting as an antimicrobially active carminative to relieve colic or griping. It is used to flavor Benedictine and Chartreuse liqueurs (Bisset and Wichtl 1994). *Angelica archangelica* contains photosensitizing furanocoumarins, so it should not be consumed in large quantities. The main constituent of the aromatic essential oil is beta-phellandrene, and there are many minor components (Duke 1985).

Potential: The potential as a food plant is probably very limited due to low productivity in the north and lack of demand. The presence of a significant amount of volatile oil suggests it might be worth further investigation as an aromatic.

Caraway

Other Names: Cree: *sīcisis;* French: *anis canadien.*

Scientific Name: *Carum carvi* L.

Description: A smooth, hollow-stemmed biennial growing up to 1 m tall. The leaves are three to four times pinnately divided into very narrow lobes up to 15 mm long. Bracts are absent or

(R. Marles)

sometimes small and threadlike at the base of the long stalked umbel, and each of the 7-15 secondary umbels. White (rarely pink) flowers develop into pairs of oval, thin, strongly ribbed seeds (actually mericarp-type fruits) about 4 mm long, with the characteristic caraway smell.

Habitat: A Eurasian escapee from cultivation found on roadsides and waste ground across Canada and northern USA.

Food Uses: The seeds can be used to flavor bannock (Leighton 1985).

Medicinal Uses: Caraway seeds are one component, perhaps as a flavoring, of a tea given to children to treat coughs (C54), to quiet a crying child (Leighton 1985), or to relieve an upset stomach or colic (Strath 1903).

Properties: Caraway seeds (100 g fresh weight, 10% moisture) contain: food energy (333 kcal), protein (24.9 g), fat (14.6 g), total carbohydrate (49.9 g), crude fiber (15.9 g), thiamine (0.38 mg), riboflavin (0.38 mg), niacin (3.6 mg), and minerals (ash: 7.8 g), including Ca (689 mg), P (568 mg), Na (17 mg), K (1351 mg), and Fe (16.2 mg) (Kuhnlein and Turner 1991). The fruit contain 3-7% essential oil, primarily (+)-carvone and (+)-limonene. The essential oil promotes gastric secretion, stimulates appetite, and relieves spasms, so it is useful as a stomach remedy and to relieve colic and griping. The oil has antifungal activity stronger than that of the commercial drug nystatin (Bisset and Wichtl 1994). The spasm-relief activity could also explain the use to treat coughs.

Potential: Caraway is already grown as a commercial spice crop in Canada, and a number of trials are underway to develop good annual varieties with significant essential oil productivity (Wahab 1997). The essential oil is in demand for aromatherapy (Rogers 1997).

Water Hemlock

Other Names: Cree: *machīskatask-wak, maciskatask*; English: cowbane; French: *carotte à moreau*; Slave: *yagodī*.

Scientific Name: *Cicuta maculata* L. Also *C. virosa* L. (common synonym: *C. mackenzieana* Raup.), *C. douglasii* (DC.) Coult. & Rose, *C. bulbifera* L.

Description: The common water hemlock (*C. maculata*) is a marsh plant growing up to 2 m tall from a swollen bulbous rootstock that if sliced lengthwise often shows partitioned chambers inside and a yellowish, poisonous exudate. The stems are smooth, often purplish, and give rise to sheathing-stalked, compoundly pinnate leaves (usually two to three

Cicuta maculata L. (R. Marles)

times pinnate or pinnate/three-part) with broad, lance-shaped, coarsely saw-toothed to sparsely toothed leaflets. There are usually no bracts at the base of the 10-cm-wide compound umbel (each umbel has 18-28 umbelets each with 12-25 flowers), although all have bracts at the base of each separate umbelet of the compound umbel. The flowers are small and white, and develop into pairs of yellowish, oblong, slightly flattened seeds (mericarps), each of which has five thick brown ribs and oil tubes in between the ribs. The other species have minor differences in height, the size and complexity of the leaf and umbel divisions, and fruit size.

Habitat: Common in wet and marshy places, such as sloughs or stream edges, throughout the northern hemisphere.

Medicinal Uses: These plants are known to be deadly poisonous (C24, C25; Lamont 1977). They are easily confused with other members of the carrot family by inexperienced people, with fatal results. The root has been dried, powdered, and made into a liniment applied externally (Leighton 1985). Lamont (1977) identified *Sium suave* Walt., *C. douglasii*, and *C. virosa* as plants whose roots can be mixed with tobacco and smoked to relieve a headache, making the true identity of the medicinal plant questionable, in light of the known toxicity of *Cicuta* species.

Properties: This is considered to be one of the most violently poisonous plants of the world's northern temperate zone. Even a single piece of root the width of a finger can be fatal to an adult, with symptoms of poisoning occurring from 15-60 minutes after ingestion and death often occurring before help can arrive. If the victim survives the first few hours, usually that person will recover. All parts of the plant are toxic due to the presence of a complex highly unsaturated fatty alcohol known as cicutoxin (Turner and Szczawinski 1991).

Potential: The danger of poisoning if ingested is too great to recommend any casual use for this plant. Strangely enough, cicutoxin has shown activity against leukemia experimentally and is being investigated as a possible anticancer agent (Harborne and Baxter 1993).

Cow Parsnip

Other Names: Cree: *puk-wanatik, pakwānāhtik* ("leaf plant," i.e., big leaves), *askīskatask, askīwīskātask, ōskātaskwistikwān, piygwa-nā(h)tik* ("hollow inside"); French: *berce*; Slave: *etsoʰ, deko naydī* ("cough medicine").

Scientific Name: *Heracleum maximum* Bartr., common synonym: *H. lanatum* Michx.

Description: A coarse perennial growing up to 2 m tall, with hairy stems, large hairy leaves divided into three broad, toothed segments, an unpleasant odor,

(C. Clavelle)

and a large compound umbel of white flowers giving rise to pairs of disk-shaped, winged dry fruits marked with distinctive dark lines of oil tubes.

Habitat: Common in shady woodlands and moist places throughout central and northern North America and eastern Asia.

Food Uses: Young stems can be roasted over hot coals and eaten when they go limp (M6). The young stems must be peeled before being eaten raw or roasted (Siegfried 1994). The leaf stalk can be peeled and eaten fresh (Lamont 1977; Leighton 1985) and the roasted stem pith can also be eaten (Leighton 1985). The rhizomes can be eaten fresh or cooked like a potato (C60). The seeds can be added to flavor home brew (Lamont 1977).

Medicinal Uses: The fresh or dried root can be placed in the mouth against an aching tooth and the juice can be swallowed (C47, C57; Siegfried 1994). The root (fresh or dried) can be grated and mixed with warm water to make a paste applied to swollen legs twice a day for only half an hour; blistering might occur (M6). The root can be part of a medicinal tea for treating cancer (M9). To treat an aching body or sore body parts the plant can be dried, chopped, and rubbed on the affected area, or it may be boiled and the cooled decoction used to bathe sore parts ("sore bones"), and some of the decoction can be drunk (C23, C27, C44). This can also be used to treat colds (C23, C27). The root decoction can be drunk to treat coughs (Lamont 1977). To treat arthritis the roots can be gathered in the fall when they are mature, cleaned, dried, and boiled to make a decoction that can be drunk, and the roots can also placed in bath water and the affected body areas can be soaked (C52). The steam from boiling the roots and leaves can be inhaled to make all the sickness come out of the body (C38). The root can be mixed with other herbs and applied as a poultice and/or wash to treat painful limbs, an aching head, or "worms in the flesh" (Leighton 1985).

Technological Uses: The hollow stems can be used as a snorkel to swim underwater without being seen (M9). The Chipewyan crush the root and mix it in trap bait for bears (Morice 1910).

Properties: Cow parsnip greens contain (per 100 g fresh weight, 91% moisture): protein (1.6 g), riboflavin (0.11 mg), and minerals (ash: 1.5 g), while the peeled stalks (per 100 g, 95% moisture) contain: food energy (20 kcal), protein (0.4 g), fat (0.2 g), total carbohydrate (3.8 g), crude fiber (0.9 g), thiamine (<0.01 mg), riboflavin (0.12 mg), niacin (0.3 mg), vitamin C (3.5 mg), vitamin A (7.5 RE), and minerals (ash: 0.6 g), including Ca (28 mg), P (19 mg), Na (0.5 mg), Mg (11.7 mg), Cu (0.4 mg), Zn (0.4 mg), Fe (0.3 mg), and Mn (0.1 mg) (Kuhnlein and Turner 1991). Although nutritious in limited quantities, cow parsnip roots and foliage contain furanocoumarins such as 8-methoxypsoralen which are photosensitizers: they can cause rashes and skin discoloration from either topical application, handling, or after excessive consumption, followed by exposure to ultraviolet radiation in sunlight (Turner and Szczawinski 1991).

Potential: Although of limited potential as a vegetable, the furanocoumarins are of great medicinal interest because they are tuberculostatic and antibacterial and are used by dermatologists to treat vitiligo and psoriasis. However, there is a risk with therapeutic use because when photoactivated, these chemicals can cause damage to the cell's DNA (Harborne and Baxter 1993). The essential oil is in demand for aromatherapy (Rogers 1997).

Water Parsnip

Other Names: Cree: *sīwas-kātask* ("sweet carrot"), *sī-waskacāskwos* ("sweet little carrot"), *ōskātask*, *kowchus-kowitoy*; French: *berle douce*; Slave: *hlue tlaʰleʰ*.

Scientific Name: *Sium suave* Walt.

Description: A perennial marsh plant growing up to 2 m tall from a stout rhizome, with smooth hollow stems, singly pinnate leaves with narrow, sharply saw-toothed leaflets and many small bracts at the base of the compound umbel of white flowers that develop into dry fruits that are 3 mm long, oval, flattened, promi-

(R. Marles)

nently ribbed, and splitting into two at maturity. Note that the similar and deadly poisonous water hemlock (*Cicuta* spp.) has compoundly rather than simply pinnate leaves with broader toothed leaflets and usually no bracts at the base of the compound umbel, although both have bracts at the base of each separate umbelet of the compound umbel. Confusion of water parsnip and water hemlock can be a fatal mistake.

Habitat: Water parsnip is very common in sloughs, swamps, and wet meadows across Canada, the USA, and Asia. Water hemlock has virtually the same range in North America.

Food Uses: The sweet-tasting roots can be eaten raw as a health food (C2, C3; Leighton 1985) or cooked (Leighton 1985; Richardson, cited in Leighton 1985). There is danger in misidentification; see the warning below.

Medicinal Uses: In addition to the tonic aspect of eating the roots (C2, C3), they can be eaten raw or boiled with other herbs and the decoction drunk to treat chest congestion (C54), and can be part of compound decoctions used to treat heart trouble, headaches, and fever (C54). Lamont (1977) collected voucher specimens of *Sium suave, Cicuta douglasii,* and *C. virosa* as plants whose roots can be mixed with tobacco and smoked to relieve a headache, making the true identity of the medicinal plant questionable, in light of the known toxicity of *Cicuta* species. Water parsnip may have been part of a compound medicine to treat cancer (Siegfried 1994).

Properties: Budd et al. (1987) suggest that water parsnip may be slightly poisonous, and it has been implicated in numerous cases of livestock poisoning. However, extensive use by Aboriginal people of the roots and young stems for food suggests that there could be some toxicity in the flowering tops and not other parts; another strong possibility is confusion of this plant with water hemlock (Turner 1978). Since the two plants are easily confused, harvesting of this plant should be left to very experienced people.

Potential: The risk of poisoning through misidentification suggests that use of this plant should not be promoted.

APOCYNACEAE (Dogbane Family)

Spreading Dogbane

Other Names: Cree: *totosapowask* ("milk plant"); French: *herbe à pouce, gobe-mouche.*

Scientific Name: *Apocynum androsaemifolium* L.

Description: A somewhat bushy perennial herb growing up to 1.5 m tall from a rhizome, with many branches that exude an acrid milky sap when broken. The opposite leaves are oval in outline, and the small, pink, bell-shaped flowers grow from the leaf axils and branch tips. The fruit is a long, narrow pod splitting along one side to release hairy-tipped seeds.

(C. Clavelle)

Habitat: Common in woodlands on light sandy soil throughout North America, except in the southeastern USA.

Medicinal Uses: A tea can be made from the whole plant to increase lactation in nursing mothers (M6; Leighton 1985). The cooled tea can also be used as an eyewash to treat sore eyes from smoke or snow blindness (M6; Leighton 1985).

Properties: The presence of a milky sap probably explains the traditional use to increase lactation, by the "doctrine of signatures" concept. However, this is a dangerous practice because spreading dogbane is known to contain steroid glycosides, including K-strophanthoside, K-strophanthin-beta, and cymarin (Hetherington and Steck 1997; Farnsworth 1999), which act on the heart and thus increase blood pressure. Dogbane has been implicated in livestock poisonings, although these are not common because the plant tastes very bitter. Although it has been used as a heart stimulant and was listed in the USA National Formulary until 1960, this herbal medicine should be used only under the supervision of a health professional (Duke 1985; Dobelis 1986). The milky sap may cause a skin rash (Turner and Szczawinski 1991); therefore preparations of the plant cannot be recommended for topical treatment.

Potential: Because of the risk of toxic effects with improper use, it is unlikely there will be a significant market for this herb.

ARALIACEAE
(Ginseng Family)

Wild Sarsaparilla

Other Names: Chipewyan: *gajíé* ("rabbit berry"); Cree: *wāposōcēpīhk* ("rabbit root"), *wāposocīpihk, wāpōsogībī;* French: *salsepareille.*

Scientific Name: *Aralia nudicaulis* L.

Description: A perennial herb growing from a creeping rhizome, with a single stem that divides into three stems each of which produces three or five oval, pointed, finely toothed leaflets. The greenish flowers are produced in an umbel on a leafless stem that is lower than the leaves and develop into black berries.

Habitat: Common in shady rich woodlands across Canada and northern USA.

Medicinal Uses: The rhizome can be chewed or made into a tea to treat heart pain (D22), chronic chest trouble (tuberculosis?) (D9), upset stomach (D29), liver problems (D29), a sore throat (C21, C22), teething sickness (Leighton 1985), and venereal disease (Richardson, cited in Leighton 1985).

(R. Marles)

It should be collected in the autumn (D29). The root can be used as a "forti-fier" (M9). The root can be chewed and applied topically to prevent infec-tion of the gums (Leighton 1985) or to treat infections in wounds (Siegfried 1994), or it can be mixed with other herbs in a poultice used to treat infected wounds (C54; Richardson, cited in Leighton 1985; Welsh, cited in Leighton 1985). A decoction of the whole plant can be used to treat pneumonia in children and of the fruiting stalk to stimulate lactation (Leighton 1985).

Properties: Wild sarsaparilla greens have (per 100 g fresh weight): protein (0.4-1.2 g), Ca (97-182 mg), P (22-30 mg), K (79-225 mg), Mg (34-46 mg), Cu (0.1 mg), Zn (0.4-2.7 mg), Fe (1.5-3.9 mg), Mn (6.0-28.8 mg), and Cl (2.4 mg) (Kuhnlein and Turner 1991). The root aqueous and ethanolic extracts were found to be inactive against strains of the bacteria *Mycobacterium tuberculo-sis*, *Escherichia coli*, and *Staphylococcus aureus*. Two triterpenes, alpha- and beta-amyrin, and some ubiquitous sterols are the only compounds to have been isolated from the roots, and a screening test for alkaloids was positive, but in other species of *Aralia* many triterpene saponins are known (Farnsworth 1999).

Potential: Too little work has been done on this species. The many signifi-cant uses of this and other species of *Aralia* and the information available on the chemistry of the genus suggest a high priority for further investigation. See Barl et al. (1996) for further information on sourcing and selling.

Devil's Club

Other Names: French: *bois piquant.*

Scientific Name: *Oplopanax horridus* (Sm.) Miq.

Description: A coarse and very spiny shrub growing up to 3 m tall, with very large palmately lobed leaves and a terminal cluster of umbels of greenish flowers that develop into scarlet berries.

Habitat: Found in moist woods and rocky thickets of the Canadian and USA Pacific Northwest, extending into central Alberta and the Rocky Mountains of Idaho and Montana, with a disjunct population around lakes Superior and Michigan.

(R. Marles)

Medicinal Uses: The root can be used with other plants in a decoction to treat diabetes (C31, M9), as a diuretic, and to prevent birth (M9).

Properties: An extract of the inner bark of devil's club has been shown to have antibacterial activity against *Bacillus subtilis* (gram-positive), *Staphylococcus aureus* (gram-positive) including both methicillin-sensitive and methicillin-resistant strains, *Mycobacter phlei* (gram-positive, non-acid-fast), *Pseudomonas aeruginosa* H188 (gram-negative), and *Salmonella typhimurium* TA98 (gram-negative) (McCutcheon et al. 1992); and antifungal activity against *Aspergillus fumigatus, Fusarium tricuictum, Microsporum cookerii, Microsporum gypseum, Saccharomyces cerevisiae, Trichoderma viridae,* and *Trichophyton mentagrophytes* and partial inhibition against *Candida albicans* (McCutcheon et al. 1994). The same extract partially inhibited the cell-damaging effects of respiratory syncytial virus (McCutcheon et al. 1995). Very promising activity was shown for this extract against *Mycobacterium tuberculosis* and isoniazid-resistant *Mycobacterium avium*. The constituents responsible for the antibacterial, antifungal, and antiviral activities are mainly a series of at least five polyacetylenes, including falcarinol and falcarindiol, compounds known from both the Araliaceae and the Apiaceae (Kobaisy et al. 1997). The traditional use by other Canadian Aboriginal cultures as an antidiabetic and case studies regarding blood-sugar-lowering activity have been reviewed (Marles and Farnsworth 1995).

Potential: Several groups are rumored to be working on this plant's antidiabetic activity, but very little has actually been published. The most significant potential would appear to be its promise as an antibiotic against the bacteria that cause tuberculosis and other antibiotic-resistant bacteria.

ASTERACEAE
(Aster Family)

Yarrow

Other Names: Chipewyan: *t'á"chay delgai* ("holy flower"); Cree: *wapunewusk* ("white flower"), *wapanowask, wapānaskiy(h)k, astēskotawān, astawēskōtawan* ("to put out a campfire," i.e., relieves burning pain), *mistī-gonīmaskīgiah* ("head medicine"), *miski-gonimaski, oskānīmaskīgī, osgunīmasgigah* ("bone medicine"), *wīcipōwānīwistikwān, kāwāpistikwānīkāpawik, āmowask*; English: milfoil; French: *herbe à dindes*; Slave: *dath eto" atselī* ("it has little leaves").

Scientific Name: *Achillea millefolium* L. *Achillea sibirica* Ledeb. is not always distinguished from *A. millefolium* by elders.

Achillea millefolium L. (R. Marles)

Description: Common yarrow (*A. mille-folium*) is an aromatic perennial herb growing up to 1 m tall, with finely divided feathery leaves, often with silky hairs, and a somewhat flat-topped inflorescence of composite flower heads with white to pink flowers having about five ray florets and 10-30 disk florets. Siberian or many-flowered yarrow (*A. sibirica*) has less deeply divided leaves.

Habitat: Common in moist meadows and openings in the boreal woods of the parklands throughout the northern hemisphere.

Medicinal Uses: To treat headaches, the leaves and/or flowers can be dried and placed in the nostrils (C21, C22, C24, C25, C38, C42, C43, C44; Leighton 1985) or boiled with other plants and both the steam inhaled and the decoction drunk (C43). The fresh flower heads can be chewed and applied to bee stings, cuts (C11, C17, M9; Siegfried 1994), sores (C11, C17, M9), and burns (Leighton 1985), or placed in the nostril to stop a nosebleed (C23, C24, C25, C27, C39, C52, D26; Siegfried 1994). The flower decoction can be drunk as a spring tonic, to regain lost appetite (C17), to treat menstrual cramps or heavy menstruation, to aid in childbirth to relieve labor pains and to stop hemorrhaging (C17, D26; Siegfried 1994), or, when concentrated (lots of flower heads boiled 1.5 h), to treat a cough or liver ailments (Lamont 1977).

The flower can also be a good medicine for treating sinus or chest congestion (C27). The dried flower heads can be boiled and the decoction can be used as a wash for skin rashes or sores (C17, C48, M9). The dried leaves can be boiled to make a decoction that can be drunk to treat diabetes (C24, C25; Siegfried 1994). A decoction of the aboveground parts can be drunk to treat a sore chest (C10). A decoction of the whole plant can be drunk to relieve diarrhea (C28) or mixed with another plant and the tea drunk as a painkiller (C20). To treat arthritis or aching bones, the whole plant can be added to hot bath water in which the patient soaks, and a twice-boiled decoction of the plant can be drunk after the bath (C38). The above-ground parts may be applied to the head as a poultice to treat headaches including migraines (C23, C27, C39, C52; Leighton 1985), for which it can be sometimes mixed with other herbs (C20). It can also be used as a poultice to treat a sore back (C44), or to other areas to treat pain (C54). The leaves may be chewed and applied to burns (C28), cuts to stop the bleeding (C41; Welsh, cited in Leighton 1985), or bee stings (C41). An infusion of the leaves can be used as a wash for pimples or mosquito bites (D9). Yarrow can be mixed with lard and applied to infected sores (C17). An ointment made with the roots of this plant mixed with another plant can be rubbed on sore, aching bones or swellings to relieve the pain, and a decoction of the same mix can be drunk to help reduce the swelling (C43). The seeds and the roots can be boiled and the steam used to treat sore eyes (C43). The flowers or leaves can be burned and the smoke inhaled to treat a headache (D6, D29). The smoke can also be used to fumigate a room in which someone is sick (D32). The root can be part of a compound decoction drunk to treat fever or teething sickness and may be applied to a tooth fresh or drunk as a decoction to treat a toothache; the flowers can be part of a compress to clean the gums of a teething infant (Leighton 1985).

Technological Uses: The fragrant leaves could be mixed with mint leaves and other materials in a trap bait for lynx (D9, D23, D29; Leighton 1985). Other plants used in trap baits include whitlow-grass (*Draba breweri* S. Wats. var. *cana* (Rydb.) Rollins, Brassicaceae, common synonym: *D. lanceolata* Royle) for martens, blueberries (*Vaccinium uliginosum* L., Ericaceae) for martens, white geranium (*Geranium richardsonii* Fisch. & Trautv., Geraniaceae) for fishers, Maydell's oxytrope (*Oxytropis maydelliana* Trautv., Fabaceae) for hoary marmots, stiffstem saxifrage (*Saxifraga hieraciifolia* Waldst. & Kit. ex Willd., Saxifragaceae) for martens, reflexed saxifrage (*Saxifraga reflexa* Hook.) for foxes, small blacktip groundsel (*Senecio lugens* Richards., Asteraceae) for foxes, and blunt-leaved orchid (*Platanthera obtusata* (Banks ex Pursh) Lindl.,

Orchidaceae, common synonym: *Habenaria obtusata* (Banks ex Pursh) Richards.) for beaver (Lamont 1977).

Properties: Yarrow leaves contain a number of nutrients including (per 100 g fresh weight): protein (3.8 g), Ca (225 mg), P (76 mg), Na (59 mg), K (645 mg), Mg (53 mg), Cu (0.7 mg), Fe (13.1 mg), and Mn (4.0 mg) (Kuhnlein and Turner 1991). The leaves contain up to more than 1% essential oil, and the flower heads contain even higher amounts. Yarrow is genetically very diverse, which results in widely varying composition and amounts of the monoterpenes and sesquiterpenes in the essential oil, plus triterpenes, polyacetylenes, coumarins, tannins, flavonoids, and alkaloids (Bradley 1992). The chemistry is quite well studied, with more than 120 different compounds identified (Barl et al. 1996; Farnsworth 1999). There is a long list of alkaloids, including achiceine, betonicine, stachydrine, and trigonelline, and volatile oil constituents, including azulene, borneol, camphor, and chamazulene, reported. Some of the alkaloids have weak fever-reducing and blood-pressure-lowering effects, and salicylic acid is also present (Duke 1985). The roots contain bioactive alkamides. Yarrow is used in numerous proven phytotherapy products in Europe: internally as an anti-inflammatory, for spasm and colic relief, as a stomach tonic, and as a bile production stimulator, and externally for treating wounds and inflammations of the skin and mucous membranes (Bisset and Wichtl 1994). For wound treatment, the ability to check bleeding is due to the alkaloid achilleine, anti-inflammatory activity is due to chamazulene and prochamazulenes (Bradley 1992), and broad-range antimicrobial activity is probably due to the monoterpenes and polyacetylenes (Bisset and Wichtl 1994).

Potential: Yarrow has proven effective as a medicinal herb and is considered safe by Health Canada for internal consumption (Blackburn 1993), although allergic reactions sometimes occur in people sensitive to the daisy family (Bisset and Wichtl 1994). It is already widely grown as a vigorous ornamental in Canada, so with selection for more standard medicinal properties, yarrow has potential as a herbal product. The essential oil is in demand for aromatherapy (Rogers 1997), and dried flowers for flower arrangements (Barl et al. 1996; Mater Engineering 1993). Mater Engineering (1993) categorizes yarrow as a Priority Level 1 product for further development and describes the market in some detail. See Barl et al. (1996) for further production, processing, and marketing information.

Field Sagewort

Other Names: Chipewyan: *Déné k'áze 'eya ha nadíé* ("person's throat hurts for this the medicine"); English: plains wormwood; French: *armoise rouge, aurone sauvage*; Slave: *kotzezī naydī*.

Scientific Name: *Artemisia campestris* L. Also *A. arctica* Less., *A. tilesii* Ledeb.

Description: Field sagewort (*A. campestris*) is an aromatic biennial or perennial herb up to 60 cm tall with a prominent taproot and crown that produces a basal rosette of leaves that are finely divided into narrow segments. Numerous heads of small flowers with yellow petals, often tinged with purple, are produced on

Artemisia campestris L. (R. Marles)

stems with very small leaves. Arctic sagebrush (*A. arctica*) is a similarly taprooted species with a dense tuft of branches up to 60 cm tall from the woody crown, pinnately divided, mostly basal leaves (hairiness of stems and leaves is highly variable), and a narrow, open inflorescence with slender stalks supporting mostly solitary nodding flower heads up to 1 cm in diameter with distinctive black-edged green bracts under the flower head. In some varieties the inflorescence is more densely spikelike. Tilesius' wormwood (*A. tilesii*) is a perennial up to 1.2 m tall, with a strong rhizome giving rise to fuzzy branches with long lance-shaped, sparsely toothed leaves up to 20 cm long that have a dense white wool underneath, and a pyramidal inflorescence of numerous yellow flower heads.

Habitat: Field sagewort is common in sandy woods, shores, and openings in the boreal forest and parkland. It is found throughout Canada, most of USA, Greenland, northeastern Europe, and Asia. Arctic sagebrush is found at low elevations in Alaska, Yukon, western Northwest Territories, and northern British Columbia, in the mountains from British Columbia south to California, and in northeastern Asia. Tilesius' wormwood occurs infrequently in open woods, river flats, and badlands from Alaska, Yukon, the North-west Territories, and northern British Columbia, east to northern Ontario, and in scattered locations at higher elevations in northern USA, northeast-ern Europe, and northern Asia.

Medicinal Uses: Field sagewort root can be chewed and the juice swallowed to treat a sore throat (D22) or as an emetic "when you have a bad system" (D29). Arctic sagewort root decoction can be drunk to treat soreness of the lower back (Lamont 1977). Tilesius' wormwood flower decoction can be drunk to treat liver problems (Lamont 1977).

Properties: The closely related common mugwort (*A. vulgaris* L.) leaves con-tain (per 100 g fresh weight, 87% moisture): food energy (35 kcal), protein (5.2 g), fat (0.8 g), total carbohydrate (4.5 g), crude fiber (2.2 g), thiamine (0.15 mg), riboflavin (0.16 mg), niacin (3.0 mg), vitamin C (72 mg), Ca (82 mg), P (40 mg), and Fe (1.5 mg) (Kuhnlein and Turner 1991). Common mugwort essential oil has more than 100 identified compounds including a variety of aromatic monoterpenes and bitter sesquiterpenes. The major con-stituent of the volatile oil is cineole; thujone is also present (Duke 1985). It is only rarely used today as a bitter aromatic to stimulate gastric secretion and treat flatulence, and other therapeutic uses in folk medicine have not been scientifically substantiated, but the essential oil does have considerable re-pellent activity and is antibacterial and antifungal (Bisset and Wichtl 1994).

Potential: Field sagewort might be useful as a source of essential oil. See also the following species.

Pasture Sage

Other Names: Cree: *mostosowehkuskwa* ("good tasting cow plant"), *moostoos-wehkuskwa, mōstōsowīkask*; English: fringed sagewort; French: *armoise*.

Scientific Name: *Artemisia frigida* Willd. Also *A. ludoviciana* Nutt (prairie sage).

Description: Pasture sage (*A. frigida*) is a silvery-gray aromatic perennial with a woody crown and root, growing up to 50 cm tall but often spreading to form a mat, with fuzzy young stems, basal leaves that are divided into feathery, very narrow segments, upper leaves that are less divided, and an inflorescence of yellowish hairy composite heads in a narrow leafy cluster. Prairie sage (*A. ludoviciana*) has much broader, only slightly lobed white woolly leaves and brownish flower heads.

Habitat: Pasture and prairie sages are common in meadows and pastures throughout the prairies and parklands of western Canada (introduced into the east), the northern and midwestern USA, central eastern Europe, and the plains of Asia.

Artemisia frigida Willd. (C. Clavelle)

Medicinal Uses: The aromatic leaves can be rubbed on the skin as an insect repellant (C59, M6). The boiled leaves may be used as a poultice to treat skin problems including promoting healing of burns with less scarring (C13). The leaf tea can be drunk to relieve back pain caused by kidney trouble, to rid the body of intestinal worms, as a diuretic (a handful of leaves to five cups of water boiled and then cooled) to treat bladder infections and other urinary disorders and to relieve the body of toxins, and as a tonic to promote healing, and it may also be used as a gargle to treat a sore throat (° cup of sage to 2 cups of water), as a wash for wounds and (warm or cold) to clear blurred vision, and as a bath (2 handfuls of dried or fresh leaves in 2 gallons of water) for sore feet, rheumatism, or arthritis (M6). The leaves may be chewed to freshen the breath (C59). The leaf decoction can be drunk to treat fever and associated headache (Leighton 1985).

Technological Uses: The aromatic leaves can be used in trap lures (Leighton 1985).

Ritual Uses: Sage is an important incense used alone or with sweet-grass (*Hierochloe odorata* (L.) Beauv., Poaceae). It may be burned in a ceremonial pipe or in a small dish and then the smoke can be washed over the patient to cleanse the person spiritually before other treatment (C5, C13, D26, M6, M7, M8). Sage leaves may be chewed to bring luck, so it is sometimes called "bingo medicine" (C59).

Properties: Prairie sage leaves contain (per 100 g dry weight, 7% moisture): protein (10.8 g), fat (3.8 g), crude fiber (25.3 g), vitamin A (60 RE), Ca (859 mg), and P (177 mg). See previous species for further details. The leaves have proven insect-repellent activity (Dobelis 1986).

Potential: Sage might find a niche in the market for natural insect repellents given that it is as effective as the leading synthetic repellent, DEET, the safety of which has long been controversial. The essential oil is in demand for aromatherapy (Rogers 1997).

Lindley's Aster

Other Names: Cree: *mistaskewusk, amowusk* ("bee plant"); French: *aster.*

Scientific Name: *Aster ciliolatus* Lindl.

Description: A tall, stout perennial herb growing from a thick rhizome, with mostly smooth stems up to 1 m tall, stem leaves that are oval with a long winged petiole, and a branched inflorescence of composite flowers consisting of pale blue ray florets and yellow disk florets.

Habitat: Common in woodlands throughout the parklands and boreal forest of Canada and northern USA.

Medicinal Uses: The scented roots can be made into a tea used to treat pinkeye (conjunctivitis), and can be ground and applied topically to stop bleeding in open cuts (M6; Anderson 1982).

Properties: This species does not appear to have been studied scientifically, but other species have been shown to be inactive against viruses, and most species tested are also inactive against bacteria, but do have anti-inflammatory activity. A wide variety of constituents have been isolated from asters, including monoterpenes, sesquiterpenes, diterpenes, triterpenes, saponins, flavonoids, coumarins, phenylpropanoids, and polyacetylenes (Farnsworth 1999).

Potential: Not enough is known about this species, although the literature suggests some support for the traditional uses.

(R. Marles)

Smooth Aster

Other Names: Cree: *mistahisak-wiwask* ("big head flower").

Scientific Name: *Aster laevis* L.

Description: A stout, tall perennial herb growing from a rhizome, with smooth, waxy stems, thick, waxy, lance-shaped leaves, and clusters of composite flower heads with blue or purple ray florets and yellow disk florets.

Habitat: Common in grasslands, shrubby areas and open woods across Canada and most of the USA.

Medicinal Uses: The root can be chewed to treat toothaches and the pain of teething, and can be made into a tea used to treat fevers (induces sweating) and to aid "the organs to return to natural functioning" for women in recovery after childbirth (C17).

(J.D. Johnson)

Properties: This species does not appear to have been studied scientifically, but other species have been shown to have antispasmodic and anti-inflammatory activities, which might lend support to the traditional uses (Farnsworth 1999). See the other two species of *Aster* for a brief overview of the chemistry.

Potential: Not enough is known about this species, but the complex chemistry of asters suggests it might be worth investigating. It is also an attractive flower, so there might also be some potential as an ornamental.

Purple-stemmed Aster

Other Names: Chipewyan: *Déné tthí 'eya ha nadíé* ("person's head hurts for this the medicine" = "aspirin"), *tlh'ogh thetsën* ("big sweet-grass"); Cree: *mistasakewusk* ("big arrow"), *mistahīsakwīwask, mstahiysāgiywusk, pāwistiko(h)maskīhkīh, bigonbimaskgigiah, pikōnbīmaskīgīah (maskigiah =* "medicine"), *pikwanpīmāskīgah;* French: *aster ponceau.*

Scientific Name: *Aster puniceus* L.

Description: A stout, purplish-stemmed branching herb growing from a thick rhizome, with hairy stems and leaf midribs, long lance-shaped, sharp-toothed leaves, and numerous flower heads with blue to purplish rays.

(R. Marles)

Habitat: Fairly common in swamps and marshy ground in Canada and the USA east of the Rocky Mountains.

Medicinal Uses: The aboveground parts can be dried and then boiled and the decoction drunk repeatedly to treat kidney problems (C23, C27, C34), chills, and cold sweats (C44). The aboveground parts could also be used for treating headaches, but should be collected when in flower (D22). The decoction with another plant can be drunk to treat difficulty with breathing (C43). The roots can be dried, mixed with tobacco and smoked, or powdered and inhaled, to treat headaches (D22, D23, D32) or chewed and applied to a sore tooth (Leighton 1985). The roots can also be used in a heart medicine, a diuretic and emetic tea (D29), and a medicine for sore kidneys (D3, D22), fever, teething sickness, failure to menstruate, recovery after childbirth, and facial paralysis (Leighton 1985). The roots may be mixed with other plants and smoked to treat "insanity" (D23). The roots can be burned on the hot rocks in a sweat lodge to ease breathing due to the heat there (D26). The purple color of the lower stems is considered to be important as an indication of the plant's medicinal value (C63). Dried purple aster roots can be used combined with other plants in a decoction for a relaxing and sleep-aiding medicine (M9), in a decoction for treating kidney problems (Siegfried 1994), and in a different combination to facilitate childbirth (C14).

Properties: Analyses of five different species of aster leaves reported in Kuhnlein and Turner (1991) give the following ranges of nutrients (per 100 g fresh weight, 90% moisture): protein (0.6-2.3 g), crude fiber (1.3-1.5 g), and minerals (ash: 1.2-1.3 g), including Ca (11-130 mg), P (9-72 mg), Na (0.2-0.6 mg), K (92-511 mg), Mg (29-46 mg), Cu (0.1 mg), Zn (0.4-0.6 mg), Fe (0.1-1.5 mg), Mn (0.3-0.6 mg), Mo (<0.1 mg), and Cl (9.8-23.7 mg). Purple-stemmed aster has confirmed anti-inflammatory activity in the whole plant. It contains aurapten-type coumarins, polyacetylenes, terpenoids of various types, flavonoids, phenylpropanoids, and saponins. Other species have been shown to have antispasmodic and antitumor activity, antibiotic activity against amoebic infections, and, of special significance, strong activity from the aerial parts or flowers against *Mycobacterium tuberculosis* (Farnsworth 1999).

Potential: The extensive use of this aster in traditional medicine, its complex chemistry, and its proven pharmacological activities all suggest that this plant would be worth investigation as a possible drug.

Ox-eye Daisy

Other Names: Cree: *iskwew owehowina*; French: *marguerite.*

Scientific Name: *Chrysanthemum leucanthemum* L.

Description: An erect, rather strong-smelling perennial with short rhizomes, usually growing in patches, with few branches, narrow-toothed leaves, and large daisylike flower heads (white ray florets, yellow disk florets) occurring singly on the ends of long stalks.

Habitat: A garden escapee native to Eurasia but commonly found in roadsides, waste areas, and meadows across North America.

Medicinal Uses: The flowers and leaves can be mixed with other plants to make a tea that soothes nerves in adults and hyperactivity in children (M6).

Properties: The leaves (100 g fresh weight) contain: riboflavin (0.39 mg) and vitamin C (29.3 mg) (Kuhnlein and Turner 1991). Ox-eye daisy contains a number of polyacetylenes with possible antibacterial activity, the coumarin scopoletin, and the flavonoids apigenin and acacetin (Hetherington and Steck 1997). Scopoletin has hypotensive (lowers blood pressure), spasm relief, antibacterial, and antifungal activities, acacetin has histamine-release inhibition activity, and apigenin has anti-inflammatory, hypotensive, diuretic, and smooth-muscle-relaxing properties (Harborne and Baxter 1993).

Potential: This flower is already widely cultivated as an ornamental and is well-known as a herbal remedy.

(R. Marles)

Canada Thistle

Other Names: Chipewyan: *tlh'oslini* ("bad grass = weed"); Cree: *kamina-kuse, kaweminukuse*; French: *chardon des champs*.

Scientific Name: *Cirsium arvense* (L.) Scop.

Description: A tall, persistent perennial growing from deep running rhizomes, usually in large patches, with deeply toothed, prickly leaves and a branched inflorescence of pinkish purple (occasionally white) flower heads producing large quantities of hairy seeds.

Habitat: A very common weed of farmers' fields, roadsides, and waste places, native to Eurasia but found across North America.

(R. Marles)

Medicinal Uses: The fleshy white root can be dried, powdered, and mixed with warm animal grease as a poultice for aching joints (M6).

Properties: Canada thistle contains the flavonoids rutin and tricin, plus pectolinarigenin and cirsimaritin (Hetherington and Steck 1997). It also contains sesquiterpenes, triterpenes, and polyacetylenes, and has been reported to have anti-inflammatory, spasm relief, and blood-pressure-lowering activities (Farnsworth 1999). Rutin has radical scavenger activity. Tricin inhibits the growth of other plants' roots, which is why Canada thistle is such a troublesome weed.

Potential: If a medicinal value can be established for Canada thistle, which seems possible, there are many farmers who would welcome the harvesting of this weed from their fields.

Gumweed

Other Names: Cree: *kāpa-sakwāk maskīhkīh*; French: *epinette de prairie.*

Scientific Name: *Grindelia squarrosa* (Pursh) Dunal.

Description: A biennial or perennial, branching, smooth-stemmed plant growing up to 60 cm high, with finely toothed oblan-ceolate (narrow base, wider toward the tip) leaves and a characteristic inflorescence

(R. Marles)

of yellow-rayed composite flower heads with very gummy and sticky green bracts underneath.

Habitat: Common on dry prairies and somewhat saline flats or slough edges from the southern Mackenzie District, south through Alberta, into southern British Columbia, east along the margins of the boreal forest to Quebec, and across most of the USA except the southeast.

Medicinal Uses: The flower heads can be brewed into a tea used to treat migraine headaches, a cure learned from the native people of southern Alberta. It could also be used to treat a venereal disease (M9).

Properties: Gumweed resin contains a number of diterpene grindelic acid derivatives, and the plant also contains matricarianol, 0.3% essential oil (largely borneol), tannins, saponins, and the alkaloid grindeline (Duke 1985). It is reported to have anti-inflammatory, antispasmodic, antibacterial, and antifungal activities (Farnsworth 1999). According to Hetherington and Steck (1997), the grindelic acid derivatives are probably the main active compounds, the plant is possibly active in treating asthma and bronchitis, and several patents have been granted for uses of gumweed substances.

Potential: Gumweed appears to have some potential as a medicinal plant. The essential oil is in demand for aromatherapy (Rogers 1997).

Sneezeweed

Other Names: Cree: *cācāmōsikan* ("it makes you sneeze").

Scientific Name: *Helenium autumnale* L. var. *montanum* (Nutt.) Fern., common synonym: *H. montanum* Nutt.

Description: A perennial with a stout, erect, smooth to slightly fuzzy stem up to 1 m tall, narrowly elliptical leaves that are sometimes slightly toothed and have distinctive extensions down the stem as narrow wings, and numerous flower heads at the ends of branches, 2-3 cm across, with a high rounded yellow disk and yellow ray florets that bend backwards.

(C. Clavelle)

Habitat: Common in moist meadows and beside streams in the prairies and parklands across Canada and most of the USA.

Medicinal Uses: The dry yellow disk florets can be crumbled and inhaled into the nose to make you sneeze in order to treat a headache (C11, C20).

Properties: Sneezeweeds contain a number of sesquiterpene lactones including helenalin and flavonoids (Hetherington and Steck 1997). Sneezeweeds have been reported to be fatally toxic to cattle, horses, sheep, and mules, but no human poisonings have been recorded (Mulligan and Munro 1990).

Potential: In light of the toxic effects on livestock, this plant should be investigated further before any recommendations are made regarding its use as a medicinal. Improved varieties are being grown as garden flowers (Hetherington and Steck 1997).

Nuttall's Sunflower

Other Names: Cree: *owtiyhiymeskiyhkiy, mītiyhiymeskiyhkiy*; French: *soleil*.

Scientific Name: *Helianthus nuttallii* Torr. & Gray.

Description: A perennial herb up to 2 m tall with thickened fleshy roots, slightly hairy stems, lance-shaped, very rough hairy leaves up to 15 cm long, opposite when low on the stem but sometimes becoming alternate higher up, with short winged stalks, smooth or slightly toothed edges, and one to several flower heads with a yellow or light brown disk up to 3 cm wide and long yellow ray florets.

Stiff sunflower (*Helianthus pauciflorus* Nutt.)
(R. Marles)

Habitat: Occasionally found in moist meadows and slough margins across southern Canada and western USA.

Medicinal Uses: The mature root decoction can be drunk to treat heart problems (Siegfried 1994).

Properties: There are a number of sesquiterpene lactones in *Helianthus* species (Hetherington and Steck 1997).

Potential: Due to the presence of the sesquiterpene lactones, this species is worth examining for medicinal properties. It also has an attractive flower.

Colorado Rubber-Plant

Other Names: None known.

Scientific Name: *Hymenoxys richardsonii* (Hook.) Cockerell.

Description: A perennial herb growing from a coarse woody taproot that often has a woolly crown, with fleshy leaves divided into three to seven narrow segments, arising from the base and to a lesser extent from the stems, and a few composite flower heads with bright yellow three-toothed ray florets.

Habitat: Common on open prairie and dry rocky hillsides of southern Alberta and Saskatchewan and in the USA south through the midwestern states to Texas.

(J.D. Johnson)

Medicinal Uses: Obtained by travel or trade, the root of this plant can be ground into a powder and used as a snuff to induce sneezing to "clear one's head" and relieve head colds and headaches (C60).

Properties: This species has been reported to cause poisoning of sheep and to a lesser extent goats and cattle. There are no reports of human poisoning (Mulligan and Munro 1990).

Potential: In light of its toxic effects on livestock, this plant should be investigated further before any recommendations are made.

Pineapple Weed

Other Names: French: *herbe à crapaud*; Slave: *kozoⁿthalī*.

Scientific Name: *Matricaria discoidea* DC., common synonym: *M. matricarioides* (Less.) Porter.

Description: A short annual herb with finely divided leaves, a composite inflorescence of only greenish yellow disk florets (no white ray florets as in the similar wild chamomile), and a distinctive pineapple smell when crushed.

Habitat: A weed commonly found in waste areas, roadsides, and driveways, it is native to Eurasia but introduced into most of Canada and the USA.

(R. Marles)

Medicinal Uses: The dried plant can be steeped in boiling water to make a tea drunk to treat insomnia or calm the nerves. It can also be sweetened with honey and given in a bottle to calm a fretting baby (M6) or drunk to treat urinary problems associated with the kidneys (Siegfried 1994). It may also be used to treat eye infections by squeezing the fresh juice out of a small flower directly into the eye (C6).

Technological Uses: The leaves can be mixed with other materials in trap bait for lynx (D29).

Properties: Pineapple weed leaves contain up to 0.45% essential oil, and almost twice that amount in the flowers. The essential oil consists mainly of beta-farnesene, geranyl isovalerate, germacrene, and myrene (Hetherington and Steck 1997). A close relative of pineapple weed is German chamomile (*M. recutita* L.), the flowers of which are a well-known herbal tea product with proven anti-inflammatory, spasm relief, ulcer-protecting, bactericidal, and fungicidal activity. Chamomile contains a complex mixture of active ingredients, including essential oil with alpha-bisabolol and its oxide derivatives, chamazulene, chamaviolin, spiroethers, and polyacetylenes, and also numerous flavonoids, sesquiterpene lactones, and coumarins. It is widely used and effective topically against inflammations and internally against gastrointestinal complaints (Bisset and Wichtl 1994). It is also considered to be mildly sedative and is used in modern British phytotherapy to treat mild sleep disorders, particularly in children (Bradley 1992).

Potential: Health Canada (1996) has published a labeling standard for Roman chamomile (*Chamaemelum nobile* (L.) All., Asteraceae) as a single medicinal ingredient (flower heads) digestive aid. Pineapple weed would not be allowable under these regulations because it is not the same species, but the potential is there for it to be developed as a drug or essential oil source.

Arrow-leaved Coltsfoot

Other Names: Cree: *piskehte pusk-wa, nigutinepia, mōsōtawakayipak* ("moose ear leaf"), *yuwskiy(h)tiypuk* ("soft leaves"); French: *pétasite*; Slave: *sa^h yenoshetī* ("bear eats it"), *tsa^hle (mbe) thone, dath eto^n tsho* ("it has big leaves").

Scientific Name: *Petasites sagittatus* (Banks ex Pursh) A. Gray.

Description: A perennial herb with a creeping rhizome, large arrow-

Vine-leaved coltsfoot (*Petasites ×vitifolius* Greene) (R. Marles)

shaped leaves that are green on top and densely white and woolly underneath, and a dense terminal cluster of composite flower heads composed of white disk florets.

Habitat: Fairly common in moist woods, meadows, bogs, and slough margins across Canada and south into the mountainous western and northern USA.

Medicinal Uses: The whole moist leaf can be used as a poultice on skin sores (M9; Siegfried 1994) and burns to draw out infections (M9), for "worms in the flesh," or for itchy skin (Leighton 1985). The root decoction can be used to treat or prevent infections (Siegfried 1994). The flower head decoction can be drunk to treat a cough (Lamont 1977).

Properties: Sweet coltsfoot or butterbur (*P. hybridus* (L.) P. Gaertn., B. Meyer, & Scherb.) leaves contain esters of eremophilane-type sesquiterpene alcohols, flavonoids, triterpenoid saponins, an essential oil with dodecanal as the main odoriferous substance, and pyrrolizidine alkaloids. Because of the presence of pyrrolizidine alkaloids, which are toxic to the liver, carcinogenic, and mutagenic, in varying amounts in all parts of the plant, this plant should never be used internally. The leaf does have pain-relieving properties, due at least in part to the sesquiterpene petasin and related compounds (Bisset and Wichtl 1994).

Potential: Although there may be some effectiveness of the leaf as a poultice, the probability of toxic effects if taken internally will probably hinder commercial development as a herbal medicine. Despite this, Mater Engineering (1993) categorizes coltsfoot as a Priority Level 2 product for further development and describes the market in some detail.

Canadian Goldenrod

Other Names: Cree: *chachamos kakew* ("it makes one sneeze"); French: *verge d'or géante.*

Scientific Name: *Solidago canadensis* L.

(R. Marles)

Description: A stout erect perennial growing from a stout rhizome, up to 2 m tall, with a smooth stem bearing alternate, thin, long, sharply toothed and pointed leaves without stalks and a large pyramidal inflorescence of yellow flower heads on spreading, downward curving branches.

Habitat: Found in meadows, damp thickets, borders of woods, and roadsides across Canada and the USA, including Alaska and Hawaii.

Medicinal Uses: The leaves and stems can be boiled and the decoction drunk to treat kidney and bladder problems or constipation. When cold it may also be used as a wash to dry weeping sores (D15).

Technological Uses: At any time of the year galls on the stems can be cut open and the grubs inside can be used as fish bait or even cooked as an emergency food (M5).

Properties: Goldenrod leaves contain a complex mixture of active ingredients, including flavonoids, bisdesmoside saponins, diterpenes, volatile oil, phenolpropanoid acids such as caffeic, chlorogenic, and hydroxycinnamic acids, phenolic glycosides, complex polysaccharides, and tannins. Some of the flavonoids and saponins have diuretic activity, other saponins have antifungal activity, some of the phenolic glycosides have anti-inflammatory activity, some extracts show blood-pressure-lowering activity, and some of the complex polysaccharides have shown preliminary activity against cancer cell assays. There are differences in the spectrum of activity between *S. canadensis* and *S. gigantea* Ait., leading to problems when species are mixed in commercial lots of the drug, which is not uncommon (Bisset and Wichtl 1994).

Potential: Goldenrod is a herb with interesting medicinal properties which require further investigation. There could be a market for a certified pure and standardized herbal product. The essential oil is in demand for aromatherapy (Rogers 1997).

Tansy

Other Names: Chipewyan: *tlh'ogh tsën* ("grass that smells"); French: *tanaisie.*

Scientific Name: *Tanacetum bipinnatum* (L.) Schultz-Bip. ssp. *huronense* (Nutt.) Breitung, common synonym: *T. huronense* Nutt. Also *T. vulgare* L., which is more commonly encountered.

Description: A perennial herb growing from a stout rhizome, with very aromatic, deeply toothed feathery leaves (one to three times pinnatifid) that are hairy in Huron tansy (*T. bipinnatum*) and smooth in common tansy (*T. vulgare*). The composite flower heads consist almost entirely of yellow tubular disk florets (ray florets are inconspicuous in Huron tansy and absent in common tansy).

Tanacetum vulgare L. (R. Marles)

Habitat: Common tansy is a weed introduced from Eurasia, found in roadsides, ditches, and waste places throughout Canada and most of the USA except the far south. Huron tansy is a much less common native species found growing on sand dunes, gravel bars, and shorelines in scattered locations across Canada and northeastern USA.

Technological Uses: The fragrant leaves of Huron tansy can be mixed with meat and other materials to make trap bait (Chipewyan: *eni*) for white fox (D22) or lynx (D29).

Properties: Common tansy has a number of aromatic compounds, including camphor, umbellulone, and essential oil containing beta-thujone, (-)-chrysanthenone, *E*-chrysanthenyl acetate, *E*-chrysanthenol, vulgarones A and B, and numerous other minor components (Hetherington and Steck 1997). The dried leaves are an effective insect repellent (Dobelis 1986). Some chemical races of tansy but not others contain thujone in the volatile oil (up to 95%). Thujone is toxic and can cause convulsions and psychotic effects in people, and overdoses of tansy tea or oil of tansy have caused serious toxic effects with symptoms including rapid, feeble pulse, severe inflammation of the stomach lining, violent spasms, convulsions, and even fatalities (Turner and Szczawinski 1991).

Potential: There are at least 10 documented chemotypes (Hetherington and Steck 1997), so any commercial development (such as for essential oil extraction) would require chemical assays and careful genetic selection to assure a reasonably standard and safe product that is thujone-free. The thujone-free essential oil is in demand for aromatherapy (Rogers 1997).

Dandelion

Other Names: Cree: *meoska-mewuskos* ("spring plant"); French: *pissenlit*; Slave: *eto^n hleko^n* ("smells sweet").

Scientific Name: *Taraxacum officinale* G.H. Weber ex Wiggers.

Description: A robust perennial with leaves and flower stalks arising from the crown of a deep fleshy taproot. The

(R. Marles)

leaves are coarsely toothed, with triangular lobes and a large terminal lobe, and produce white latex when broken. The flower heads are composed entirely of bright yellow ray florets that produce seeds with an umbrella of bristles to carry them on the wind.

Habitat: A very common weed of lawns, roadsides, and waste places, introduced from Europe and found throughout North America.

Food Uses: The young leaves can be boiled and eaten, and the latex can be sucked from the leaves (Lamont 1977).

Medicinal Uses: The leaf decoction can be drunk to "purify the blood," for the treatment of anemia, jaundice, and also for nervousness (M6). The root decoction can be drunk as a diuretic to "clean out the blood stream" (C39, C42). The leaves and roots can be taken to promote the flow of bile in liver disease (M6). The milky latex can be used for a mosquito repellent (M5).

Properties: Dandelion greens contain the following nutrients (per 100 g fresh weight, 85% moisture): food energy (45 kcal), protein (2.7 g), fat (0.7 g), total carbohydrate (0.2), crude fiber (1.6 g), thiamine (0.19 mg), riboflavin (0.28 mg), vitamin C (35 mg), vitamin A (1400 RE), and minerals (ash: 1.8 g), including Ca (209 mg), P (64 mg), Na (73), K (422 mg), Mg (51.5 mg), Cu (0.3 mg), Fe (4.1 mg), Mn (0.7 mg), and Cl (329 mg) (Kuhnlein and Turner 1991). The leaf contains bitter germacranolide sesquiterpene lactones, triterpenes, phytosterols, *p*-hydroxyphenylacetic acid, coumarins, carotenoids, and vitamin D. It has proven diuretic and bile-production-stimulating activities (Bradley 1992). The root contains bitter eudesmanolide sesquiterpene lactones, triterpenes, sterols, carotenoids, flavonoids, caffeic acid, and mucilage. It has established effectiveness as a diuretic and stimulant of bile secretion (Bisset and Wichtl 1994).

Potential: Dandelion leaves are considered by Health Canada to be safe when consumed as a food (Blackburn 1993). Dandelion root is already marketed as a registered diuretic drug in Canada (e.g., by Nature's Way, drug identification number 00827789). However, much of the herb is imported from the USA, which a glance at just about anyone's lawn would suggest is hardly necessary. It is already being cultivated in several states, such as Texas, Florida, New Jersey, Arizona, and California (Foster 1993), and could also be cultivated in Canada. Barl et al. (1996) provide information on cultivation and marketing. There are commercial products containing dandelion root roasted and used as a coffee substitute and some demand for the young leaves and flowers in gourmet salad mixtures (Mater Engineering 1993). Mater Engineering (1993) categorizes dandelion as a Priority Level 1 product for further development and describes the market in some detail.

BETULACEAE
(Birch Family)

Green Alder

Other Names: Chipewyan: *k'ái lisën* ("willow that smells"); Cree: *atōs-pīah, atōsbīah, atōspī, māthatōspī, mithkwatōspi, miskwatōspi, mihkwa-tōspi*; French: *aulne, bois à rames*; Slave: *ke, hoe^h*.

Scientific Name: *Alnus viridis* (Vill.) Lam. & DC. ssp. *crispa* (Ait.) Turrill, common synonym: *A. crispa* (Ait.) Pursh Also *A. incana* (L.) Moench ssp. *rugosa* (Du Roi) Clausen and *A. incana* (L.) Moench ssp. *tenuifolia* (Nutt.) Breitung, common synonyms: *A. rugosa* (Du Roi) Spreng., *A. tenuifolia* Nutt.

Description: Green alder (*A. viridis*) is a dense shrub up to 3 m tall with twigs that are sticky and fuzzy when young, egg-shaped, irregularly

Alnus viridis (Vill.) Lam. & D.C. with prominent male catkins (R. Marles)

finely toothed leaves that are often sticky on the underside, and woody catkins that develop at the same time as the leaves and produce tiny nutlets surrounded by a wing. River or speckled alder (*A. incana*) grows up to 8 m tall and has larger leaves (4-10 cm vs. 2-8 cm) with some fuzziness underneath, the catkins develop before the leaves emerge, and the nutlets have no wings.

Habitat: Green alder is common in dry, open coniferous woods, sand hills, and the edge of bogs across Canada, south in the mountains to California in the west, and across northeastern USA, western Greenland, northeastern Europe, and Asia. River alder is found along streams and lake edges, and in valleys across Canada, northern and western USA, and Eurasia.

Food Uses: The dried cones may have been chopped finely and mixed with tobacco as an extender (D9).

Alnus viridis (Vill.) Lam. & D.C. with female cones (R. Marles)

Medicinal Uses: The green female catkins can be boiled to make a medicinal tea for treating venereal disease (not specified) in men (D24, D29), the stem can be boiled to make an emetic for treating an upset stomach (D9), and the roots can be used in a decoction drunk to relieve menstrual cramps (D23). It can also be used to treat scalding from boiling water (C44). Alder can be part of a compound decoction used in a steam treatment to bring about menstruation (Leighton 1985). River alder (*A. incana*) inner bark decoction can be used to wash sore eyes, and bark removed by scraping downward can be used as a laxative (Leighton 1985).

Technological Uses: Alder bark and stem pieces can be chopped and boiled to make a red-brown dye for hides (C23, C24, C25, C27, C44, D6; Lamont 1977; Leighton 1985; Siegfried 1994), birch bark baskets (Leighton 1985), quills (Lamont 1977; Welsh, cited in Leighton 1985: red-orange from the inner bark, yellow from the catkins), arrows (Lamont 1977), and fishnets (D6; Lamont 1977; Siegfried 1994). According to D6, the dyed twine is harder for the fish to see and they cannot avoid being caught. However, dyeing might weaken the net (D29). Alder wood can be carved to make a pipe, bottoms and lids for small birch bark containers, and small bows for bird or squirrel hunting, and the natural curve that is commonly found at the base of the tree can be used in carving a tool to peel bark from trees (Lamont 1977). Dry alder wood can be burned to smoke meat (Lamont 1977). Rotten alder wood can be burned with peat moss to smoke hides during tanning (D30; Lamont 1977). Rotten wood can also be burned to make a smudge to chase away mosquitoes (Lamont 1977). River alder wood charcoal can be mixed with pitch to seal canoe seams, and the bark decoction can be used to soak toboggan boards to soften them for bending (Leighton 1985).

Properties: Alder bark contains up to 20% tannin, a hyperoside-type flavonoid glycoside, triterpenes, and a reddish dye compound. The wood is elastic, soft, fairly light, and easily worked, and has been used in carvings and shoe manufacture (Duke 1985). The tannins give it some astringency as a healing agent (Dobelis 1986). The buds are rich in resin and the wood contains pinosylvin, a stilbene-type compound that is toxic to fungi and bacteria and discourages snowshoe hares from chewing on the stems (Harborne and Baxter 1993).

Potential: There is a demand among interior decorating firms for tree tops, which are used to produce natural-looking semiartificial trees (real trunks and branches, silk leaves). Branches are in demand for baskets, wreaths, bird cages, decorative furniture, and specially preserved leafy branches for decorative purposes. The "cones" are also in demand as decorative items (Mater Engineering 1993). Alder is important ecologically as a nitrogen-fixing colonizer of disturbed sites, suggesting possible use in land reclamation.

Bog Birch

Other Names: Chipewyan: *íⁿt'áⁿbaⁿd-haze* ("little round leaf"); English: dwarf birch, glandular birch; French: *bouleau de savane*; Slave: *dī thīli, dī yoshetī* ("grouse eat it").

Scientific Names: *Betula nana* L., *B. pumila* L., and hybrids: *B. ×sargentii* Dugle.

Description: A slender shrub with glandular, sometimes fuzzy twigs, small roundish, shiny leaves with blunt-toothed margins, slender pollen catkins that hang down, and round woody female catkins that produce tiny winged seeds.

Habitat: Fairly common in marshes, sloughs, and bogs across the boreal forest and in the mountains of western and northeastern North America.

Betula ×sargentii Dugle (R. Marles)

Medicinal Uses: Fresh twigs can be chewed and put on a deep cut to stop the bleeding (D29). The stems and leaves can be boiled to make a weight-loss tea (D14).

Technological Uses: A bundle of branches can be used as a broom (D6).

Properties: Bog birch leaves contain (per 100 g fresh weight, 58% moisture): protein (8.1 g) and total carbohydrate (8.5 g), while the shoots contain protein (1.3 g), Ca (62 mg), P (11 mg), Na (0.2 mg), K (40 mg), Mg (44 mg), Cu (0.1 mg), Zn (1.6 mg), Fe (0.9 mg), Mn (5.0 mg), and Cl (0.1 mg) (Kuhnlein and Turner 1991). Birch twigs are astringent, accounting for their effectiveness in treating wounds, and they contain some methyl salicylate, which would help to relieve pain (Dobelis 1986).

Potential: The most likely commercial use for bog birch is for cut branches in flower arrangements, because the leaves are small and attractively shaped.

Paper Birch

Other Names: Chipewyan: *k'i*; Cree: *wuskwi-atik, wāsk-wayahtik* ("birch bark tree"), *wasgwah, waskwaha, wāsk-wāh, waskway, owkimawa(h)-tik*; English: white birch; French: *bouleau blanc*; Slave: *kī(aʰ)*.

Scientific Name: *Betula papyrifera* Marsh. Also *B. neoalaskana* Sarg.

Betula papyrifera Marsh. (N. Tays)

Description: A tree up to 30 m high with white bark that has conspicuous brown lenticels (pores) and peels off in horizontal strips, leaves with saw-toothed edges, and pendant catkins. Paper birch (*B. papyrifera*) has fuzzy twigs and egg-shaped leaves that have tufts of hairs in the vein axils underneath. Alaska birch (*B. neoalaskana*) has glandular twigs and triangular leaves whose undersurface has glands but not tufts of hairs. They are often considered varieties of one species.

Habitat: Common along rivers, in openings, and in moist sites in the boreal forest, aspen parkland, and mountains across Canada and northern USA. Alaska birch has a more narrow northerly distribution overlapping that of paper birch.

Food Uses: The inner bark (cambium layer and associated young phloem and xylem) (Chipewyan: *k'i k'a* = "birch fat") can be eaten in early spring as a sweet treat and starvation food (C23, C27, C52, C60, D3, D6, D24, D26, M6; Leighton 1985; Welsh, cited in Leighton 1985). It can also be boiled to make a drink (C23, C24, C25, C27). The sap (Chipewyan: *k'i tue*) can be collected and drunk as a health food (C6, C13, C60, D26; Lamont 1977) or boiled down to make a sweet syrup similar to maple syrup (C23, C27, C44, C52, D3, D9, D11, D24, D29, M6; Ross 1862; Macoun 1882; Lamont 1977; Leighton 1985; Welsh, cited in Leighton 1985; Siegfried 1994). The leaves or root inner bark can be boiled to make a beverage (Cree: *watapi*) (M6; Leighton 1985).

Medicinal Uses: The leaves can be chewed and plastered on wasp stings to extract the poison (D6). To treat a woman who cannot conceive a child, birch bark can be collected from the east side of the tree (where the sun rises) and boiled with another plant, and the decoction can be drunk (C35, C36). The bark can be applied as a poultice for aching bones (C37, C40). The powdery outer layer (lichens and dead periderm) can be sprinkled on a sprained ankle before bandaging it (C23, C27). A sleeve of bark from the trunk can be used as a cast for a broken arm or leg (C44), a sprained ankle (C23, C27), or swollen limbs (C27, C35, C36). The bark must be collected only in the summer time (C27). A piece of the sweet bark can be given to a baby who is teething (C44). The bark is part of a compound decoction drunk to treat tuberculosis and other lung troubles (Strath 1903). The outer bark can be steamed and peeled to produce thin sheets suitable for bandages (M5). The reddish inner bark tea steam can be inhaled to treat asthma (C13) and it can be drunk for "women's troubles," can be given to babies when they are teething (M6), and can be used as a gargle for tonsillitis, sore throats, and colds (C6, M1). The inner bark can be boiled and used as a poultice to treat burns and wounds (C60, M1, M6; Leighton 1985) or in an ointment with pitch and grease for sores and rashes (Leighton 1985). The buds (Strath 1903) or wood (Welsh, cited in Leighton 1985) can be used to treat gonorrhea. The buds can also be mixed with lard to make an ointment for treating skin sores and infections (Siegfried 1994). The wood decoction can be used to wash fresh or infected wounds (Siegfried 1994). The wood is part of compound remedies for back pain and teething sickness, to stimulate sweating or lactation, or to treat "women's troubles" (Leighton 1985). The roots can be used with other plants in a decoction drunk to relieve menstrual cramps (D23) or in a different mix for a heart medicine (D9). The dry, finely powdered rotted wood can be used for baby powder (M6; Leighton 1985).

Technological Uses: Sheets of bark (Chipewyan: *k'i t'uzé*, Cree: *wāskway*) are harvested before June when they can be easily stripped from the tree (C1, C4), soaked in water to make them flexible, and made into baskets (Chipewyan: *k'i tili*) and bowls (C1, C4, C51, D3, D17, D28, M6, M9; Churchill pers. comm.; Ebner pers. comm.; Hall pers. comm.; Leonard pers. comm.; Pikios and Winter pers. comm.; Fidler 1792; Hearne 1795; Franklin 1823; Ross 1862; Morice 1909; Mason 1913; Curtis 1928; Birket-Smith 1930; Leechman 1948; Munsterhjelm 1953; Jenness 1963; Oswalt 1966; Lamont 1977; Idiens 1979; Brandson 1981; Leighton 1985; Siegfried 1994). Canoes (Chipewyan: *ts'i*) are also made from birch bark (C44, C51, D5, D11, D24, M6; Hearne 1795; Ross 1862; Morice 1910; Goddard 1912; Waugh 1919; Blanchet 1928; Birket-Smith 1930; Breynat 1948; Adney and Chapelle 1964; Li 1964; Oswalt 1966; Gillespie 1976; Leighton 1985). Few of the elders still

◄ Cree toy canoe
of birch bark (N. Tays)

▼ Birch bark fishing
net shuttle and spacer
(R. Marles)

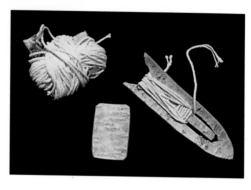

alive remember how to make
a birch bark canoe because
of the long availability of
commercially made canoes
(D24).

Other items made from
birch bark include sleds
(C44), tepee covers (Leighton 1985), food platters,
boxes with lids, cups, moose
callers (conical trumpets),
writing or drawing material, net weaving shuttles and spacers (C38), toy
canoes (C38; Siegfried 1994), and torches (C17, C34, C60, D6, D24, M6, M9;
Churchill pers. comm.; Ross 1862; Morice 1910; Curtis 1928; Birket-Smith
1930; Smith GW 1973; Lamont 1977; Jarvenpa 1980; Leighton 1985). An important use of birch bark practiced by some Aboriginal artists is to create
pictures by biting very thin layers of folded bark (Lamont 1977; Leighton
1985; seen in the Saddle Lake Museum, Alberta). Thin layers of dry birch
bark are commonly used as kindling for a fire (D24, M6; Lamont 1977;
Leighton 1985; Siegfried 1994). Inner bark from young birch trees can be
made into a yellow-red dye for porcupine quills (Lamont 1977).

Birch wood is used to make light, strong snowshoe frames (Chipewyan:
ay) (C44, D1, D3, D7, D10, D11, D24, M4; Isham 1743; Graham 1775; Hearne
1795; Ross 1862; Petitot 1868; Morice 1910; Birket-Smith 1930; Davidson 1937;
Oswalt 1966; Sharp 1973; Crowe 1974; Lamont 1977; Irimoto 1981; Leighton
1985; Siegfried 1994). The wood must be collected in the fall when the sap
is no longer running (C35, C36). During summers on the barren grounds
the snowshoe frames served as small tent poles (D6, D33; Hearne 1795;
Leighton 1985). Birch wood is also commonly used to make toboggans and
sleds because, as with making snowshoe frames, birch can be soaked with
boiling water and then readily bent into an appropriate curve which will

Chipewyan snowshoe frame of birch being webbed with wet caribou rawhide (R. Marles)

set permanently when dried (D1, D3, D11, D21, D23, M4; Macdonell 1760; Fidler 1792; Ross 1862; Morice 1910; Blanchet 1928; Munsterhjelm 1953; Lamont 1977; Irimoto 1981; Leighton 1985; Siegfried 1994). Canoe paddles (Chipewyan: *t'oth*) are also made of birch wood (C40, D3, D25; Leighton 1985). There are two Chipewyan traditional styles, a stout single-bladed paddle with a narrow handle for paddling and poling a family canoe (Chipewyan: *gha^nghólé ts'ié*) and a double-bladed paddle (Chipewyan: *elhats'én t'odhé*) used with light hide-covered one-man hunting canoes (Chipewyan: *nalzé ts'iaze*) similar to an Inuit kayak (D3, D25; Hall pers. comm.; Hearne 1795; Ross 1862; Jenness 1963; Crowe 1974).

Other items made from birch wood include canoe carrying boards (Chipewyan: *bek'e ts'i gheti^nlh*) made from flexible green wood (D24, D33), bows (Chipewyan: *i^nlhtí^n*) and arrows (Chipewyan: *k'á*) (D9; Curtis 1928; Birket-Smith 1930; Siegfried 1994), drum frames (Chipewyan: *elgheli*) (D3, D6; Birket-Smith 1930; Siegfried 1994), axe handles (Chipewyan: *tthe^nlh chëné*) (Ross 1862; Irimoto 1981; Siegfried 1994), snowshoe webbing needles (Chipewyan: *ay tlh'ul chëné*) (D11), canoe ribs (Chipewyan: *ts'i eghos*) (D6; Siegfried 1994), wooden nails (Chipewyan: *dechën hotsálh*) for canoe gunwales (Chipewyan: *ts'i eghí*) (D3, D5, D11; Li 1964), handles for dog whips (Chipewyan: *el ttháidh lhi^n*) (D3), grease lamp bowls (Chipewyan: *nú^n tlhesé*) (D11), spoons and hammers (Leighton 1985), hide scrapers (Siegfried 1994), berry mashers, and hide stretching frames (Lamont 1977). Ceremonial rattles (Chipewyan: *deldhére*) can be made by bending a strip of birch wood into a figure "9" and covering it with caribou hide that encloses some pebbles (D3, D21, D24; Hall pers. comm.; Birket-Smith 1930; Brandson 1981). A sweat lodge frame can be made from twelve birch branches (C24, C25). Rotted birch wood can be used to dye hides reddish-brown, can be burned to smoke fish (M6; Leighton 1985), and can be used as baby powder (Leighton 1985).

Properties: The nutrient value of the sap or syrup may be similar to that of maple syrup (see under *Acer negundo* L., Aceraceae). The inner bark of *B. nana* L. was found to have 3.1 g of protein, 14 g of total carbohydrate and 11 mg of vitamin C per 100 g fresh weight. Paper birch twigs and leaves contain (per 100 g fresh weight, 48% moisture): protein (4.9 g), fat (5.5 g), crude fiber (11.6 g), vitamin A (157 RE), and minerals (ash: 1.6 g), including Ca (434 mg), P (118 mg), Fe (7.3 mg), and Mn (10.5 mg) (Kuhnlein and Turner 1991). Birch leaves contain up to 3% flavonoids, plus sesquiterpene oxides, up to 0.5% vitamin C (ascorbic acid), and triterpene alcohols. Birch leaf tea is used in modern phytotherapy in Germany as a diuretic for irrigation therapy of the urinary tract against bacterial infections, inflammation, and renal gravel (Bisset and Wichtl 1994). Birch twigs are astringent, accounting for their effectiveness in treating wounds, and contain some methyl salicylate, which would help to relieve pain (Dobelis 1986). Birch bark has antibacterial and antifungal properties (Farnsworth 1999) and is a rich source of the triterpenes betulin and betulinic acid (at least 20% of the dry weight) (Harborne and Baxter 1993).

Potential: The value of birch wood is well known. There is a significant tourist and gallery market for well-made birch bark baskets and bark-biting artwork. The black birch (*B. lenta* L.) of eastern USA was a commercial source of oil of wintergreen, but the oil is now produced synthetically, reducing what was becoming a serious risk of overharvesting (Dobelis 1986). The essential oil is in demand for aromatherapy (Rogers 1997). There is a market among interior decorating firms for birch tree tops for natural-looking semi-artificial trees (real trunks and branches with silk leaves). Birch branches are used for baskets, wreaths, bird cages, decorative furniture, and specially preserved leafy branches for decorative purposes. There is also a strong demand for birch bark in the form of flat sheets, strips, or sleeves, and hollowed birch logs for floral arrangements, accent pieces for decoration (e.g., picture frames), lamp bases, bird feeders, flower pots, and candles (Mater Engineering 1993). Betulin has antiviral activity against the AIDS virus (Sun et al. 1998) and betulinic acid is active against melanoma (Pisha et al. 1995) and malignant brain tumors (Fulda et al. 1999), indicating a very significant potential for birch bark as a source of important drugs.

Beaked Hazelnut

Other Names: Cree: *pakanak, pakan, pukan, pukānā(h)tik, pakān* ("nut"); French: *noisettier.*

Scientific Name: *Corylus cornuta* Marsh.

Description: A tall, much branched shrub with smooth bark, oval and coarsely toothed leaves, and flowers in separate long male catkins and tiny female catkins. The fruit that develops is a nut surrounded by a tube of fused, hairy bracts that project in a "beak" up to 3 cm beyond the nut.

Habitat: Plentiful in woods, thickets, and moist hillsides across Canada, with extensions into western, central and eastern USA.

(R. Marles)

Food Uses: The nuts are eaten raw when fresh or stored for winter use (C29, C50; Leighton 1985; Siegfried 1994).

Technological Uses: The nuts can be boiled for 30 to 60 minutes to produce a green dye (C29). The bark can be boiled to make a reddish brown dye for moose hide (M1).

Ritual Uses: To prevent newborn babies from becoming ill during teething, very small branches are woven together with a very thin bit of sinew and placed around the baby's neck, where it is worn constantly until it eventually falls off of its own accord (C6).

Properties: Hazelnuts (*C. americana* Walt., 100 g fresh weight, 6% moisture) provide: food energy (634 kcal), protein (12.6 g), fat (62.4 g), total carbohydrate (16.7 g), crude fiber (3.8 g), thiamine (0.46 mg), riboflavin (0.10 mg), niacin (1.1 mg), vitamin C (1.0 mg), vitamin A (7 RE), and minerals (ash: 3.6 g), including Ca (209 mg), P (337 mg), Na (2.0 mg), K (704 mg), and Fe (3.4 mg) (Kuhnlein and Turner 1991).

Potential: Although hazelnuts are not cultivated in most regions of Canada, and the wild ones are smaller than those obtained from the grocery store, their flavor is excellent. The only problem with harvesting from the wild is that they often contain insect grubs. Wild hazelnuts thus have limited potential for development.

BORAGINACEAE
(Borage Family)

Lungwort

Other Names: Cree: *ogu-malask* ("king's plant"); English: tall bluebells; Slave: *eto^n tsha* ("big leaf").

Scientific Name: *Mertensia paniculata* (Ait.) G. Don.

Description: A perennial herb with hairy stems up to 80 cm tall bearing alternate lance-shaped leaves with smooth edges and hairs on both sides, and a few terminal clusters of purplish blue tubular flowers. The fruit is a wrinkled nutlet.

Habitat: Found in moist woodlands and shady stream banks from British Columbia to western Quebec and northern USA.

Food Uses: The large basal leaves can be sun dried, crushed, and mixed with tobacco for smoking (Lamont 1977).

Medicinal Uses: This plant can be part of a compound medicine for treating heart trouble (M9).

Properties: Aerial parts of two other species of *Mertensia* were found to contain potentially toxic pyrrolizidine alkaloids (Farnsworth 1999), so its use as a medicine cannot be recommended until more is known.

Potential: The flowers are very attractive, so it might be worth attempting cultivation as an ornamental.

(R. Marles)

CAMPANULACEAE
(Bluebell Family)

Harebell

Other Names: Chipewyan: *degai mari bet'ánchayé* ("Holy Mary's flower"); Cree: *kuskwasonapiskos* ("thimble plant"), *sewayonakunis, mitīhīmaskīhkīh*; English: bluebell; French: *cloches, clochettes bleues.*

Scientific Name: *Campanula rotundifolia* L.

Description: A perennial with round basal leaves that quickly wither away, leaving only long narrow stem leaves when the beautiful blue bell-shaped flowers appear.

Habitat: Common in dry meadows, on hillsides, and in open woods across Canada and most of the USA except the southeast, and across northern Eurasia.

(R. Marles)

Medicinal Uses: The roots can be used in medicinal teas to treat influenza, fever, lung trouble, or heart trouble (D9, D29). The root can also be chewed to treat angina attacks and irregular heart beat and for strengthening a heart weakened by birth defects or previous heart attacks (D26, M6; Leighton 1985).

Properties: Harebell contains flavonoid glycosides (luteolin derivatives) and triterpenes including ursolic acid (Hetherington and Steck 1997). Luteolin has anti-inflammatory and antibacterial properties, while ursolic acid has been reported to have cytotoxic and leukemia-fighting activities (Harborne and Baxter 1993).

Potential: Harebell is an attractive flower that can be grown as an ornamental, and scientific evidence lends support to its use as a herbal medicine.

CAPRIFOLIACEAE
(Honeysuckle Family)

Northern Bush-Honeysuckle

Other Names: Cree: *maskōcīpihk*; French: *herbe bleue.*

Scientific Name: *Diervilla lonicera* P. Mill.

Description: A shrub up to 1 m tall with opposite leaves that are up to 12 cm long, simple, short-stalked, oval with a long point, mostly hairless, and finely toothed, and yellow (often red-tinged) flowers that are narrow, funnel-shaped, about 2 cm long, in axillary and terminal clusters of one to five, developing into slender seed capsules.

Habitat: Found infrequently in rocky or dry woodlands and clearings from central Saskatchewan east to the Maritimes and south through the eastern USA.

Medicinal Uses: The cooled decoction or infusion of root or stem can be used as a wash for sore eyes or drunk to promote lactation (Leighton 1985).

Properties: Diervilloside has been isolated from the leaves (Hetherington and Steck 1997).

Potential: This attractive plant could be cultivated as an ornamental.

(J.D. Johnson)

Twining Honeysuckle

Other Names: Cree: *sīpāhtik, sī-paminukusīatik, sīpaminitasīatik, sīpāminakasīwā(h)tik, gāganōnskīwaskwah* ("long hair plant"), *gagīnawonskiwaskwah, pay(h)payā(h)tik* ("hole in the middle"); English: limber honeysuckle; French: *chèvrefeuille*; Slave: *kotzedetlelī, detsinka naydī.*

Scientific Name: *Lonicera dioica* L.

(C. Clavelle)

Description: A twining, ascending, or reclining vine or shrub with light-colored shreddy bark, oval leaves that are opposite and often joined at their bases, especially the upper ones, and have a waxy or fuzzy undersurface, and a terminal cluster of tubular, two-lipped flowers that are yellow when young, turning reddish later, and finally developing into red berries.

Habitat: Fairly common in open woodlands and on rocky slopes from southeastern British Columbia to western Quebec, and south in the midwest and northeastern states.

Medicinal Uses: The stem nodes can be cut off and discarded and the internodes boiled to make a drink taken as a diuretic (C11, C54; Lamont 1977; Leighton 1985), to treat heart ailments (Siegfried 1994), or with other plants in decoctions to treat postpartum blood clotting and venereal disease (Leighton 1985). The plant can be soaked in water which is then used to wash the hair to make the hair grow longer (C24, C25). The root can be cut, peeled, and boiled, and the decoction drunk to treat chronic bladder problems, such as when someone can't stop urinating (C38, C44). Honeysuckle roots can be peeled downward (away from the stem) and boiled for an hour, then one-third of a cup of the decoction drunk to relieve constipation (Lamont 1977).

Technological Uses: Hollow stem sections can be used as pipe stems for toy pipes made from rose hips or, more recently, corn cobs, or as straws (Leighton 1985).

Properties: There are a number of iridoid loganin and secologanin derivatives in the leaves and bark (Hetherington and Steck 1997). Loganin acts a bitter tonic and laxative (Harborne and Baxter 1993).

Potential: Secologanin is a specific precursor of several major types of indole alkaloids and could therefore be useful to the pharmaceutical industry for semisynthesis of drugs (Harborne and Baxter 1993).

Bracted Honeysuckle

Other Names: Cree: *payipahtik, pipahtikwa* ("hollow stem wood"); English: black twinberry; French: *chèvrefeuille.*

Scientific Name: *Lonicera involucrata* (Richardson in Franklin) Banks ex Spreng.

Description: A shrub up to 3 m tall, sometimes with downy stems, with oval leaves that have some glandular dots and a downy undersurface, and pairs of yellow flowers with large leaflike bracts at their bases. The fruit is a large purple-black berry with an unpleasant taste.

(R. Marles)

Habitat: Fairly common in moist woodlands of the boreal forest from British Columbia to western Quebec and northern USA.

Medicinal Uses: Pieces of the stem can be gathered when mature in late summer, dried, and boiled to make a decoction drunk to treat venereal disease (M6).

Properties: See twining honeysuckle.

Potential: See twining honeysuckle.

Snowberry

Other Names: Cree: *mahekunimin* ("wolf berry"), *mahekun menes, māyikaniminanahtik* ("wolf berry plant"), *mahikanimin*; English: waxberry, wolfberry; French: *graine d'hiver, graine de loup, belluaine.*

Scientific Name: *Symphoricarpos albus* (L.) Blake. Also *S. occidentalis* Hook.

Description: A slender, freely branching shrub up to 1.5 m tall, with opposite, thin, oval, occasionally wavy-toothed leaves and clusters of a few pink and white bell-shaped flowers in the upper leaf axils or branch tips. The fruit is a distinctive white, waxy, two-seeded berry, 6-10 mm in diameter. Western snowberry

Symphoricarpos occidentalis Hook. in flower
(C. Clavelle)

(*S. occidentalis*) is a more robust shrub, with stamens and styles that protrude from the flower's corolla, and the fruit turns purplish instead of white on drying. The two species occur together and intergrade to a limited extent, so they should probably be treated as different varieties of the same species (Boivin 1967).

Habitat: Common in bushy areas and open rocky woodlands of southeastern Alaska and the southern Northwest Territories, across Canada to Quebec and perhaps introduced into the Maritimes, and the northern USA. Western snowberry's distribution overlaps common snowberry's to a large extent, but extends further south to Texas.

Medicinal Uses: The berries can be crushed or boiled whole to make a wash for sore eyes (D19; Leighton 1985). The root and stem decoction can be given to a child to treat teething pain (D19) or fever associated with teething (Leighton 1985), used as a wash and drunk to treat skin rashes (D19; Leighton 1985), or mixed with another plant to make a remedy for venereal diseases (D19; Leighton 1985). The branches and leaves can be boiled to make a diuretic decoction given to humans (C10) or horses (C11). For treatment of kidney problems in humans, the leafy stems can be part of a compound decoction (C10). It can also be part of a compound love potion (C29).

Properties: Snowberry fruit contains several flavonoid glycosides, and the leaves and roots contain some alkaloids including chelidonine, a narcotic characteristic of the poppy family, numerous terpenoids (Hetherington and Steck 1997), saponins, coumarins, and tannins. Many cases of poisoning from eating snowberries have been documented, especially among children. Symptoms include vomiting and other gastrointestinal irritation, dizziness and delirium, blood-stained urine, and sedation to a semicomatose state, even death, depending on the amount eaten (Turner and Szczawinski 1991).

Potential: Snowberry is clearly poisonous. Although it can be grown as an ornamental, there does not seem to be much development potential for this plant.

Symphoricarpos albus (L.) Blake in fruit (R. Marles)

Mooseberry

Other Names: Chipewyan: *deníjíé* ("moose berry"), *ts'utseljíé*; Cree: *moosomina* ("moose berry"), *mōsomina, muwsuwmin, moosominahtik, mōsōminā(h)tik*; English: low bush-cranberry, squashberry, pembina; French: *pimbina*; Slave: *mathīlīu.*

Scientific Name: *Viburnum edule* (Michx.) Raf.

Description: A shrub growing up to 2 m tall with opposite, oval, coarsely toothed leaves that may be shallowly three-lobed at the apex, small clusters of a few white flowers developing into bright red berries (drupes) with a very acidic taste and strong smell.

Habitat: Common in moist, heavily wooded areas throughout Canada and northern USA, extending further south at higher elevations.

Food Uses: The berries can be eaten fresh but are very sour, so they can be left on the bush as an emergency winter food or cooked to make a jelly (C5, C13, C16, C21, C22, C51, D6, D9, D15, D29, M1, M4; Diamant pers. comm.; Lamont 1977; Jarvenpa 1979; Leighton 1985; Siegfried 1994). Sometimes the bark can be smoked (D15).

Medicinal Uses: The twig tips can be chewed to treat a sore throat, the unopened buds can be rubbed on lip sores to heal and dry them, and a tea made from the roots can be used to ease the pain of teething and as a gargle

(R. Marles)

for a sore throat (D15; Leighton 1985). The tea can also be used as a blood purifier (M9). The ripe fruits can be boiled to make a cough medicine (Lamont 1977).

Technological Uses: Pipe stems can be made from the hollowed out branches (D15, M9).

Properties: The fruit (100 g fresh weight, 89% moisture) contains: food energy (39 kcal), protein (0.1 g), fat (0.4 g), total carbohydrate (9.4 g), crude fiber (3.8 g), vitamin C (13.4 mg), vitamin A (6 RE), and minerals (ash: 0.5 g), including Ca (24 mg), P (23 mg), Na (0.6 mg), Mg (11 mg), Cu (0.1 mg), Zn (0.1 mg), Fe (0.3 mg), and Mn (0.1 mg). *Viburnum opulus* L. fruit has 0.02-0.08 mg of riboflavin per 100 g fresh weight, 89% moisture, decreasing with ripeness (Kuhnlein and Turner 1991). The bark of *Viburnum prunifolium* L. contains a biflavone called amentoflavone, a number of triterpenes and coumarins, salicin and derivatives, and tannins (Bisset and Wichtl 1994). The tannin and salicin content could support many of the traditional uses described here.

Potential: The fruit has limited market potential due to low demand.

High bush-cranberry

Other Names: Cree: *nepiminana, nīpiminān* ("summer berry"); English: pembina.

Scientific Name: *Viburnum opulus* L. var. *americanum* (Mill.) Ait., common synonyms: *V. trilobum* Marsh., *V. opulus* ssp. *trilobum* (Marsh.) Clausen.

Description: A shrub growing up to 4 m tall, with broad, palmately veined, deeply three-lobed, and coarsely toothed leaves, bearing flat-topped sprays of numerous white

(R. Marles)

flowers that develop into orange to red, very juicy but sour fruits.

Habitat: Fairly common in moist, dense woods across Canada, northern USA, and Eurasia.

Food Uses: The berries are added to pemmican only if other, sweeter berries (e.g., blueberries or saskatoons) are not available (D15). The fruits can be eaten fresh, pressed for juice, or preserved as jams or jellies (C50) although they do not smell very nice.

Medicinal Uses: A tea made from the bark can be used as a diuretic and can be given to mothers after birth to prevent infection from the afterbirth (D15). The bark tea can also be given to treat insomnia (D15, M9).

Properties: See the previous species for nutrient and phytochemical properties. The bark extract has been shown to relieve spasms, relaxing uterine muscles, and is effective in treating the uterine pain of menstrual cramps and

High-bush cranberry in late autumn
(R. Marles)

failure to menstruate, but the active ingredients are still unknown (Dobelis 1986; Bisset and Wichtl 1994).

Potential: The fruit has limited market potential due to low demand. The medicinal potential is supported by scientific evidence but remains to be developed.

160

CHENOPODIACEAE
(Goosefoot Family)

Lamb's-Quarters

Other Names: Cree: *wīthiniwpakwātik*; French: *chou gras, poulette grasse*; Slave: *eto^n dītlī* ("leaf is blue").

Scientific Name: *Chenopodium album* L.

Description: An annual erect herb up to 80 cm tall, with longitudinally grooved and reddish-splotched stems, oval, coarsely toothed or wavy leaves with a mealy surface, the flowers arising from the leaf axils and stem tips in dense clusters that have a bluish tinge, producing black shiny seeds.

Habitat: One of the most common weeds of gardens, roadsides, waste ground, and other disturbed sites across North America and Eurasia.

(R. Marles)

Food Uses: The leaves can be eaten raw or cooked (C60; Siegfried 1994).

Medicinal Uses: A decoction of the plant can be taken internally or applied externally as a wash to treat painful limbs (Leighton 1985).

Properties: Lamb's-quarters, a relative of spinach and Swiss chard, is well known as an edible plant. The greens contain the following nutrients (per 100 g fresh weight, 88% moisture): food energy (34 kcal), protein (3.3 g), fat (0.6 g), total carbohydrate (5.7 g), crude fiber (1.5 g), thiamine (0.18 mg), riboflavin (0.49 mg), niacin (1.4 mg), vitamin C (98.3 mg), vitamin A (1277 RE), and minerals (ash: 2.3 g), including Ca (309 mg), P (76 mg), K (874 mg), Mg (177 mg), Cu (0.2 mg), Zn (0.7 mg), Fe (1.2 mg), and Mn (1.1 mg) (Kuhnlein and Turner 1991). They should be consumed only in moderation because they contain soluble oxalates that can bind to and reduce body levels of calcium when eaten in large quantities, and that may also cause photosensitization (Turner and Szczawinski 1991).

Potential: Lamb's-quarters has had a limited market as a potherb, and this use could be promoted as an environmentally friendly way to deal with a troublesome weed.

Strawberry Blite

Other Names: French: *blette*; Slave: *tsa dzhī* ("beaver berry").

Scientific Name: *Chenopodium capitatum* (L.) Aschers.

Description: An annual herb with either erect or spreading stems up to 50 cm tall, pale green triangular leaves up to 10 cm long with coarsely toothed or wavy edges, and flowers in round, fleshy red clusters resembling strawberries at the leaf axils or in terminal interrupted spikes.

Habitat: Found infrequently but conspicuously on stony ground around woodland bluffs, clearings, burns, and other disturbed areas across Canada, in mountainous western and northern USA, and Europe.

(D. Cahoon)

Technological Uses: The flower clusters can be crushed with water and applied as a red dye to rawhide (M9; Lamont 1977) or quills (Lamont 1977).

(J.D. Johnson)

Properties: The red pigment in strawberry blite is due to the same anthocyanins found in beet root, emphasizing their relationship within the same family (Marie-Victorin and Rouleau 1964).

Potential: There might be a market among weavers and other artisans interested in natural dyes.

Red Samphire

Other Names: Cree: *sīwītākan* ("salt"); English: glasswort, sand-fire, swamp-fire; French: *corail, passe-pierre.*

Scientific Name: *Salicornia rubra* A. Nels., common synonym: *S. europaea* L.

Description: A small annual herb growing up to 25 cm tall, with jointed, round, succulent stems that have a membranous-edged collar at the upper end of each joint, opposite branches, leaves reduced to tiny, broadly triangular scales at the nodes, and very tiny flowers in opposite groups of three sunk into the stem tissue of flowering spikes up to 5 cm long. The plant turns bright crimson at maturity.

Habitat: Common and easily spotted in late summer or early autumn as a red plant along saline slough shores or ditches across Canada, western USA, and Eurasia.

Food Uses: The plants can be washed well, then boiled and the decoction can be evaporated in a frying pan to produce salt for food use (C1, C4, C20).

Properties: A number of flavonoids have been reported in red samphire (Hetherington and Steck 1997).

Potential: Plants that grow well in saline areas are of interest for reclamation of brine spill sites associated with the oil drilling industry.

C. Clavelle

CORNACEAE (Dogwood Family)

Bunchberry

Other Names: Chipewyan: *jíkonaze*; Cree: *pihew mina* ("grouse berry"), *kawiskowimin* or *kāwiscōwimin* ("itchy chin berry"), *kawastuwiymin, githu-kistomina* ("itchy beard berry"), *sāsākominān, sāsāguwmin*; English: dwarf dogwood, pigeon berry; French: *quatre-temps, rougets*; Slave: *glo^n dzhī* ("squirrel berry"), *tsīe alī*.

(R. Marles)

Scientific Name: *Cornus canadensis* L.

Description: A low-growing herb from a rhizome with a whorl of elliptical leaves (four on sterile stems, six on flowering stems), a cluster of tiny greenish flowers surrounded by four white bracts, and orange to red berries (drupes).

Habitat: Very common in shady woodlands throughout the boreal region of Canada, mountainous western and northern USA, Greenland, and eastern Asia.

Food Uses: The fruit is sometimes eaten fresh, mainly as an emergency food since the berries are not very palatable (D6, M6; Diamant pers. comm.; Lamont 1977; Leighton 1985; Siegfried 1994). The Cree name comes from the facial irritation caused by the tiny white hairs on the fruit (Siegfried 1994). If the berries are rubbed on the skin they give a prickly feeling (D6).

Medicinal Uses: Bunchberry tea can be taken to treat a "sore heart" (heartburn? Lamont 1977).

Properties: The fruit (100 g fresh weight, 81% moisture) contains the following nutrients: food energy (52 kcal), protein (0.6 g), fat (0.8 g), total carbohydrate (16.6 g), crude fiber (5.2 g), thiamine (0.01 mg), riboflavin (0.03 mg), niacin (0.5 mg), vitamin C (2.1 mg), vitamin A (4 RE), and minerals (ash: 0.5 g), including Ca (52 mg), P (19 mg), Na (0.4 mg), Mg (12 mg), Cu (0.1 mg), Zn (0.1 mg), Fe (0.6 mg), and Mn (0.1 mg) (Kuhnlein and Turner 1991). There are a number of triterpenes, sterols, and anthocyanins known from bunchberry (Hetherington and Steck 1997).

Potential: The anthocyanin derivatives of pelargonin and cyanin have some potential as natural red food coloring (Harborne and Baxter 1993). The fruit is not delicious enough to create a market.

Red Osier Dogwood

Other Names: Chipewyan: *k'ái k'ozé* ("willow which is red"); Cree: *mehkwa pemakwa, mikwapamuk, mīhkwa pēmakwa, mīkōbīmāka, mikwanbimaka, mikwapimakwah, mithkwāpīmak, miskwāpīmak, mi(h)kwapiymak, mikwa piskaw* ("red wood"), *nipsiy wasaskwetow, pīmīhkwāhtik* ("red plant"), *mīhkwanīpisīya* ("red bark"), *mikobimuk* ("red bush"); English: red willow; French: *hart rouge*; Slave: *(d)aʰ dakalī* ("little white" = berries).

Scientific Name: *Cornus sericea* L., common synonym: *C. stolonifera* Michx.

Description: A shrub up to 3 m tall with deep red, aromatic bark, opposite oval, pointed leaves with smooth edges, and flat-topped clusters of small white flowers that develop into bitter white berries.

Habitat: Common in moist wood and on riverbanks across Canada, western and northern USA, and northern Mexico.

Food Uses: The coarse red outer bark can be scraped off and discarded, then the soft green inner bark can be shaved off, dried, and mixed with tobacco to give it a pleasant aroma when smoked for pleasure (it also extends the supply of tobacco) (C21, C22, C23, C24, C25, C27, C35, C36, C47, C52, C57, C58, D3, D9, D24, D29, D32; Munsterhjelm 1953; Lamont 1977; Leighton 1985; Siegfried 1994). It may be mixed with dried prairie sage (*Artemisia ludoviciana* Nutt., Asteraceae) or dried bearberry leaves (*Arctostaphylos uva-ursi* (L.) Spreng., Ericaceae) for smoking (M1, M6). Morice (1909)

(R. Marles)

Red osier dogwood stems being woven into a Dakota basket (R. Marles)

165

says that the inner bark of a viburnum is mixed with tobacco by the north-eastern Chipewyan. This could refer to low- or high bush-cranberry (*Viburnum edule* (Michx.) Raf., *V. opulus* L., Caprifoliaceae) but more likely to red willow. Macoun (1882) says that all the Indians of the plains mix the inner bark of red osier dogwood with tobacco, so this practice may have spread among many cultures.

Medicinal Uses: A tea made from the roots can be drunk to treat dizziness (D29). A tea made from the stem may be taken for chest trouble (perhaps tuberculosis from which this contributor suffers: D33), as an emetic and for coughs and fevers (Holmes, cited in Leighton 1985) or to cure an inability to urinate (D32). A decoction made from bark scraped from the branch tips down toward the base is believed to be laxative, while that prepared from bark scraped from the base up toward the tips of the branches is believed to be emetic (Siegfried 1994). The peeled bark can be mixed with another plant and boiled, and a cloth can be soaked in the solution and then applied to sore eyes (C23, C24, C25, C27). The fruit or stem pith can be made into a wash to treat snow blindness or cataracts (Leighton 1985). A decoction of the ripe fruit can be taken to treat tuberculosis (Lamont 1977). The root can be mixed with other herbs in a decoction given to children to stop diarrhea (C26).

Technological Uses: The red bark can be used to trim birch bark baskets (M6; Lamont 1977; Leighton 1985). Thicker stems have been used to make ribs for spruce bark canoes (Lamont 1977). The dry stems can be burned to smoke moose hides (C52). The bark can be used to dye hides brown or, if mixed with rust, black (Welsh, cited in Leighton 1985; Holmes, cited in Leighton 1985).

Ritual Uses: The dried bark can be mixed with other plants and burned in a pipe to pray (M9). To make a dream-catcher charm, a whole thin red branch can be soaked and then bent into a circle, wrapping around more than once if necessary to use the whole length, tied with sinew, and allowed to dry. It is then webbed with sinew or rawhide and decorated (C59).

Properties: The bark of *C. florida* L. contains gallotannins, the iridoid glucoside cornin, flavonoids including kaempferol and quercetin, and the triterpene ursolic acid. The root contains tannins (3%), gallic acid, and betulinic acid (Duke 1985). The tannin content might explain part of the efficacy as a medicine. The iridoid glucoside cornin (verbenalin) acts as a weak parasympathomimetic (stimulates the nervous system's division responsible for resting and digesting activities) and has smooth-muscle-contracting and laxative properties (Harborne and Baxter 1993). The bark also contains cornic acid which, according to Willard (1992), has an action similar to but milder than ASA.

Potential: Currently the main use of this shrub is as an ornamental due to its attractive red branches, strongly veined leaves, and white berries. It could see more use in basket-making and other handicrafts. Not enough is known of the medicinal properties to make a judgment. There is also some demand for red osier dogwood as a dried or preserved floral product (Mater Engineering 1993). Mater Engineering (1993) categorizes red osier dogwood as a Priority Level 1 product for further development and describes the market in some detail. See Barl et al. (1996) for information on sourcing and selling.

ELAEAGNACEAE
(Oleaster Family)

Silverberry

Other Names: English: wolf-willow; French: *chalef changeant*.

Scientific Name: *Elaeagnus commutata* Bernh. ex Rydb.

Description: A shrub with rusty twigs and distinctive alternate, oval silver leaves. The flowers are silver on the outside, yellow inside, and develop into silver berries with a large stony seed.

Habitat: Very common in dry meadows, valleys, and shores across Canada and central USA.

Food Uses: The fruit is mealy and dry, but is eaten by the Cross Lake Cree (Diamant pers. comm.).

(R. Marles)

Properties: The fruit (100 g fresh weight, 86% moisture) provides: food energy (51 kcal), protein (1.3 g), fat (0.9 g), total carbohydrate (10.9 g), crude fiber (0.5 g), thiamine (0.03 mg), riboflavin (0.05 mg), niacin (0.4 mg), vitamin C (10 mg), vitamin A (1 RE), and minerals (ash: 0.7 g), including Ca (7.0 mg), P (20 mg), and Fe (0.4 mg) (Kuhnlein and Turner 1991).

Potential: There is not likely to be any market for the fruit. The essential oil is in demand for aromatherapy (Rogers 1997).

Buffaloberry

Other Names: Cree: *kinipikomina* ("snake berry plant"), *kinēpikōminānahtik* ("snake berry tree"), *kinīpikōminā(h)tik emskuwmnā(h)tik*; English: soapberry; French: *graines de boeuf*; Slave: *tsena hoe*[h].

Scientific Name: *Shepherdia canadensis* (L.) Nutt.

Description: A shrub with brown branches covered with tiny scales, opposite elliptical leaves with both white and reddish brown star-shaped hairs on the undersurface, small brown flowers and bright red (in some varieties yellow) fruit (drupes) that may be slightly hairy.

Habitat: Fairly common in open woods and along river edges across Canada. It is distributed from Alaska to Oregon, south to New Mexico in the mountains, and east across northern USA to the Atlantic coast.

Food Uses: The fruits are bitter but are eaten by the Cross Lake Cree (Diamant pers. comm.). They can be whipped with icing sugar and eaten as a foamy pudding (C51, M6; Siegfried 1994), but if too much is eaten it will cause diarrhea (C51; Siegfried 1994). This is apparently only a recent practice here, and older people said they were previously never eaten because of their bitterness (Siegfried 1994). They can also be eaten cooked with grease or sugar (Lamont 1977).

(R. Marles)

Medicinal Uses: The leaves and stems can be boiled to make a decoction drunk as a purgative and emetic (C20) to relieve constipation and "clean you out." It can be drunk to treat tuberculosis (M6, M9) and can be used as a wash for cuts, swellings, and skin sores of impetigo (M6; Leighton 1985) and to treat aching limbs or joints, such as in arthritis (Leighton 1985). A tea made from the new shoots can be drunk to prevent miscarriages and can be used as a wash for easing arthritis (M6, M9; Leighton 1985); it can also be taken to treat venereal diseases and coughing up blood (M6; Leighton 1985). The root can be used in a heart medicine (D29). An infusion of inner bark collected by scraping downward can be used as a laxative (Leighton 1985). A decoction of fresh, split roots and peeled and split stems and twigs can be given to babies to reduce a fever, or used as a rub or rinse on their sore mouths (Lamont 1977).

Properties: Buffaloberries or soapberries (100 g fresh weight, 81% moisture) have the following nutrients: food energy (72 kcal), protein (1.8 g), fat (0.7 g), total carbohydrate (6.6 g), crude fiber (1.1 g), Ca (16 mg), P (21 mg), Na (0.5 mg), Mg (8.0 mg), Cu (0.3 mg), Zn (1.4 mg), Fe (0.5 mg), and Mn (0.2 mg) (Kuhnlein and Turner 1991). Due to the fruit's saponin content, they should only be consumed in moderation (Turner and Szczawinski 1991).

Potential: The bitterness of the berry is considered by many to be an acquired taste, so there is not a great demand for soapberries.

EMPETRACEAE
(Crowberry Family)

Crowberry

Other Names: Chipewyan: *tsá^{n}lht'éth*;
Cree: *askīmināsiht*; English: curlew-
berry; French: *graines à corbigeaux*;
Slave: *dzhīa^h tethe* ("watery berries").

Scientific Name: *Empetrum nigrum* L.

Description: A prostrate, matted
shrub with numerous narrow, spreading, evergreen leaves, small solitary
purple flowers, and large, shiny, juicy
black berries.

Habitat: Fairly common in sandy or
acidic gravel ridges, rocky soils,
tundra, and bogs throughout the
circumpolar and circumboreal regions and the Pacific states of the USA.

(R. Marles)

Food Uses: The berrylike drupes are eaten fresh (Diamant pers. comm.;
Birket-Smith 1930; Thompson, cited in Hopwood 1971; Lamont 1977;
Leighton 1985) or cooked and strained to make a syrup (D6, D9). This is the
most popular fruit among the Inuit (Porsild and Cody 1980).

Medicinal Uses: The roots can be boiled with other plants to make a decoction drunk to treat coughs (D29). The leafy branches can be chewed, or applied topically with grease or as a decoction to treat a fever especially in
children (Leighton 1985).

Properties: The fruit (100 g fresh weight, 89% moisture) provides: food energy (35 kcal), protein (0.2-0.6 g), fat (0.7-1.4 g), total carbohydrate (2.4-9.5
g), crude fiber (1.4-5.9 g), thiamine (<0.01 mg), riboflavin (<0.01 mg), niacin
(0.1 mg), vitamin C (51 mg), and minerals (ash: 0.2-0.7 g), including Ca (9.0-
40 mg), P (9.5-11 mg), Na (2.5-3.9 mg), K (46-87 mg), Mg (7.9-11.3 mg), Cu
(1.0 mg), Zn (0.1 mg), Fe (0.4-2.4 mg), and Mn (0.4-2.1 mg) (Kuhnlein and
Turner 1991).

Potential: This low shrub makes an excellent, attractive ground cover, and
the fruit could be examined for potential value-added product development.

ERICACEAE
(Heather Family)

Bog Rosemary

Other Names: Slave: *tli^nte dedzhine, kothentelī naydī, kotsu^ndago dakalī* ("white Labrador tea").

Scientific Name: *Andromeda polifolia* L.

Description: A shrub often 10 cm but up to 30 cm tall, with alternate, evergreen, oblong leaves 1-3 cm long whose edges are rolled to-

(R. Marles)

ward their waxy white undersurface, and a terminal umbel of a few nodding, urn-shaped pink flowers 5-7 mm long with five short lobes on the petal tube, producing a seed capsule that splits down the middle of each of the five seed chambers. It looks similar to bog laurel (*Kalmia polifolia* Wang., Ericaceae), but can be distinguished by its alternate leaves and urn-shaped flowers, while bog laurel has opposite leaves and wheel-shaped flowers.

Habitat: A circumboreal species found in bogs, muskeg, or swamps of most of Canada, Alaska, northwestern and northeastern USA, Greenland, and northern Eurasia.

Medicinal Uses: The stem and root decoction can be drunk to treat a stomachache accompanied by body aches and a cough (Lamont 1977).

Properties: Bog rosemary leaves contain a number of minerals including (per 100 g fresh weight): Ca (330 mg), P (50 mg), K (330 mg), Mg (90 mg), Cu (26 mg), Zn (2.2 mg), Fe (13.8 mg), Mn (53.1 mg), Mo (<0.1 mg), and Cl (16.1 mg). However, bog rosemary also contains a poisonous compound called andromedotoxin, which if consumed in large concentrations can be harmful, causing vomiting and even death; caution is advised (Kuhnlein and Turner 1991).

Potential: Bog rosemary has potential as an ornamental shrub because of its very attractive flowers and foliage. There is probably no potential for it as a herbal medicine because of its toxicity.

Alpine Bearberry

Other Names: Chipewyan: *jíze naghé* ("whiskey-jack's eye"); French: *herbe à caribou, raisin-d'ours alpin*; Slave: *dzhīa^h de^h*.

Scientific Name: *Arctostaphylos alpina* (L.) Spreng.

Description: A trailing shrub with shreddy bark, thin, spoon-shaped, round-toothed, slightly leathery leaves, yellow-green urn-shaped flowers, and shiny black berries.

Habitat: Found occasionally in rocky and gravelly tundra, bogs, and muskeg across the arctic and boreal forest of Alaska, northern Canada, mountains of Maine and New Hampshire, Greenland, and Eurasia.

Food Uses: The berries are eaten fresh (Lamont 1977) or as a jam, but are not very popular because they have little flavor (D6, D9, D29).

Properties: The fruit has 52.5 mg of vitamin C and 30 RE of vitamin A per 100 g fresh weight (Kuhnlein and Turner 1991).

Potential: Although abundant in certain locations, there would never be enough for sustainable harvesting of the fruit from the wild. It would make a very attractive ground-cover species, so the agronomics should be investigated.

(R. Marles)

Red Bearberry

Other Names: Slave: *oⁿka dzhī.*

Scientific Name: *Arctostaphylos rubra* (Rehd. & Wilson) Fern.

Description: A matted, trailing shrub up to 30 cm tall with shreddy bark similar to alpine bearberry (*A. alpina*), but the

(J.D. Johnson)

spoon-shaped, round-toothed leaves are thinner, less wrinkled, and readily deciduous, turning purplish red in autumn and then withering. There are two to four white flowers in a terminal cluster, developing into very juicy scarlet fruit.

Habitat: Fairly common in mossy places in open coniferous woodland and on peaty soils and rocky tundra across northern Canada, Alaska, and Asia.

Food Uses: The fruit can be eaten fresh or cooked (C64; Lamont 1977).

Properties: The fruit has 0.5 g of protein, 5.9 g of total carbohydrates, and 82.3 mg of vitamin C in 100 g fresh weight (85% moisture content) (Kuhnlein and Turner 1991).

Potential: Although abundant in certain locations, there would never be enough for sustainable harvesting of the fruit from the wild. It would

make a very attractive ground-cover species, so the agronomics should be investigated. Once under cultivation, the juicy fruit could be examined for its market potential as a value-added food product such as a jam.

(J.D. Johnson)

Common Bearberry

Other Names: Chipewyan: *délhni, déni* ("crane food" = berries), *'íⁿt'áné* (= leaves); Cree: *āchiygasipuk, muskomina* (= berries), *muskominanatik* (= berry bush), *pithīkōmin, kinnikinnick* (= leaves); English and Algonkian: *kinnikinnick;* French: *raisin-d'ours;* Slave: *netene.*

Scientific Name: *Arctostaphylos uva-ursi* (L.) Spreng.

Description: A prostrate, much-branched shrub forming large mats, with spatula-shaped, smooth-edged, evergreen leaves, pinkish white urn-shaped flowers, and dull red mealy berries.

Habitat: Common in woodlands on sandy hills, exposed rocks, eskers, and riverbanks throughout the boreal region as far north as the tree limit, in Canada, western and northern USA, Greenland, Iceland, and northern Eurasia.

Food Uses: The fruit, although rather dry and mealy, can be eaten and may be cooked in lard with other foods (D6, D9; Curtis 1928; Diamant pers. comm.; Lamont 1977; Leighton 1985; Siegfried 1994). The leaves can be dried and added to tobacco or used as a substitute (D3, D6, D9, D32, M6; Hearne 1795; Morice 1909; Curtis 1928; Lamont 1977; Leighton 1985; Siegfried 1994). *Kinnikinnick* means "mixture" in Algonkian languages and is used to refer to any of several plants mixed with tobacco as extenders.

Medicinal Uses: A tea made from the roots can be drunk to treat a persistent cough (D29) or with other herbs to slow excessive menstrual bleeding (Leighton 1985). The stem decoction can be drunk to prevent miscarriage, to speed a woman's recovery after childbirth, or to bring on menstruation (Leighton 1985). The leaf decoction can be drunk to treat bladder and kidney problems (M6). The fruit with grease can be given to a child to treat diarrhea (Leighton 1985.)

Technological Uses: The dense heartwood of the central root in a large plant can be carved into a pipe bowl (Siegfried 1994).

Properties: The fruit (100 g fresh weight, 75% moisture) contains: food energy (92 kcal), protein (0.7 g), fat (1.1 g), total carbohydrate

(R. Marles)

175

(22.4 g), crude fiber (14.8 g), and minerals (ash: 0.6 g), including Ca (37 mg), P (35 mg), Na (0.5 mg), Mg (17 mg), Cu (1.3 mg), Zn (0.5 mg), Fe (0.7 mg), and Mn (0.2 mg). The leaves (100 g fresh weight, 49% moisture) contain: protein (1.7 g), fat (3.1 g), crude fiber (4.2 g), vitamin A (21 RE), and minerals (ash: 1.0 g), including Ca (221 mg), P (39 mg), Fe (12.7 mg), and Mn (0.6 mg) (Kuhnlein and Turner 1991). The leaves contain a number of hydroquinone derivatives, especially arbutin, methylarbutin, and some esters, abundant gallotannins and catechol tannins, flavonoids (especially hyperoside), triterpenes, iridoid glycosides, and phenol-carboxylic acids. The leaves are effective as a urinary tract disinfectant because of antibacterial activity of the hydroquinone sulfate ester and/or free hydroquinone liberated from arbutin or related compounds in slightly alkaline urine, and due to *p*-hydroxyacetophenone released from the glycoside piceoside. Because of the tannins it is also quite astringent (Bradley 1992; Bisset and Wichtl 1994). Note that bearberry leaves are not diuretic (Bradley 1992; Bisset and Wichtl 1994) but can be mixed with other herbs to provide the necessary diuretic irrigation therapy for urinary tract infections, so long as the other ingredients do not cause an acid urine that would prevent the antimicrobial compound production (Bisset and Wichtl 1994). Large doses of the leaf tea have been reported to have an oxytocic effect (causing contraction of uterine and other smooth muscles) but are risky because large doses or prolonged administration provide excessive tannin and hydroquinone, which can have acute toxic effects such as convulsions and chronic impairment of the liver (Duke 1985).

Potential: In Canada, bearberry leaves are registered, incorrectly it would seem, as a diuretic drug (e.g., Nature's Way, drug identification number 00827800). Despite the fact that this is a very common herb of the boreal forest floor, much of the bearberry leaf drug material is imported from the USA. There is definite market potential for this plant, which can also be used as a very attractive ground-cover species for landscaping. Mater Engineering (1993) categorizes bearberry as a Priority Level 2 product for further development and describes the market in some detail. See Barl et al. (1996) for information on sourcing and selling.

Creeping Wintergreen

Other Names: Cree: *āps-chiypukos* ("tiny leaves"); English: teaberry, creeping snowberry; French: *petit thé, oeufs-de-perdrix.*

Scientific Name: *Gaultheria hispidula* (L.) Muhl. ex Bigelow.

Description: A tiny shrub growing as a mat, with very slender, creeping, reddish fuzzy stems up to 40 cm long, alternate, evergreen ellipti-

(R. Marles)

cal leaves 3-6 mm long which have brown bristly hairs underneath, and a few tiny (2 mm long), cup-shaped white flowers growing singly from leaf axils, with four sepals joined at the base and a petal tube with four short lobes, producing an edible white berrylike fruit with tiny dark hairs and a mild wintergreen flavor.

Habitat: Found occasionally in bogs, muskeg, and wet coniferous woods across Canada, into Washington and Idaho in western USA, and across northeastern USA.

Food Uses: The leaves can be added to tea for flavor (Siegfried 1994).

Medicinal Uses: The leaf decoction can be drunk to treat high blood pressure or in combination with other herbs to treat a fever, and the boiled leaves are cooled and applied to a baby's gums to sooth them (Siegfried 1994).

Properties: The shoots contain (per 100 g fresh weight): protein (5.9 g), Ca (640 mg), P (120 mg), K (680 mg), Mg (410 mg), Cu (0.5 mg), Zn (3.5 mg), Fe (26.2 mg), Mn (300 mg), Mo (<0.1 mg), and Cl (44.2 mg) (Kuhnlein and Turner 1991). The leaves contain oil of wintergreen, of which a major constituent is methyl salicylate, an effective pain reliever, fever reducer, and anti-inflammatory (Dobelis 1986). The hydroquinone derivative arbutin, gallotannins, and a number of aromatic alcohols are also present (Duke 1985).

Potential: The traditional uses are validated by scientific evidence, but the rarity of this plant and ready availability of synthetic substitutes indicates that there is little market potential.

Bog Laurel

Other Names: Chipewyan: *nágodhts'ëlé*; English: pale laurel; French: *crevard de moutons*.

Scientific Name: *Kalmia polifolia* Wangenh.

Description: A small shrub with two-edged twigs, opposite lance-shaped leaves with their edges rolled under and a white undersurface due to a layer of very fine waxy hairs, and flowers in terminal clusters, with a five-lobed sepal tube and pink to reddish petal tube that is rotate (wheel-shaped: a short tube that flares out horizontally to make a flat disk), giving rise to spherical capsules. Some people confuse this plant with Labrador tea (*Ledum groenlandicum* Oeder, Erica-

(R. Marles)

ceae) which grows in the same habitat, but bog laurel has a smooth white leaf undersurface while Labrador tea's leaf undersurface is covered by a rusty wool, and bog laurel has pink rotate flowers while Labrador tea has white flowers with separate petals.

Habitat: Common in bogs and wet acidic meadows across Canada, northern USA, and California.

Medicinal Uses: The leaves have been chewed or made into a tea taken to treat diarrhea (D7, D29).

Properties: Bog laurel contains a poisonous resin called andromedotoxin, consisting of a series of diterpenoid grayanotoxins (Harborne and Baxter 1993), which if consumed in large concentrations can be harmful, causing vomiting and even death; caution is advised. Not only have livestock deaths been reported, but people have died mistaking this plant for Labrador tea. For this reason, it is very important to distinguish bog laurel from Labrador tea, which has only very small amounts of andromedotoxin (Kuhnlein and Turner 1991; Turner and Szczawinski 1991). Arbutin and tannic acid may also contribute to the toxicity (Duke 1985).

Potential: Bog laurel is an attractive ornamental shrub that should not be used medicinally.

Labrador Tea

Other Names: Chipewyan: *nágodhi, naghodhi, nagodhe*; Cree: *muskeko-pukwa, muskekopakwa, muskakopukwu* ("medicine tea"), *maskīkowāpoy* ("muskeg tea"), *maskēkopakwa, mas-kēkopakwatī* ("muskeg leaf tea"), *meskiy(h)kowpuk, mōkōpukwatikwah, mocopawkwatikwa, tīmaskīk, kākī-kīpak*; French: *thé du Labrador*; Slave: *kotsuⁿdago(aʰ)*.

Scientific Name: *Ledum groenlandicum* Oeder, common synonym: *L. palustre* L. var. *latifolium* (Jacq.) Michx. Also *L. palustre* L. ssp. *decumbens* (Ait.) Hultén, *L. glandulosum* Nutt.

Description: A stout erect, aromatic shrub with alternate evergreen leaves, their edges rolled under and rusty hair underneath, a terminal umbel of white flowers with a very

Ledum groenlandicum Oeder in bloom
(R. Marles)

small five-toothed sepal tube and five separate petals, and fruit a small fuzzy capsule tipped with a persistent style. Marsh or northern Labrador tea (*L. palustre* L. ssp. *decumbens*) is distinguished from common Labrador tea by its very narrow leaves with more rolled edges, flowers with 8-11 stamens instead of 5-7 stamens, and smaller seed capsules which are bent abruptly downward. There is also a glandular Labrador tea or trapper's tea (*L. glandulosum* Nutt.) whose leaf edges are only slightly rolled and the undersurface of which is covered with small granular resin glands. It hybridizes with Labrador tea where their ranges overlap on the southwestern edge of the boreal forest.

Habitat: Labrador tea is very common in muskeg, bogs, and wet coniferous woods across Canada, northern USA, and Greenland. Northern Labrador tea, as the name suggests, is found in the northern parts of the circumpolar boreal forest, subarctic and arctic tundra. Glandular Labrador tea is found in moist woods of the southern Rocky Mountains.

Food Uses: The leaf infusion or decoction is widely known as a beverage (C1, C2, C3, C4, C20, C24, C25, C32, C35, C36, C38, C39, C44, C57, C60, D6, D7, D9, D29, M9; Fidler 1792; Morice 1909; Birket-Smith 1930; Leechman 1948; Lamont 1977; Leighton 1985; Siegfried 1994).

Medicinal Uses: The leaves can be either chewed and the juice swallowed or made into a tea drunk to treat stomach flu and diarrhea (D6, D7), chills and bad breath (C38), pneumonia, difficulty urinating (Leighton 1985), or headaches (Lamont 1977). The leaf decoction boiled three times can be taken to treat heart ailments or used warm as a bath to treat arthritis of the hands (Siegfried 1994). With other herbs the leaf tea can be taken to treat colds, infants' teething pain, as a "system cleanser" (C13), to treat whooping cough (Leighton 1985), or to treat kidney ailments (Siegfried 1994). The leaf tea is said to quiet nervous people or relieve tension, and powdered leaves can be applied to burns (D12; Siegfried 1994: leaf powder mixed with lard) or wet eczema (D12). The cooled above-ground parts decoction can be used to soak joints affected by arthritis (C20). To treat colds or chest pains, two whole plants can be boiled with another plant and the decoction can be drunk (C23, C27, C39, C44). To treat excessive hair loss, first soak a plant in water, then boil it, let the decoction cool, then use some to wash your hair and drink some (C23, C27, C39). To treat a migraine headache the leaves can be boiled and the decoction can be drunk, and some of the leaves can be saved, dried, wrapped in a cloth, and applied to the head overnight (C52). The cooled leaf decoction can be drunk to treat a burning sensation during urination (C23, C37). To treat eye infections the plant can be boiled with a little salt until the water turns red, then a cloth is soaked in the hot liquid and laid as hot as can be tolerated over the eyes (C39). The leaf decoction with a little salt added can also be used as an eye wash to treat dry eyes (C42). The leaves can be applied to wounds to treat infections (C35, C36; Holmes, cited in Leighton 1985), an

Ledum groenlandicum Oeder foliage
(R. Marles)

umbilical scab to promote healing, or to cracked nipples, dried and the powder applied to a baby's skin to treat rashes, added to pitch ointment to treat burns, or boiled and the liquid used to wash burns, itchy skin, sores, or chapped skin (Leighton 1985). The peeled root decoction can be used to treat colds and clean out the stomach (C38).

Ritual Uses: Labrador tea can be spilled over the hot rocks in a sweat lodge as an aromatic (C24, C25).

Properties: The leaves contain the following nutrients (per 100 g dry weight, 42% moisture): protein (4.2 g), fat (0.7 g), total carbohydrate (8.7 mg), thiamine (0.01 mg), riboflavin (0.40 mg), niacin (92 mg), vitamin C (98.2 mg), Ca (215 mg), P (93 mg), Na (3.7 mg), Mg (73 mg), Cu (2.4 mg), Zn (2.4 mg), Fe (184 mg), Mn (45.4 mg), Mo (0.2 mg), and Cl (31 mg). The leaves also contain catechin tannins, flavonoids including quercetin, hyperoside, arbutin, and 0.3-2.5% volatile oil consisting of camphor, palustrol, and many other monoterpenes and sesquiterpenes (Duke 1985; Farnsworth 1999). In *L. groenlandicum* the main volatile oil constituent is germacrone, but in *L. palustre* it is ledol, so there are unique qualities to the essential oil from the two species (Hetherington and Steck 1997). Labrador tea leaves also contain a small concentration of the poisonous compound andromedotoxin, which if consumed in large concentrations can be harmful, causing headaches, vomiting, and even death. Therefore Labrador tea should only be consumed in dilute infusions taken infrequently (Kuhnlein and Turner 1991).

Potential: Labrador tea is an attractive shrub with ornamental potential. Because of its potential in the floral industry, Mater Engineering (1993) categorizes labrador tea as a Priority Level 3 product for further development and describes the market in some detail. The leaf tea should probably not be promoted commercially because of the risks associated with overconsumption, although it is possible that selective breeding could reduce the andromedotoxin content to an inconsequential level. The essential oil is in demand for aromatherapy (Rogers 1997).

Blueberry

Other Names: Chipewyan: *tsá^{n}lh-choth*; Cree: *inimena, enimina, īyi-nomin* ("person berry"), *iynimin, ithīnīmina* ("Indian berry"), *sīpīkōmin* ("blue berry," i.e., translated from English); English: bilberry, whortle-berry, huckleberry; French: *bleuet*; Slave: *inkethi*.

Vaccinium uliginosum L. fruit (R. Marles)

Scientific Name: *Vaccinium myrtil-loides* Michx., common synonym: *V. angustifolium* Ait. var. *myrtilloides* (Michx.) House. Also *V. uliginosum* L. and *V. caespitosum* Michx.

Description: Small shrubs with alternate, elliptical leaves that have smooth or slightly serrate edges, and small clusters of white to pink bell-shaped flowers that develop into blue to blue-black berries with a bloom. Dwarf blueberry (*V. caespitosum*) is shorter (25 cm) and has smooth, thin, shiny, finely toothed leaves and five lobes on the pink petal tube; velvetleaf blue-berry (*V. myrtilloides*) has moderate height (40 cm), hairy twigs and leaves, and white flowers at the ends of the branches; bog blueberry (*V. uliginosum*) is the tallest (60 cm) and has thicker, dull, smooth leaves without teeth and clusters of flowers along the branches with four lobes (usually) on the pink petal tube.

Habitat: Common on acidic soil in peat bogs, moist woods, and clearings throughout the boreal forest. The bog blueberry is a circumboreal species; in North America, from the tundra through Canada's boreal region into the mountains of the western states, and also into the northeastern USA. The velvetleaf blueberry has a narrower range, being restricted to North America, from the southern Northwest Territories across Canada's forest regions and into northern USA. The dwarf blueberry is widely distributed across Canada and the western and northern USA.

Food Uses: Blueberries are one of the most important fruit due to their flavor and abundance. They are eaten fresh, cooked with sugar or in bannock, or canned (C6, C7, C9, C13, C18, C23, C27, C60, D3, D6, D28; Diamant pers. comm.; Mackenzie 1801; Curtis 1928; Birket-Smith 1930; Lamont 1977; Jarvenpa 1979, 1980; Leighton 1985; Siegfried 1994). Traditionally they are preserved by cooking in lard which is then allowed to solidify (D3) or by drying in birch bark baskets over a low fire (C23, C27, D6; Siegfried 1994), but not frozen because they become too watery and lose flavor (D3). The dried berries can be added to pemmican (Welsh, cited in Leighton 1985; Siegfried 1994). The dried leaves can be boiled to make a beverage (M1).

Medicinal Uses: Eating blueberries helps acne (M9). Blueberry syrup can be used to treat vomiting (M6). The stem can be boiled to make a drink taken to prevent pregnancy or in combination with other plants to prevent miscarriage, bring blood after childbirth, bring on menstruation, slow excessive menstruation (M6; Leighton 1985), or make a person sweat (Leighton 1985). The root decoction can be drunk to facilitate expulsion of the afterbirth (Siegfried 1994). The whole plant can be one component of an anticancer medicine (M6). The root can be boiled to make a decoction taken for headaches (D29).

Technological Uses: The berries can be used to dye porcupine quills (Welsh, cited in Leighton 1985).

Properties: The fruit of *V. myrtilloides* (100 g fresh weight, 88% moisture) contains: food energy (41 kcal), protein (0.8 g), fat (0.7 g), total carbohydrate (9.1 g), crude fiber (1.5 g), thiamine (0.03 mg), riboflavin (0.05 mg), niacin (0.5 mg), vitamin C (14 mg), vitamin A (1 RE), and minerals (ash: 0.2 g), including Ca (13 mg), P (14 mg), Na (0.3 mg), K (90 mg), Mg (9.5 mg), Cu (0.1 mg), Zn (0.3 mg), Fe (0.2 mg), Mn (0.3 mg), and Mo (<0.1 mg). The fruit of *V. uliginosum* (100 g fresh weight, 88% moisture) contains: food energy (45 kcal), protein (0.7 g), fat (0.6 g), total carbohydrate (10.6 g), crude fiber (3.3 g), and minerals (ash: 0.2 g), including Ca (19 mg), P (13 mg), Mg (8.0 mg), Cu (0.2 mg), Zn (0.3 mg), Fe (0.2 mg), and Mn (2.7 mg). The fruit of *V. caespitosum* has 15 mg of vitamin C per 100 g fresh weight. The leaves of *V. myrtilloides* provide 0.12 mg of riboflavin, 4.5 mg of Cu, 20.3 mg of Zn, 0.2 mg of Fe, and 2.3 mg of Mn per 100 g fresh weight (Kuhnlein and Turner 1991). The closely related species, *V. angustifolium* Ait. and *V. corymbosum* L., are the cultivated blueberries (Simpson and Ogorzaly 1995). As a medicinal herb, the leaves of *V. myrtillus* L. contain catechol tannins, leucoanthocyanins, flavonoids (mostly quercetin glycosides), phenol-carboxylic acids, quinolizidine alkaloids, and iridoids. Used externally it is effective as an astringent, and it is being investigated for internal use against diabetes due to its content of chromium and flavonoids (Bisset and Wichtl 1994).

Potential: Blueberry fruit has an established market and supply lines that would be difficult for northern communities to compete with except locally (Morgan 1999), but there may be the potential for value-added food or beverage products. Medicinally there is not enough evidence yet to confirm its usefulness and major pharmaceutical companies are already active in investigating its potential (Hammond pers. comm.).

Bog Cranberry

Other Names: Chipewyan: *tunelhésaze* ("little fog [hard to see]"); Cree: *we'sagimena, maskekōmin*; English: swamp cranberry, mossberry; French: *airelle canneberge, atocas*; Slave: *dzhīa^h tethe* ("watery berries"), *de^h enda* ("crane's eye").

Scientific Name: *Vaccinium oxycoccos* L., common synonyms: *Oxycoccus microcarpus* Turcz., *O. quadripetalus* Gilib.

Description: A tiny creeping shrub with threadlike stems, small oval leaves with margins strongly rolled under, pink flowers with petal lobes bent back, and juicy red berries.

Habitat: Frequent in muskeg and bogs, from the Pacific Northwest of Canada and USA to Labrador and northeastern USA, Iceland, and Eurasia.

Food Uses: The fruit is eaten fresh (D29, Diamant pers. comm.; Lamont 1977; Leighton 1985), preferably after a frost (Curtis 1928), or cooked (D6; Leighton 1985).

Properties: The fruit (100 g fresh weight) provides: protein (0.4 g), total carbohydrate (3.6 g), vitamin C (5.5 mg), Cu (0.1 mg), Zn (0.2 mg), Fe (0.8 mg), and Mn (1.7 mg) (Kuhnlein and Turner 1991).

Potential: This species and the closely related *V. macrocarpon* Ait. are cultivated for juice and jelly production (Simpson and Ogorzaly 1995). Low productivity and lack of easy access to markets in the north will probably limit the market potential of wild cranberries.

(R. Marles)

Mountain Cranberry

Other Names: Chipewyan: *naⁿtlh'ér, jíé súⁿlhiné*; Cree: *wesakemina* ("bitter berry"), *wīsaki(h)min, wiysukiymin*; English: bog cranberry, cowberry, lingonberry; French: *berris, graines rouges, airelle.*

Scientific Name: *Vaccinium vitis-idaea* L. ssp. *minus* (Lodd.) Hultén.

Mountain cranberry in bloom (R. Marles)

Description: A low evergreen shrub up to 20 cm tall, with trailing stems producing some erect branches, spoon-shaped leathery leaves with rolled edges and black dots of hairs underneath, and terminal clusters of pink to white bell-shaped flowers that develop into dark red berries with the characteristic acidic taste.

Habitat: Common in dry bogs, rocky tundra, and sandy woodlands throughout the boreal forest of Canada, New England, Greenland, Iceland, and northern Eurasia.

Food Uses: Mountain cranberries are smaller but with a flavor similar to or even superior to commercial cranberries. They are harvested in late fall (or even in early spring) and eaten raw (they taste better after a frost), mixed in pemmican, fried in lard, cooked and canned, or strained to make a jelly (C12, C24, C25, C50, D3, D6, D9, D24, D29; Diamant pers. comm.; Hearne 1795; Mackenzie 1801; Curtis 1928; Birket-Smith 1930; Lamont 1977; Jarvenpa 1979, 1980; Irimoto 1981; Leighton 1985; Siegfried 1994). Cranberries can be stored for a whole year in birch bark baskets in a cache under the muskeg (C24, C25; Siegfried 1994). The dried leaves can be added as an extender to tobacco (D3; Birket-Smith 1930; Munsterhjelm 1953).

Mountain cranberry in fruit (R. Marles)

Medicinal Uses: Eating the berries can be good for you because they "clean out your stomach" (C24). The berries can be eaten to relieve a bad fever that is suffered in the spring (D29). The roots and stems can be boiled and the decoction drunk to treat bladder problems (C6, D27).

Technological Uses: A red dye (e.g., for porcupine quills) can be made from the boiled berries (D27; Welsh, cited in Leighton 1985). The ripe berries can be strung to make a necklace (Leighton 1985).

Properties: The fruit (100 g fresh weight, 82% moisture) provides: food energy (62 kcal), protein (0.7 g), fat (0.7 g), total carbohydrate (14.9 g), crude fiber (1.4 g), thiamine (0.02 mg), riboflavin (0.08 mg), niacin (0.4 mg), vitamin C (21.2 mg), and minerals (ash: 0.5 g), including Ca (13 mg), P (11 mg), Na (<0.1 mg), K (98 mg), Mg (6.6 mg), Cu (0.1 mg), Zn (6.1 mg), Fe (0.2 mg), Mn (2.9 mg), and Mo (<0.1 mg) (Kuhnlein and Turner 1991). The leaves contain arbutin and thus have urinary antiseptic properties as described for bearberry leaves (*Arctostaphylos uva-ursi* (L.) Spreng., Ericaceae), and like bearberry leaves, they probably do not have the diuretic properties claimed for them, which would come from other herbs in a mixture (Dobelis 1986; Bisset and Wichtl 1994). Cranberry fruit juice is clinically proven to be useful in treating urinary tract infections. This is not due to acidification of the urine as was originally thought (the acidity does not change enough to have an appreciable antibacterial effect), but due to the presence of two types of active compounds. Fructose inhibits adhesion of type 1-fimbriated *E. coli* bacteria, and certain proanthocyanidin-type condensed tannins, restricted in their distribution to cranberries and blueberries, prevent adhesion of P-fimbriated *E. coli* bacteria to the urinary tract epithelium (Foster and Tyler 1999). The fimbriae are fringes of lectins (sugar-binding proteins) on the surface of the bacterium that it uses to attach itself to the surface it will grow on. Thus, when the function of the fimbriae is blocked by the fruit sugar or special tannin, the bacteria cannot adhere and continue to grow in the urinary tract and can be flushed out with diuretic irrigation therapy.

Potential: There is an established market for cranberry fruit and juice, but due to well-established supplies for the commercial market and limits on productivity and market access in the north, competition might hinder development.

FABACEAE
(Bean Family)

American Milk-Vetch

Other Names: Cree: *kāsīsīkwānī-pathisihk* (*sīsīkwan* = "rattle"); English: rattlepod, locoweed; Slave: *kozo^n^ dakalī*.

Scientific Name: *Astragalus americanus* (Hook.) M.E. Jones, common synonym: *A. frigidus* (L.) Gray var. *americanus* (Hook.) S. Wats.

Description: A perennial woody stem base gives rise to several annual, slightly hairy stems up to 1 m tall, with conspicuous stipules (small leaflike projections) at the nodes, pinnate leaves with 7-15 oblong leaflets, slightly hairy on their under-surfaces, and several long slender

Canadian milk-vetch (*Astragalus canadensis* L.) (C. Clavelle)

inflorescences of yellowish white pea-type flowers that develop into inflated oval seed pods about 2 cm long, which hang down and rattle with the seeds inside.

Habitat: Found in moist woods, bogs, fens, forest openings, and riverbanks from southeastern Alaska and Yukon, south through western Canada into Montana, Wyoming, Colorado, and South Dakota, with a limited spread eastward into Ontario and Quebec.

Food Uses: The root could be eaten only in very small amounts during times of starvation (Lamont 1977).

Medicinal Uses: The root can be chewed and the juice swallowed to treat a stomachache, cramps, or stomach flu (Leighton 1985).

Technological Uses: The seed pods have been given to babies as rattles (Lamont 1977).

Properties: Some milk-vetches are desirable as forage crops due to their high protein content and for soil-building because certain bacteria associated with their roots can turn nitrogen gas from the air into ammonia, which can then be used by surrounding plants as a nitrogen fertilizer. However, some are toxic due to the presence of derivatives of nitropropionic acid or of selenium accumulated from the soil (Turner and Szczawinski 1991). The chemistry of *A. americanus* is not known, although many other species have been studied extensively (Hetherington and Steck 1997; Farnsworth 1999). The root of *A. membranaceus* Moench has a long history of use as a medicine in China, and has been shown to have immune stimulating, antiviral, and cardiac effects possibly beneficial in cases of myocarditis or congestive heart failure (Boon and Smith 1998).

Potential: Not enough is known about this species to make a judgment. It deserves further investigation.

American Alpine Sweet-Vetch

Other Names: English: sweet-broom; French: *sainfoin alpin*; Slave: *Déné thae*[h] ("Slave carrot").

Scientific Name: *Hedysarum alpinum* L. var. *americanum* Michx.

Description: An erect perennial herb growing up to 80 cm tall, with a few somewhat hairy branches, small brown leaflike stipules where the leaf stalks join the stem, leaves divided pinnately into 11-21 oblong leaflets up to 3 cm long, and numerous slender columns of pink to reddish purple flowers which have sepals shaped like a five-lobed cup and petals shaped like a pea flower. The pod is flat, may be smooth or

(J.D. Johnson)

slightly fuzzy, and has three to five bulges, breaking crosswise between each of the seeds rather than splitting lengthwise like a pea pod would.

Habitat: Common in moist open woods, tundra, parkland, or gravel slopes across Canada, in the mountains of Montana and Wyoming, east through the Maritimes to Maine, New Hampshire, and Vermont, and in northern Eurasia.

Food Uses: The roots can be boiled in a soup, or eaten raw in times of starvation (Lamont 1977).

Medicinal Uses: Small pieces of the sun-dried roots can be burned and the smoke trapped with a blanket over the head to treat sore eyes (Lamont 1977).

Properties: The roots contain 29 mg of vitamin C per 100 g fresh weight (Kuhnlein and Turner 1991). The plant contains the xanthones mangiferin and isomangiferin (Hetherington and Steck 1997). These compounds have anti-inflammatory, liver protecting, central nervous system stimulant, and antiviral activities (Harborne and Baxter 1993).

Potential: There is one French patent on this plant as a source of mangiferin (Hetherington and Steck 1997). There seems to be some potential as a medicine.

Alfalfa

Other Names: English: lucerne; French: *luzerne, lentine.*

Scientific Name: *Medicago sativa* L.

(R. Marles)

Description: A fairly erect perennial herb up to 80 cm tall, much-branched, with leaves divided into three egg-shaped leaflets up to 35 mm long, sharply toothed toward the apex. The typical pea-type flowers are in a dense oblong spray and are usually bluish violet to purple, occasionally whitish, up to 10 mm long, developing into pods that are usually coiled one to three times.

Habitat: A native of Eurasia that has escaped from cultivation and is now very common in fields and waste places and along roadsides throughout most of North America.

Medicinal Uses: The above-ground parts can be steeped in hot water to make a drink for treating arthritis or ulcers. This is a remedy learned from a German woman (C20).

Properties: Alfalfa greens provide the following nutrients (per 100 g fresh weight, 83% moisture): food energy (52 kcal), protein (6.0 g), fat (0.4 g), total carbohydrate (9.5 g), crude fiber (3.1 g), thiamine (0.15 mg), riboflavin (0.18 mg), niacin (0.5 mg), vitamin C (152 mg), vitamin A (341 RE), and minerals (ash: 2.3 g), including Ca (690 mg), P (110 mg), Na (110 mg), K (650 mg), Zn (0.9 mg), and Fe (5.4 mg) (Kuhnlein and Turner 1991). The leaves also contain tannins (up to 2.8%), and coumestrol and several related compounds which have been reported to have an estrogenic effect (Duke 1985). There is some evidence for a cholesterol-lowering effect of alfalfa seed consumption (Boon and Smith 1998). The leaves and seeds are an excellent source of nutrients, particularly for vitamins C, D, E, and K (Dobelis 1986). However, as with most foods, moderation is important because alfalfa contains a non-protein amino acid, l-canavanine, which may play a role in causing blood abnormalities (pancytopenia) and in inducing or reactivating systemic lupus erythematosus in persons having a predisposition to that condition who consume large amounts of alfalfa sprouts or take large quantities of alfalfa tablets (Foster and Tyler 1999).

Potential: The nutritive value is well established and it is widely used as a forage crop and as sprouts at salad bars. Its medicinal value is not established.

White Sweet-clover

Melilotus albus Medik. (C. Clavelle)   *Melilotus officinalis* (L.) Lam (C. Clavelle)

Other Names: French: *trèfle d'odeur blanc*; Slave: *Dénélī naydī* ("man medicine").

Scientific Name: *Melilotus albus* Medik., common synonyms: *M. alba* Desr., *M. alba* Medik. Also *M. officinalis* (L.) Lam, yellow sweet-clover.

Description: White sweet-clover is an annual or biennial introduced forage herb growing up to 2.5 m tall, with leaves divided into three leaflets, each of which is toothed almost to the base, and long, spikelike sprays of small (4-5 mm long) white pea-type flowers that develop into short, thick, straight, smooth pods containing just one or a few yellow seeds. Yellow sweet-clover has yellow flowers, pods that are wrinkled, and olive green or purple spotted seeds, but vegetatively is very similar to white sweet-clover.

Habitat: Sweet-clovers are introduced Eurasian forage crops now commonly escaped in fields, roadsides, and waste ground throughout North America.

Medicinal Uses: The entire plant of white sweet-clover can be boiled with barley seeds and 1 cup of the decoction can be drunk once per week for a month as a general tonic. This remedy was learned from a Ukrainian woman (C57).

Ritual Uses: Yellow sweet-clover can be part of a "man medicine" love charm (Lamont 1977).

Properties: Yellow sweet-clover seeds have 34.6 g of protein, 6.0 g of fat, and 4.0 g of minerals (ash) per 100 g fresh weight (Kuhnlein and Turner 1991). The leaves of yellow sweet-clover contain coumarin and its derivatives (hence the sweet smell), flavonoids (especially kaempferol and quercetin derivatives), and oleanolic-acid-derived saponins. The infusion is effective internally as an antiphlebitis remedy and reduces inflammatory and congestive edema. It treats venous insufficiency by increasing venous return and improving lymph kinetics. Externally it has demonstrated acceleration of wound healing (Bisset and Wichtl 1994). If sweet clover is allowed to become moldy, the mold fungus converts plant coumarins, which are not particularly toxic to humans or cattle, into bishydroxycoumarin (dicoumarol), an enzyme inhibitor that prevents normal blood clotting, causing cattle to die from internal bleeding (Duke 1985).

Potential: Although its use as a forage crop is well established, there is also scientific support for sweet-clover's use as a herbal medicine.

Alsike Clover

Other Names: Cree: *moostos mechewin* ("cattle food"); French: *trèfle alsike.*

Scientific Name: *Trifolium hybridum* L.

Description: A perennial much-branched herb with long-stalked, smooth leaves divided into three oval leaflets, pink, slender pea-type flowers in long-stalked heads, and two to four greenish to black seeds in small pods.

Habitat: A Eurasian species that has escaped from cultivation as a forage crop; common in waste places and roadsides across most of North America.

Red clover (*Trifolium pratense* L.)
(R. Marles)

Food Uses: The flowers may be boiled and eaten (C60).

Medicinal Uses: The leaves can be boiled to make a tea drunk as a "blood purifier," "blood thinner," or treatment for eczema (M6) or psoriasis (M6, M9).

Properties: The leaves of red clover (*T. pratense* L., 100 g fresh weight, 78% moisture) contain: protein (5.0 g), thiamine (0.56 mg), vitamin C (71 mg), vitamin A (1330 RE), Ca (64 mg), P (4.0 mg), K (70 mg), Mg (9.0 mg), Cu (0.2 mg), Zn (2.5 mg), Fe (16.3 mg), and Mn (1.5 mg) (Kuhnlein and Turner 1991). Red clover flowers are used in modern British phytotherapy externally in various preparations to treat psoriasis, eczema, and rashes, and internally as a mild antispasmodic and expectorant for coughs and bronchitis. The leaves contain caffeic acid derivatives, coumarins, and isoflavones (1% dry weight), mainly formononetin and biochanin, with lesser amounts of genistein, daidzein, pratensein, and several others. The leaves' coumarin derivative, coumestrol, and the isoflavones have been shown to cause estrogenic disorders in cattle feeding largely on red clover (Bradley 1992; Duke 1985). Red clover is listed as Generally Regarded as Safe (GRAS) by the US FDA (Bradley 1992).

Potential: The nutritional value of clover is expected of an important forage crop, but it also appears to have some interesting medicinal properties that warrant further investigation. Turner and Szczawinski (1991) recommend moderation in eating clovers, because some health problems have been reported from eating large amounts. Humans do not digest foods in the same way as cattle (because they do not have a rumen), so the fact that cattle eat a lot of clover is not relevant here.

GROSSULARIACEAE (Currant Family)

Wild Red Currant

Other Names: Chipewyan: *jítlh'oghaze* ("little grassy berry"); Cree: *mīthicīmin, meriychiymin*; French: *gadellier;* Slave: *dzhīaʰ dehoneʰ, dzhīaʰ dethī.*

Scientific Name: *Ribes glandulosum* Grauer. Also *R. triste* Pall., common synonym: *R. rubrum* L. var. *propinquum* (Turcz.) Trautv. & Mey.

Ribes glandulosum Grauer
(R. Marles)

Description: Skunk red currant (*R. glandulosum*) is a low spreading shrub without thorns, with leaves having five to seven lobes and a skunklike odor, white or reddish flowers in a short spray, and red, bristly berries. Swamp red currant (*R. triste*, Cree: *athīkimin* = "frog berry") has leaves without odor, fewer lobes, and smooth red berries.

Habitat: Skunk red currant is common in damp woodlands, clearings, and rocky slopes throughout the aspen parkland and boreal forest across northern and central Canada and northeastern USA. Swamp red currant is a circumboreal species found across Canada and northern USA.

Food Uses: Currants are eaten fresh (D6, D9, D29; Lamont 1977; Leighton 1985; Siegfried 1994) or cooked to make a jelly (D6; Siegfried 1994). The stem can be made into a bitter tea (Leighton 1985).

Medicinal Uses: The stem decoction of skunk red currant can be given to prevent blood clotting after birth (Leighton 1985). The bark of swamp red currant can be scraped off, dried, and then boiled to make a decoction drunk to bring on menstruation (Siegfried 1994).

Properties: The fruit of *R. glandulosum* contains 55 mg of vitamin C and *R. triste* contains 51.5 mg of vitamin C per 100 g fresh weight. Commercial currants have the following nutrients (100 g fresh weight, 86% moisture): food energy (50 kcal), protein (1.4 g), fat (0.2 g), total carbohydrate (12.1 g), crude fiber (3.4 g), thiamine (0.04 mg), riboflavin (0.05 mg), niacin (0.1 mg), vitamin C (41 mg), vitamin A (7.2 RE), and minerals (ash: 0.6 g), including Ca (25 mg), P (27 mg), Na (1.0 mg), K (198 mg), Mg (10 mg), Cu (0.1 mg), Zn (0.1 mg), Fe (0.3 mg), and Mn (0.1 mg) (Kuhnlein and Turner 1991).

Potential: The market for red currants is not very large, but value-added products might be feasible.

Black Currant

Other Names: Chipewyan: *nútsëné*; Cree: *kaskitīmin, māntuwmna(h)tik*; French: *cassis*; Slave: *ndatsene.*

Scientific Name: *Ribes hudsonianum* Richards. Also *R. americanum* P. Mill.

Description: An erect shrub without thorns, with three- to five-lobed, hairy, glandular leaves, white flowers in sprays, and smooth dark red to black berries. The northern black currant (*R. hudsonia-*

Ribes hudsonianum Richards. (R. Marles)

num) differs from the American black currant (*R. americanum*) in the minor details of having a somewhat broader flower on a longer stalk, white rather than greenish white sepals, and a few glands on the ovary.

Habitat: Northern black currant is common in moist shady woods and rocky slopes from British Columbia and Alaska to western Quebec, and, in the USA, the western, midwestern, and Great Lakes states. American black currant has a more eastern and southern distribution, east of the continental divide from central Alberta to Nova Scotia, south to New Mexico at higher elevations, and across northern USA.

Food Uses: Black currants are eaten fresh (C51, D6, D29; Lamont 1977) or cooked for jam (Leighton 1985; Siegfried 1994) and can be used with raspberries to make wine (D6) or flavor home brew (Lamont 1977). The young leaves may also be eaten in a salad (C51).

Medicinal Uses: The roots can be boiled with other plants to make a medicinal drink for bad colds (D9). The leafy stem decoction can be drunk to treat a cough (Lamont 1977) or sickness after childbirth (Leighton 1985), or to bring on menstruation, or, in combination with other plants, to treat diabetes (Siegfried 1994).

Properties: *Ribes hudsonianum* fruit has 41 mg of vitamin C and *R. americanum* fruit has 89 mg of vitamin C per 100 g fresh weight. Trailing black currant fruit (*R. laxiflorum* Pursh, 100 g fresh weight, 84% moisture) contains: food energy (59 kcal), protein (0.7 g), fat (0.6 g), total carbohydrate (14.2 g), crude fiber (5.2 g), thiamine (<0.01 mg), riboflavin (<0.01 mg), niacin (0.4 mg), vitamin C (3.3 mg), vitamin A (2 RE), and minerals (ash: 0.5 g), including Ca (51 mg), P (23 mg), Na (1.8 mg), Mg (18 mg), Cu (0.1 mg), Zn (0.4 mg), Fe (0.6 mg), and Mn (1.2 mg) (Kuhnlein and Turner 1991). The leaf of *R. nigrum* L. contains 0.5% dry weight of flavonoids: kaempferol, quercetin, myricetin and isorhamnetin glycosides. One flavonoid, sakuranetin, has been shown to have fungicidal activity. *R. nigrum* leaves are used occasionally in diuretic herbal preparations (Bisset and Wichtl 1994).

Potential: The fruits are nutritious but the demand is limited at present. In Britain, black currant syrup is popular as a dietary supplement and flavoring agent. The market potential for such a product here could be investigated.

Swamp Gooseberry

Other Names: Cree: *soominisak, sapominahtik, sikakomina*; English: prickly currant; French: *gadellier*; Slave: *tli^n dzhīa^h* ("dog berry").

Scientific Name: *Ribes lacustre* (Pers.) Poir.

Description: A very spiny low shrub with leaves that each have three to seven pronounced lobes; flowers that are small, green, or purplish, saucer-shaped, and arranged in sprays; and fruits that are reddish purple to black and hairy.

Habitat: Found occasionally in swamps and moist woods from central Alaska south to California and across Canada and northern USA.

Food Uses: The berries are eaten raw or preserved in jams (M6).

Medicinal Uses: The stem bark tea can be drunk as a treatment for diarrhea and colds, and the leaf tea can be drunk to prevent miscarriages (M6).

Properties: The fruit of *R. lacustre* (100 g fresh weight, 86% moisture) contains: food energy (59 kcal), protein (1.5 g), fat (2.3 g), total carbohydrate (9.7 g), crude fiber (3.5 g), thiamine (0.04 mg), riboflavin (<0.01 mg), niacin (<0.1 mg), vitamin C (58.2 mg), vitamin A (3 RE), and minerals (ash: 0.9 g), including Ca (68 mg), P (47 mg), Na (0.6 mg), Mg (22 mg), Cu (0.1 mg), Zn (0.2 mg), Fe (0.4 mg), and Mn (0.3 mg) (Kuhnlein and Turner 1991).

Potential: Gooseberries are not in great demand, but a niche market might be found for gooseberry jam or other value-added products.

(R. Annas)

Northern Gooseberry

Other Names: Chipewyan: *daghósjíé* ("thorn berry"), *doghosé jíé*; Cree: *sapoominak, sāpōmin* ("bitter berry"), *sābuwmin*; English: Canadian gooseberry; French: *groseillier hérissé*; Slave: *dahoze, dahothe*.

Scientific Name: *Ribes oxyacanthoides* L., common synonym: *R. setosum* Lindl. Also *R. hirtellum* Michx., common synonym: *R. oxyacanthoides* L. var. *saxosum* (Hooker) Cov.

Description: The northern gooseberry (*R. oxyacanthoides*) is a shrub growing up to 1 m high with bristly stems and longer spines at the nodes, three- to five-lobed fuzzy and glandular leaves, greenish purple or white flowers, and large, globose, smooth berries first green but turning reddish purple when ripe. The wild gooseberry (*R. hirtellum*) is very similar but has few spines or bristles on older stems, no glands on the leaves, and a wedge-shaped rather than heart-shaped leaf base.

Habitat: The northern gooseberry is common in woodlands and calcareous rocky hillsides and clearings across Canada and northern USA. The wild gooseberry is found east of the continental divide in the southern half of Canada and adjacent northern USA.

Food Uses: Gooseberries are often eaten fresh or made into jam (D6, D9, M6; Diamant pers. comm.; Hearne 1795; Mackenzie 1801; Curtis 1928; Lamont 1977; Jarvenpa 1979, 1980; Leighton 1985; Siegfried 1994).

Ribes oxyacanthoides L. (R. Marles)

Medicinal Uses: The root can be boiled and the decoction drunk to stimulate a delayed menstrual period (D29). The stem can be steeped in boiling water and the tea drunk by mothers after childbirth to stop excessive bleeding (M6). The stem decoction is part of a compound decoction drunk to treat sickness after childbirth (Leighton 1985).

Properties: Northern gooseberries (100 g fresh weight, 82% moisture) contain: food energy (58 kcal), protein (1.0 g), fat (0.3 g), total carbohydrate (14.6 g), crude fiber (1.9 g), and minerals (ash: 0.7 g) including Ca (91 mg), P (83 mg), Na (0.3 mg), K (613 mg), Mg (28.4 mg), Cu (0.1 mg), Zn (0.3 mg), Fe (0.9 mg), Mn (0.3 mg), and Mo (<0.1 mg). Commercial gooseberries (100 g fresh weight, 88% moisture) contain the vitamins thiamine (0.04 mg), riboflavin (0.03 mg), niacin (0.3 mg), vitamin C (27.1 mg), and vitamin A (29 RE) (Kuhnlein and Turner 1991).

Potential: Gooseberries are not in great demand, but a niche market might be found for gooseberry jam or other value-added products.

LAMIACEAE
(Mint Family)

Giant Hyssop

Other Names: Cree: *kā-wīkīpakahk*; French: *agastache fenouil.*

Scientific Name: *Agastache foeniculum* (Pursh) Ktze.

Description: An erect, branched perennial growing from creeping rhizomes, with smooth or minutely hairy stems up to 1 m tall, bearing opposite, pointed oval, coarsely saw-toothed leaves and dense terminal spikes of flowers that have violet or bluish sepals and blue petals. The plant has a characteristic pleasant aniselike odor.

(R. Marles)

Habitat: Common in open woodlands and semiopen grasslands throughout the parklands region and into the boreal forest. Native to British Columbia, the Prairie provinces, western Ontario, and the adjacent states, and introduced into northeastern North America.

Food Uses: The leaves can be dried and boiled to make a beverage, or added to commercial tea as a flavoring (D19; Leighton 1985).

Medicinal Uses: The dried whole plant can be boiled with another herb to make a decoction drunk to treat stomachaches (C47). The leaves can be one component of a compound medicine for treating severe coughing (D19; Leighton 1985), and the flower head can be chewed as a breath freshener (D19).

Properties: The essential oil, which is present in the foliage in yields from 0% to 3%, is quite variable, as would be expected from wild populations. It contains primarily methyl chavicol, gamma-cadinene, alpha-cadinol, spathulenol, bornyl acetate, and caryophyllene, with numerous other components in lesser amounts (Hetherington and Steck 1997).

Potential: As a fairly large and common mint, giant hyssop has promise as a source of essential oil for the perfume and aromatherapy markets (Rogers 1997). It is also used in dried floral arrangements and herbal teas (Miller 1997).

Hemp Nettle

Other Names: Cree: *amisko wehkuskwa*; French: *gratte, ortie royale.*

Scientific Name: *Galeopsis tetrahit* L.

Description: An annual, coarse, hairy herb growing up to 1 m tall, with stems usually swollen below each cluster of oval to lance-shaped, coarsely toothed

(C. Clavelle)

leaves and axillary flowers that have sharply pointed sepal teeth and petals that are pink or purple variegated with white and often two yellow spots, fused into a tube that ends with an arched upper lip and a lower lip split into three parts.

Habitat: A common weed of fields, roadsides, and waste areas in the parklands and boreal forest across Canada and northern USA, introduced from Eurasia.

Food Uses: The highly scented stems, roots, and flowers can be used to make tea and season meat (D27).

Medicinal Uses: The tea can be drunk to calm nerves and it can be given to children to reduce hyperactivity. It can also be taken as a spring tonic, to restore appetite, and to treat bad breath, while the leaves can be chewed to treat severe hiccups (D27).

Properties: The leaves of *G. segetum* Neck. contain tannins (approximately 5% of dry weight), flavonoids, and iridoids. Hemp nettle is used as an astringent, prepared as teas or drops (Bisset and Wichtl 1994).

Potential: Its use as a herbal tea additive is established in Europe, where *G. tetrahit* is considered an adulterant of *G. segetum*. There is no market for this species at this time.

Wild Mint

Other Names: Chipewyan: *tsá tlh'ogh tsëné* ("beaver grass with scent"); Cree: *amisko wehkuskwa* ("good tasting beaver plant"), *amis-kōwīkask, āmskuwiy(h)kusk, wīkask* ("pleasant tasting"), *wīkaskwah, wakaskwah*; English: field mint; French: *baume*; Slave: *eto^n detsī* ("leaf smells").

Scientific Name: *Mentha arvensis* L. Sometimes segregated into *M. arvensis* and *M. canadensis* L.

Description: An erect perennial herb with square stems, opposite, egg-shaped, saw-toothed, glandular leaves with a strong but pleasant mint odor, and pink flowers

(R. Marles)

in crowded whorls around the stem where the leaves join it.

Habitat: A circumboreal species common in sloughs and wet places across much of North America and Eurasia.

Food Uses: The leaves are used to make mint tea (C23, C24, C27, C34, C38, C57, C58, D3, D4, D23, D31; Morice 1909; Lamont 1977; Leighton 1985; Siegfried 1994).

Medicinal Uses: Mint tea can be drunk to treat a cough or cold (C13, C23, C24, C27, C34, C37, C38, C54, C60, D3, D4, D23, D31; Morice 1909; Leighton 1985; Welsh, cited in Leighton 1985), congestion (C34, C38), fever (C10, C20, C37; Welsh, cited in Leighton 1985; Siegfried 1994), chills (C54), or menstrual cramps (C10), to soothe teething babies' gums or as a tonic (C13), to treat tiredness or fatigue (C44), as a sleep aid (C20, M9), to treat children's diarrhea (C20), as a digestive aid (Holmes, cited in Leighton 1985), to treat headache (Welsh, cited in Leighton 1985), high blood pressure (Siegfried

1994), as part of compound medicines for treating cancer or diabetes (M9), or pain (C20), and as a wash for sores (M9). The whole fresh plant can be smelled, or boiled and the steam inhaled to clear the nasal passages when you have a cold (C57, C58). The flowers can be part of a mixture applied topically to gums to reduce infection or relieve a toothache, the leafy stem and flowers can be packed into a nostril to stop a severe nosebleed, and mint is part of a compound medicine to treat coughing up of blood (Leighton 1985).

Technological Uses: Mint leaves can be mixed with other plants in trap bait for lynx (D9, D23, D29), or with beaver castor in bait for red foxes (D32).

Properties: Mint leaves contain the following nutrients (per 100 g fresh weight, 81% moisture): food energy (39 kcal), protein (2.9 g), fat (1.0 g), total carbohydrate (7.7 g), crude fiber (1.1 g), thiamine (0.13 mg), riboflavin (0.25 mg), niacin (0.8 mg), vitamin C (64 mg), vitamin A (1334 RE), and minerals (ash: 1.8 g), including Ca (166 mg), P (45 mg), Na (2.0 mg), K (179 mg), and Fe (5.3 mg) (Kuhnlein and Turner 1991). Teas made with spearmint (*M. spicata* L.) or peppermint (*M. ×piperita* L., the × indicating it is a hybrid species) leaves are well known as a stomach tonic, for colic or gripe relief, and as a sedative due to their content of essential oil, in which carvone dominates in spearmint and menthol in peppermint, along with numerous other monoterpenes and some sesquiterpenes and their derivatives, plus bioactive flavonoids (Bisset and Wichtl 1994).

Potential: Some of the traditional uses are supported by the literature. Barl et al. (1996) provide a list of possible buyers. Mater Engineering (1993) categorizes wild mint as a Priority Level 1 product for further development and describes the market in some detail.

Wild Bergamot

Other Names: Cree: *apiscānakāskīsik, mostoswīkask* ("cow pleasant-tasting plant"), *kapiskotānāskīhk*; English: horse mint; French: *menthe de cheval, bergamote sauvage.*

Scientific Name: *Monarda fistulosa* L.

Description: An erect aromatic perennial growing up to 1 m tall, with square stems, opposite, lance-shaped, saw-toothed leaves that may be grayish with soft hairs or al-most smooth, and smaller green bracts under a large terminal head of flowers consisting of green sepal tubes ending in purplish teeth, and

(R. Marles)

showy rose or lilac-colored (rarely white), fuzzy, two-lipped petal tubes, the upper lip narrow and bearded at the tip, the lower lip spreading into three lobes.

Habitat: Fairly common on hillsides, in thickets and open woods, and on roadsides across southern Canada from British Columbia to western Quebec, through most of the USA, and in Mexico.

Medicinal Uses: The whole plant can be boiled and the decoction drunk by women (especially young mothers) after childbirth to "clean out the blood and heal the womb" (C11). It can also be mixed with other herbs to make a drink for treating menstrual cramps (C10), stomachaches (C47), headaches, and fever (C54).

Properties: The seeds (100 g fresh weight, 8% moisture) have 19.8 g of pro-tein, 17.4 g of fat, 26.6 g of crude fiber, and 6.7 g of minerals (ash) (Kuhnlein and Turner 1991). The leaves are very aromatic, and varieties have been selected that have an essential oil rich in either geraniol, linalool, or thymol (Gaudiel 1997).

Potential: Wild bergamot is under development as an essential oil crop at the Agriculture and Agri-Food Canada research station in Morden, Mani-toba, and at the Alberta Agriculture, Food and Rural Development Crop Development Centre, South, in Brooks, Alberta (Gaudiel 1997). The essen-tial oil is in demand for aromatherapy (Rogers 1997).

Marsh Skullcap

Other Names: French: *toque, tertianaire.*

Scientific Name: *Scutellaria galericulata* L.

Description: A slender ascending or erect perennial herb growing from creeping rhizomes, up to 80 cm tall, with opposite, oblong, wavy-margined leaves that have one or two flowers in the

(R. Marles)

axil. The flowers are blue, with sepals united into a cup with two lips, the upper of which has a crest, and petals fused into a two-lipped tube, the upper lip being arched and much longer than the sepals.

Habitat: Fairly common along stream banks, in swamps, and in wet meadows across most of North America and Eurasia.

Medicinal Uses: The leaves and flowers can be brewed into a tea used to treat ulcers (M11) and fever (C41).

Properties: Skullcap contains scutellarein, a flavonoid with reputed sedative and antispasmodic properties. However, an extract of *S. galericulata* showed no sedative or antispasmodic effect on various small animals (Foster and Tyler 1999). Large doses may cause giddiness, confusion, twitching, and stupor, so it should be treated as a medicine and not consumed excessively (Dobelis 1986), although it has been listed by Health Canada as safe when consumed as a food (Blackburn 1993). Other constituents include a bitter glucoside, volatile oil, and tannins (Duke 1985). Concern has been raised because of reports of possible liver damage from prolonged self-administration and the discovery that not all skullcap on the market is in fact skullcap. Some wholesalers were discovered to have substituted germander (*Teucrium chamaedrys* L., Lamiaceae) for skullcap (Foster and Tyler 1999). Germander has been proven to cause liver damage and is no longer recommended for internal use. It may easily be the reason for the reports of skullcap toxicity (Foster 1993).

Potential: Skullcap is in demand among herbalists despite the lack of strong scientific support. The problem of adulteration will have to be dealt with by having a botanical certification process.

LENTIBULARIACEAE
(Bladderwort Family)

Bladderwort

Other Names: French: *millefeuille des marais;* Slave: *te^h dzhīa, tue dzhī* ("water berry").

Scientific Name: *Utricularia macrorhiza* Le Conte, common synonyms: *U. vulgaris* L. ssp. *macrorhiza* (Le Conte) Clausen, *U. vulgaris* var. *americana* Gray.

(R. Marles)

Description: An aquatic perennial with coarse stems up to 80 cm long floating near the surface, submerged leaves crowded and forked or somewhat pinnately divided into fine threadlike segments bearing numerous bladders up to 5 mm long that trap tiny aquatic invertebrates, long flowering stems rising well above the water bearing 6 to 15 flowers up to 2 cm long with a two-lipped sepal tube split to the base, and a two-lipped yellow petal tube with brown stripes on the palate.

Habitat: Fairly common in lakes and sloughs across North America and Eurasia.

Medicinal Uses: A decoction can be used to wash sore legs (Lamont 1977).

Properties: The flavones apigenin, luteolin, 6-hydroxyluteolin, and diosmetin, and several carotenoid pigments have been identified from bladderwort (Hetherington and Steck 1997). These flavones have anti-inflammatory and antibacterial activity (Harborne and Baxter 1993).

Potential: There is not likely to be much economic demand for this plant, but it is ecologically important in aquatic communities.

MONOTROPACEAE
(Indian Pipe Family)

Indian Pipe

Other Names: Cree: *mīpitahmas-kīhkīh*; English: ghost flower.

Scientific Name: *Monotropa uniflora* L.

Description: A very unusual-looking herb, lacking any green color because it is parasitic, through a fungal intermediate, on the roots of neighboring conifers. The white waxy stems grow from a dense rounded mat of roots up to 30 cm tall, bear small white scale-leaves, and terminate in a single nodding, urn-shaped, white flower up to 2 cm long, with two to four (but sometimes none) irregular sepals and usually five petals, developing into a seed capsule that becomes erect as the whole plant dries and turns black at maturity.

(R. Marles)

Habitat: Found rarely in damp, deeply shaded woodlands across Canada, most of the USA except the dry southwest, Mexico, Central America, and Asia.

Medicinal Uses: The flower can be chewed to treat a toothache (Leighton 1985).

Properties: An extract of *M. uniflora* showed little or no antibiotic activity but it did have some insecticidal activity. A number of potentially bioactive monoterpenes, triterpenes, and benzenoids have been reported from another species of *Monotropa* (Farnsworth 1999).

Potential: The plant's rarity and the limited pharmacological activity shown so far suggest it has little commercial potential.

MYRICACEAE
(Bayberry Family)

Sweet Gale

Other Names: Cree: *mwākōpakwā(h)tik*; English: bog myrtle, gold-withy; French: *boissent-bon, herbe à cheval, piment royal*; Slave: *dakone.*

Scientific Name: *Myrica gale* L.

Description: A shrub growing up to 1.5 m tall, with ascending brown branches, deciduous, firm, aromatic, wedge-shaped leaves up to 5 cm long and 2 cm wide, with a toothed blunt apex and dotted with resin. The unisexual flowers, which have no sepals or petals, are aggregated into catkins

(J.D. Johnson)

that appear before the leaves in the spring, male and female on separate plants in any one year, but each plant being able to produce either. Pollen-producing catkins are thickly cylindrical, up to 2 cm long, with large brown bracts. Seed-producing catkins are egg-shaped, 1 cm long, and produce resinous wax-coated nutlets with two winglike scales.

Habitat: A circumboreal species, found along stream banks and in shallow-water swamps on acid soil, throughout most of Canada, the Pacific northwestern and northeastern states, northern Europe, and eastern Asia.

Medicinal Uses: The stem, leaf, and catkin decoction can be drunk to treat tuberculosis (Lamont 1977).

Technological Uses: The fragrant seed catkins can be gathered in the fall, dried, and used as an ingredient in trap lures (Leighton 1985).

Properties: Bayberry *(M. cerifera* L.) leaves contain (per 100 g dry weight): protein (10.8 g), fat (2.2 g), total carbohydrate (74.3 g), fiber (29.8 g), and minerals (ash: 12.7 g), plus an essential oil with alpha-pinene, myrcene, limonene, and other fragrant monoterpenes. The bark contains myricitrin, starch, gum, protein, a red dye, and tannins. The wax from the "berries" is used to make candles and is reputed to be irritant and sensitizing (Duke 1985; Harborne and Baxter 1993; Farnsworth 1999).

Potential: Sweet gale is an ecologically important wetland shrub that may also find use as an ornamental and as a fragrance source. The essential oil is in demand for aromatherapy (Rogers 1997).

NYMPHAEACEAE
(Pond Lily Family)

Yellow Pond Lily

Other Names: Chipewyan: *teghaizé, te tlh'óghé kálé;* Cree: *pwakumosikum, oskotamo, waskātamow, wāskātamo, waskutamo, ōskītīpak, waskītīpak* (= leaf); French: *grand nénuphar jaune;* Slave: *teta.*

Scientific Name: *Nuphar lutea* (L.) Sm. ssp. *variegata* (Dur.) E.O. Beal, common synonym: *N. variegatum* Engelm.

(R. Marles)

Description: A perennial aquatic plant with large heart-shaped floating leaves up to 15 cm wide that grow from a thick underwater rhizome and large yellow flowers 7 cm wide with six yellow sepals and numerous smaller petals, sometimes with reddish color inside, numerous stamens, and a large green stigmatic disk.

Habitat: Common in ponds and quiet waters in Alaska, Yukon, and British Columbia, and across Canada and northern USA.

Food Uses: The rhizomes may sometimes be eaten (C47, M6; Welsh, cited in Leighton 1985), for example, sliced and fried in fat or boiled (Lamont 1977), and beaver have been observed to eat them (D3), but other elders believe they are not good to eat (C38) or may be poisonous if cooked in a covered container (M9).

Medicinal Uses: The rhizomes can be cut into thin slices and dried before use. Rhizome slices can be chewed or made into a tea drunk to treat arthritic pain or used to bathe affected joints (D6) or to treat someone who is swollen up (C38). The rhizome (sliced, grated, or ground) may also be used to poultice boils (C20, C54, D9, D28, D32; Leighton 1985), diabetic skin ulcers (M9), infected wounds (C1, C2, C3, C20, C54, D23, D29, M6), or with other herbs as a poultice to treat sore legs or a sore back (C23, C27), foot pain (C20), sore joints, arthritis, headaches (M6; Leighton 1985), or "worms in the flesh"

◄ R. Willier and family
gathering pond lily rhizomes
(L. Monteleone)

▼ Pond lily rhizome slices
drying (L. Monteleone)

(Leighton 1985). Other uses for compound decoctions containing pond lily rhizome include a drink for helping a woman recover from childbirth (C58), for facilitating childbirth (exact use not clear) (D24), for a heart medicine (C54, D29), and for a cough medicine (D4, D9, D23).

Properties: The rhizomes contain tannins which would help to treat diarrhea and skin problems because of their astringency (Dobelis 1986). They also contain a complex mixture of quinolizidine alkaloids including nupharidine and deoxynupharidine, and sesquiterpene alkaloids including nuphenine and 3-epi-nupharamine (Hetherington and Steck 1997; Farnsworth 1999). The rhizome has a broad range of antibacterial activity including activity against mycobacteria, antifungal activity including antiyeast activity, estrogenic activity, and prostaglandin synthetase inhibition (Farnsworth 1999). Some of these alkaloids may have sedative (Harborne and Baxter 1993), blood-pressure-lowering, and spasm-relief activities (Duke 1992a).

Potential: Due to the bioactive alkaloid content, human consumption of yellow pond lily as a food should be discouraged (beaver have their own means of adaptation and metabolism). As a medicine, pond lily rhizome shows significant potential and should be investigated further.

ONAGRACEAE
(Evening Primrose Family)

Fireweed

Other Names: Chipewyan: *góⁿdhi'elé* ("fire new branch"); Cree: *hapaskwa, askapask, athkāpask, ākāpuskwah, liy(h)-kāpusk*; English: willow-herb; French: *bouquets rouges*; Slave: *guⁿ*.

Scientific Name: *Epilobium angustifolium* L.

Description: An erect, stout perennial up to 150 cm high with alternate, entire lance-shaped leaves, a terminal spray of pink flowers with four petals, and long seed capsules that split open to release seeds with silky tufts on them.

Habitat: Very common in open woods, gravel bars, recently burned woodlands, and other recent clearings, across Canada, most of the

(R. Marles)

USA except the south, Greenland, Iceland, and northern Eurasia.

Food Uses: The young leaves, stems, and flowering tops can be eaten raw or cooked (C23, C24, C25, C27, C38, D6, D24, M6, M9; Lamont 1977). The plant can also be boiled to make a beverage (C23, C24, C25, C27, C38). The mature stem has been tried as a smoking tobacco substitute (D24).

Medicinal Uses: A tea made from the whole plant can be taken to treat intestinal worms (D6, D33). The young tops can be eaten to "get the blood up if the blood is weak" (M9). The chewed leaves can be applied to bruises (M6; Leighton 1985). The root can be peeled, chewed, and applied to boils or abscesses to draw out the infection or to open wounds to prevent infection (M6; Leighton 1985). The roots are part of a compound decoction that will reveal pregnancy when drunk by causing a violent nosebleed in a pregnant woman or the start of menstruation if the woman is not pregnant (Siegfried 1994).

Technological Uses: A thick layer of fireweed plants can be used as a surface ("old timer's plywood") for fish to be cleaned on (D9). Fibers from the tall stems can be used for thread (M6; Welsh, cited in Leighton 1985). When the flowers of fireweed are in full bloom this indicates that the moose are fat enough to be hunted (C22, C23, C27; Leighton 1985).

Properties: Fireweed leaves (100 g fresh weight, 76% moisture) contain: protein (6.5 g), total carbohydrate (2.9 g), crude fiber (1.4 g), vitamin C (88 mg), vitamin A (22 RE), and minerals (ash: 1.8 g), including Ca (175 mg), P (132 mg), Na (50 mg), K (404 mg), Mg (70 mg), Cu (0.2 mg), Zn (0.9 mg), Fe (2.7 mg), Mn (<0.1 mg), and Mo (<0.1 mg). The peeled shoots (100 g fresh weight, 92% moisture) contain: food energy (17 kcal), protein (0.2 g), fat (0.3 g), total carbohydrate (4.0 g), crude fiber (0.9 g), vitamin A (4 RE), and minerals (ash: 0.5), including Ca (32 mg), P (31 mg), Na (0.6 mg), Mg (20 mg), Cu (0.7 mg), Zn (0.7 mg), Fe (0.5 mg), and Mn (0.1 mg). Dwarf fireweed (*E. latifolium* L.) leaves are an even better source of vitamins, containing (per 100 g fresh weight): thiamine (0.40 mg), riboflavin (0.54 mg), niacin (1.4 mg), vitamin C (128 mg), and vitamin A (1700 RE) (Kuhnlein and Turner 1991). Fireweed leaves contain flavonoids (especially derivatives of kaempferol, quercetin, and myricetin) and gallic-acid type tannins. Fireweed has potent anti-inflammatory activity – myricetin 3-O-β-D-glucuronide inhibits release of the prostaglandins PGI_2, PGE_2, and PGD_2. This compound is found in the leaves in maximum concentration during and just after flowering. It may find use as a topical anti-inflammatory or might have some potential in the treatment of benign prostate tumors and the associated problems of urination (Bisset and Wichtl 1994).

Potential: Fireweed products to treat skin irritations such as diaper rash are currently being marketed by Fytokem Products Inc. of Saskatoon, Saskatchewan (Fytokem Products 1999). The young leaves and flowering tops may have potential as a salad bar specialty item, and honey from fireweed flower nectar is already a commercial product. Clearly there is potential for economic development of this common herb, but agronomic studies are urgently needed.

OROBANCHACEAE
(Broom-Rape Family)

Northern Ground-Cone

Other Names: None known.

Scientific Name: *Boschniakia rossica* (Cham. & Schlecht.) Fedtsch.

Description: A parasitic brown herb totally lacking chlorophyll, with smooth stems up to 40 cm tall, solitary or in clusters, scalelike elliptical leaves, and a dense terminal spike of brown bracts and tubular flowers about 1 cm long, with a lobed sepal tube and a petal tube with a hood and a lobed lip, developing into a one-chambered seed capsule.

Habitat: Parasitic on the roots of green alder (*Alnus viridis* (Vill.) Lam. & DC., Betulaceae). Distributed through Alaska, Yukon, the western Northwest Territories, northern British Columbia, northern Alberta, and Asia.

Medicinal Uses: The thick stem base decoction can be drunk to treat a stomachache (Lamont 1977).

Properties: Although the root is reported by the Dena'ina (Tanaina) to be edible in an emergency if cooked (Kari 1995), it has been found to contain a number of potentially bioactive chemical constituents, including an alkaloid, a number of monoterpenes, triterpenes, phenylpropanoids, and a lignan. With regard to pharmacological activities, an extract of the aerial parts has been shown to have a radical-scavenging effect that might afford some protection against cancer (Farnsworth 1999).

(J. Pojar)

Potential: Although the plant has some pharmacological activity, its rarity and parasitic dependence on another plant suggest it would be difficult to develop commercially as a medicinal plant crop.

PLANTAGINACEAE
(Plantain Family)

Broad-leaved Plantain

Other Names: Cree: *muchikwanas* ("weed"), *paswēpak*; English: whiteman's foot; French: *queue de rat, grand plantain*; Slave: *yatoneto[n]* ("white-tailed deer leaf").

Scientific Name: *Plantago major* L.

Description: A perennial herb growing from a short thick rhizome, with a basal rosette of oval, five- to seven-ribbed leaves up to 30 cm long and a flowering stalk up to 30 cm tall bearing a dense narrow spike of tiny, yellowish white, four-lobed flowers that produce small seed capsules whose conical tops fall off to release the seeds.

Habitat: A common weed introduced from Eurasia; found on roadsides and waste ground throughout North America.

Food Uses: The leaves may be boiled and eaten after the long fibers have been removed (C60). The leaves could be used to make a tea, but only if nothing else was available (M6).

(R. Marles)

Medicinal Uses: The leaf infusion can be drunk to treat heart trouble (C20), cramps, stomachache, stomach flu, or constipation (M6). The stem base can be boiled and drunk to relieve fainting spells (M6). The fresh leaf can be warmed by a fire and then applied bottom side down as a poultice on wounds to draw out infections, and also to treat sores from scabies (Siegfried 1994).

Technological Uses: The leaves and flower spikes can be used as part of a trap lure mixture for foxes (Siegfried 1994).

Properties: The leaf nutrient content per 100 g fresh weight (84% moisture) is as follows: food energy (61 kcal), protein (1.6-2.5 g), fat (0.3 g), total carbohydrate (14.6 g), crude fiber (1.6 g), riboflavin (0.28 mg), niacin (0.8 mg), vitamin C (8.0-33.3 mg), vitamin A (252 RE), and minerals (ash: 1.2-1.7 g), including Ca (184-241 mg), P (41-52 mg), Na (16-25 mg), K (277-382 mg), Mg (22), Cu (0.1 mg), Fe (1.2-5.6 mg), Mn (0.4 mg), and Cl (191 mg) (Kuhnlein and Turner 1991). The leaves contain aucubin and other iridoid glycosides, allantoin, benzoic acid, salicylic acid, vanillic acid, ursolic acid, tannins, coumarins, flavonoids, and mucilage. Aucubin has potent antibacterial activity (equivalent to 600 IU of penicillin) against *Staphylococcus aureus* when released from its inactive sugar-bound form by an enzyme present in the fresh but not boiled plant material, and for internal use, aucubin dissolves well in hot water and appears to protect the liver from damage by chlorinated solvents or the mushroom poison alpha-aminitin. The tannins make the herb astringent which, along with the mucilage, helps relieve irritations of the mouth and throat. Externally the astringency, soothing effect, and antibacterial activity make it effective for treating skin infections and inflammations (Duke 1985; Bisset and Wichtl 1994).

Potential: Plantain is a common weed in Canada, so the presence of potent medicinal compounds such as aucubin suggest there is potential for further development. It is currently available in health food stores in both unprocessed and processed products (Barl et al. 1996). Mater Engineering (1993) categorizes broad-leaved plantain as a Priority Level 2 product for further development and describes the market in some detail.

POLYGALACEAE
(Milkwort Family)

Seneca Snakeroot

Other Names: Chipewyan: *dlúne ni*; Cree: *menisehkes, mesisikas, ominisihkes, sīkōtā-kanīsīkan, wenisikas, wīnsīkas, wīncīkēs*; French: *sénéca*.

Scientific Name: *Polygala senega* L.

Description: An erect perennial herb growing from a thick rhizome, up to 50 cm tall, with usually unbranched, minutely fuzzy stems and alternate oval or lance-shaped leaves with rough edges. The terminal inflorescence is a dense oblong spray of greenish white flowers 4-5 mm wide. The flower is irregularly shaped, with five sepals, the two inner ones almost round and larger than the rest, three

(R. Marles)

petals joined at their base, the middle one of which is boat-shaped and has a fringed crest, eight stamens whose filaments are fused into a split sheath joined to the petals, and a superior pistil with a long curved style.

Habitat: Fairly common in open woods and prairies throughout the parklands from southern Alberta to western New Brunswick, and across the USA east of the continental divide, except in the southeast.

Medicinal Uses: The root can be chewed and the juice swallowed to treat a sore throat (C11; Welsh, cited in Leighton 1985) or sore mouth (Leighton 1985), or the crushed or chewed root can be packed into the cavity of a sore tooth to treat a toothache (C11; Leighton 1985). The roots can be crushed and mixed with another herb to make a poultice applied to cuts to relieve pain and prevent infection (C11). The root can be used in combination with other herbs for a heart medicine and as a blood purifier (M9). The flower infusion can also be used as a blood medicine (Welsh, cited in Leighton 1985).

Properties: Seneca snakeroot contains up to 12% dry weight of a mixture of triterpene glycosides (senegasaponins A-D), and methyl salicylate and its glucoside. The saponins make it effective as an expectorant for congestion of the upper respiratory tract and emphysema (Bisset and Wichtl 1994). The saponins act by irritating the gastric mucosa to produce reflex expectoration. In large doses seneca root causes emesis, and it should not be given to people with gastritis or gastric ulcers (Bradley 1992).

Potential: There is an established market for seneca snakeroot. Prof. N. Kenkel of the University of Manitoba Botany Department has been investigating its agronomics (Moes 1997), and the Saskatchewan Herb Research Centre is developing analytical procedures for quality control (Barl et al. 1996). Mater Engineering (1993) categorizes seneca snakeroot as a Priority Level 1 product for further development and describes the market in some detail.

POLYGONACEAE (Buckwheat Family)

Mountain Sorrel

Other Names: Slave: *tsa dži* ("bear ear").

Scientific Name: *Oxyria digyna* (L.) Hill.

Description: A low perennial with a stout root, stems up to 30 cm tall, loosely sheathing leaflike stipules around the nodes, mostly basal, alternate, long-stalked, rounded heart-

(J.D. Johnson)

shaped or kidney-shaped leaves with wavy edges, a dense, narrow but branched inflorescence, and small greenish to reddish flowers with four sepals and no petals, producing hard, lens-shaped, winged fruits.

Habitat: Found occasionally on moist rocky slopes and mountain meadows from Alaska, Yukon, and the Northwest Territories to Hudson Bay, Quebec, Labrador, and Newfoundland, to Nova Scotia and New Hampshire in the east, in the mountains of western USA, Greenland, Iceland, and northern Eurasia.

Food Uses: The fresh leaves and the "fruit" (hard achenes enclosed within a fleshy calyx) can be eaten (Lamont 1977).

Properties: Mountain sorrel leaves (100 g fresh weight, 87% moisture) contain: protein (3.8 g), fat (0.9 g), total carbohydrate (7.6 g), vitamin C (40 mg), vitamin A (890 RE), and minerals (ash: 1.3 g), including Ca (116 mg), P (87 mg), Na (18 mg), Mg (75 mg), Cu (0.1 mg), Zn (0.6 mg), Fe (3.2 mg), Mn (1.7 mg), and Mo (<0.1 mg) (Kuhnlein and Turner 1991). The pleasant sour taste of the leaves, similar to rhubarb, is due to the presence of oxalic acid, which in small quantities is harmless. If consumed in excess, oxalic acid can act as an irritant poison and bind to calcium in the body, causing acute calcium deficiency and irritating the kidneys by depositing crystals of calcium oxalate (Turner and Szczawinski 1991).

Potential: It could be cultivated as a tasty additive to salads, so long as chefs are made aware that it should not be consumed in large quantities or over a prolonged period. Consumption with a creamy dairy-food-based salad dressing might help to prevent oxalic acid absorption by allowing it to be converted into insoluble calcium oxalate in the gut, after which it would be eliminated with other solid wastes.

Water Smartweed

Other Names: Cree: *kāmithkwacōāhtik, kistōtīwīcīpihk*; English: water knotweed, swamp persicaria; French: *renouée amphibie.*

Scientific Name: *Polygonum amphibium* L.

(R. Marles)

Description: A perennial herb with extensive black, branching rhizomes, alternate leaves up to 15 cm long, oblong to oval, smooth when growing in water but fuzzy and more narrowly lance-shaped and pointed when growing on dried out soil, with broad leafy collars (ocreae) around the stem nodes. The flower spikes are up to 3 cm long in aquatic and 10 cm long in terrestrial forms, bearing tiny flowers with five pink sepals and no petals, eventually producing small lens-shaped brown to black seeds (achenes).

Habitat: Very common in mud flats, slough margins, and lakeshores that may be seasonally dry, with a circumboreal distribution including most of Canada, USA except in the southeast, Iceland, and Eurasia.

Medicinal Uses: The fresh root can be applied to blisters in the mouth or dried and used in compound remedies (Leighton 1985).

Properties: The leaves and stems contain flavonoids (kaempferol, quercetin, and myricetin derivatives), tannins, saponins, and coumarin derivatives (umbelliferone and scopoletin). The tannins' astringency makes the herb useful for treating inflammations of the mouth and throat, and it has been used in European folk medicine as an expectorant. The flavonoids inhibit thrombocyte aggregation, presumably through an effect on cyclooxygenase (Bisset and Wichtl 1994; Hetherington and Steck 1997). Extracts of smartweed (*P. hydropiper* L.) have shown the ability to help stop bleeding and to lower blood pressure (Dobelis 1986). Extracts of climbing knotweed (*P. multiflorum* Thunb.) have shown progesterone-hormone-interfering, fever-reducing, antitumor (due to emodin and rhein), and sedative effects (Duke 1985). Although some knotweeds have edible leaves, all parts contain some oxalic acid, so they should not be consumed in large quantities (Turner and Szczawinski 1991).

Potential: Although there is some evidence in support of the traditional topical use, and they can be eaten, more research will be needed to find a commercial use for this common plant.

219

Bistort

Other Names: English: serpent grass; Slave: *tselī yaneshī* ("arctic ground squirrel potato"), *dedīe yaneshī* ("hoary marmot potato").

Scientific Name: *Polygonum viviparum* L.

Description: A perennial herb with a short, thick stem base and rhizome, a simple stem up to 30 cm tall, lance-shaped lower leaves and very narrow upper leaves, papery brown sheaths (ocreae) around the stem nodes, and a small narrowly cylindrical inflorescence bearing small bulbs in the lower part and higher up, flowers with pink or white sepals and no petals, developing into three-angled dull brown "seeds" (achenes).

Lady's-thumb (*Polygonum persicaria* L.)
(C. Clavelle)

Habitat: Moist woods and meadows to alpine elevations, from Alaska east to Newfoundland, and south across western and northern USA.

Food Uses: The rhizomes can be fried and eaten (Lamont 1977).

Properties: *Polygonum* sp. bulbs are reported to have the following food value per 100 g fresh weight: protein (1.7 g), fat (0.2 g), total carbohydrate (1.8 g), crude fiber (0.6 g), and minerals (ash: 0.3 g), including Ca (11 mg), P (44 mg), Na (3.8 mg), K (71 mg), Mg (33 mg), Fe (2.3 mg), and Mn (0.4 mg) (Kuhnlein and Turner 1991). *Polygonum bistorta* L. is the most commonly known bistort, with a starchy edible rhizome and young leaves that can be eaten like spinach. The rhizome also has a high tannin content, making it astringent (Dobelis 1986).

Potential: The literature supports the use as a food plant, although low productivity in the north will limit economic development unless agricultural modifications such as raised beds and cold frames are used. It is unlikely that commercial harvest from the wild could be sustainable.

Western Dock

Other Names: Cree: *osaw ochepihk* ("yellow root"), *pikwataskōpīwāhtik*; French: *doche*; Slave: *edetho^n*.

Scientific Name: *Rumex aquaticus* L. ssp. *occidentalis* (S. Wats.) Hult., common synonym: *R. occidentalis* S. Wats. Also *R. salicifolius* Weinm. (common synonyms: *R. triangulivalvis* (Danser) Rech. f. and *R. mexicanus* Meisn.) and *R. orbiculatus* Gray.

Description: A stout perennial growing up to 1.5 m tall from a taproot, with a simple red-tinged stem, long slender leaves with heart-shaped bases and narrow tips, and a long, narrow, dense inflorescence of reddish brown flowers that produce hard dry little fruits (achenes)

Rumex aquaticus L. (R. Marles)

each of which is enclosed by three persistent sepals. Willow dock (*R. salicifolius*) is distinguished from western dock (*R. aquaticus*) by being more branched with narrower leaves, a less dense inflorescence, and a bump (grain, tubercle) on each of the sepals (valves) surrounding the seed. Great water dock (*R. orbiculatus*) has tubercled valves like willow dock but larger leaves.

Habitat: Western dock is commonly found in moist areas and waste places from southern Alaska through British Columbia to California, in the Rockies to New Mexico, Texas, and east across Canada to Newfoundland, and in north-central and northeastern USA. Willow dock is even more widespread across North America except for southeastern USA, and is also found in Eurasia. Great water dock is found across southern Canada, the midwestern and northeastern USA, California, and Louisiana.

Medicinal Uses: A decoction from the whole plant can be used as a wash to treat painful joints, such as from arthritis (M6; Leighton 1985), and the root bark can be chewed and applied to serious wounds to stop the bleeding and promote healing (M6). The root can also be used in a medicine to treat high blood pressure and heart ailments (D26).

Technological Uses: Willow dock taproots can be boiled to make a yellow dye for moose hides or arrows (Lamont 1977).

Properties: Dock roots contain significant amounts of tannin, making them effective as astringents and antiseptics for wound healing. An infusion of *R. obtusifolius* L. is known to be laxative, and the yellow dye from the roots has been used elsewhere (Dobelis 1986). The laxative effect is due to the presence of anthraquinones (2.17% in *R. crispus* L.) including emodin and chrysophanic acid, derivatives of which have been used effectively topically to treat fungal infections such as ringworm, as well as psoriasis and other skin disorders. Overdoses of the root extract may cause diarrhea, nausea, and excessive urination (Duke 1985). Dock also contains oxalic acid, so should not be consumed in large quantities or for a prolonged period (Turner and Szczawinski 1991).

Potential: There are scientifically proven medicinal compounds in dock and there is a niche market for natural dye materials, so this common weedy plant should be examined further.

PORTULACACEAE
(Portulaca Family)

Tuberous Spring Beauty

Other Names: Slave: *tselī yaneshī* ("arctic ground squirrel potato"), *dedīe yaneshī* ("hoary marmot potato").

Scientific Name: *Claytonia tuberosa* Pallas ex J.A. Schultes.

Description: A perennial herb with a very slender and brittle stem up to 15 cm tall, growing from a spherical corm up to 1.5 cm in diameter buried deep below the soil surface. There are narrow-stalked lance-shaped basal leaves and a pair of opposite, stalkless stem leaves well below the inflorescence of three to five showy pink or white flowers that have two sepals and five petals with narrow bases, and develop into three-chambered seed capsules with shiny black seeds.

(Reprinted with permission of the National Research Council of Canada)

Habitat: Found on moist alpine slopes in Alaska, southwestern Yukon, and northern British Columbia, and in the mountains of eastern Siberia.

Food Uses: The starchy corms can be sliced and fried "like potatoes" (Lamont 1977).

Properties: Spring beauty tubers (*C. lanceolata* Pursh, 100 g fresh weight, 75% moisture) contain: protein (2.0 g), fat (0.2 g), total carbohydrate (22.2 g), and minerals (ash: 1.0 g) (Kuhnlein and Turner 1991).

Potential: Low productivity and abundance make harvesting in quantity from the wild impractical. It could become a specialty food if cultivated, and the flowers are attractive.

PRIMULACEAE
(Primrose Family)

Pygmyflower, fairy candelabra

Other Names: English: pygmyflower, rock jasmine; Slave: *ya^h naydi* ("lice medicine").

Scientific Name: *Androsace septentrionalis* L.

Description: A small winter annual or short-lived perennial herb with a persistent stem base producing a basal rosette of narrow pointed leaves up to 2.5 cm long

(J.D. Johnson)

which may have some fuzziness and smooth or toothed edges, and one to a few flowering stems each producing a terminal whorl of lance-shaped bracts from which an umbel of long-stalked flowers arises. The small flowers have a cup-shaped sepal tube with five lobes and a funnel-shaped, white or pink, five-lobed petal tube only as long as the sepal tube, developing into a dry, many-seeded capsule.

Habitat: A common species of dry open ground and eroded hillsides, so small it is often overlooked; distributed across northern Canada, western USA, Greenland, and Eurasia.

Medicinal Uses: The whole-plant decoction can be used to wash the hair or other affected body areas to rid the body of lice (Lamont 1977).

Properties: Pygmyflower contains the flavonoids quercetin, kaempferol, and rutin, plus caffeic acid and androseptosides (Hetherington and Steck 1997). An extract of the whole plant has estrogenic and antigonadotropic, follicle-stimulating-hormone release stimulation, and uterine stimulant effects, and has been shown to promote fertility in rabbits and rats (Farnsworth 1999).

Potential: Pygmyflower seems to have some potential as a herbal medicine for fertility regulation, although studies in humans are still lacking.

PYROLACEAE (Pyrola Family)

Pipsissewa

Other Names: Cree: *amiskwāthōw-ipak*; English: prince's pine; French: *herbe à clé, herbe à clef, herbe à peigne.*

Scientific Name: *Chimaphila umbellata* (L.) W. Bart.

(R. Marles)

Description: A perennial, slightly woody herb growing from long running rhizomes, with leaning stems growing up to 20 cm tall, leaves up to 8 cm long scattered along the stem in whorls of up to eight evergreen, shiny, thick, strap-shaped and finely toothed except on the narrowed base, and flowers about 1 cm in diameter that are white to purplish, fragrant, borne in a cluster of four to eight at the top of the stem, and developing into dry seed capsules that split open to release the seeds.

Habitat: A circumboreal species found occasionally on dry soil in coniferous woodlands from southeastern Alaska, across Canada, throughout the western and northeastern states, and in Eurasia.

Medicinal Uses: It is part of a compound decoction drunk to treat stabbing pains in the chest (possibly due to heart conditions such as angina pectoris), coughing that brings up blood, backache, and fever (Leighton 1985).

Properties: The greens contain (per 100 g fresh weight): protein (0.7 g), Ca (100 mg), P (15 mg), K (93 mg), Mg (37 mg), Cu (0.1 mg), Zn (0.6 mg), Fe (1.0 mg), Mn (3.0 mg), and Cl (2.4 mg) (Kuhnlein and Turner 1991). The leaves also contain the triterpene ursolic acid, the flavonoid quercetin, and the naphthoquinone chimaphilin (Hetherington and Steck 1997). The leaves are active as a mild urinary antiseptic (Dobelis 1986). Chimaphilin stimulates phagocytes, one of the nonspecific immune cell types, at low doses (Harborne and Baxter 1993).

Potential: An attractive plant with potential as an ornamental in addition to its potential medicinal value.

Pink Wintergreen

Other Names: Chipewyan: *sasdzaghé* ("bear's ear"); Cree: *amiskowehtawakewuskos* ("beaver ear plant"), *amiskōtawakayipak*, *miskīsikōmaskī(h)kīh, wāwipak*; French: *pyrole*; Slave: *tsa dzhī* ("beaver berry"), *dedīe dzhī* ("hoary marmot berry").

Scientific Name: *Pyrola asarifolia* Michx. Also *Orthilia secunda* (L.) House, common synonym: *Pyrola secunda* L.

Description: Pink wintergreen (*P. asarifolia*) is a perennial herb growing up to 30 cm tall, with leathery, shiny, round or kidney-shaped basal leaves and a flowering stalk bearing a slender column of pink flowers with characteristically protruding styles. One-sided wintergreen (*O. secunda*) is distinguished by its distinctly one-sided inflorescence, greenish white flowers, and more pointed leaves.

Pyrola asarifolia Michx. (R. Marles)

Habitat: Both are fairly common circumboreal species found in moist woods across Canada and in the mountainous western and northern USA.

Medicinal Uses: The leaves can be mashed with lard and put on a cut to stop bleeding and promote healing (D6, D22). The leaves may also be chewed to relieve a toothache (D29). As a diuretic to treat severe back pain from kidney trouble including kidney stones and urinary tract blockage or scanty urination, boil 5-10 plants in 1.5 quarts of water with 2-5 mint leaves and let cool, then drink 1 cup every 2-3 hours (D27). The leaf infusion can be used to wash sore eyes, and the decoction can be drunk to treat coughing up of blood (Leighton 1985).

Properties: Pyrolas have a number of flavonoid glycosides in the leaves (Hetherington and Steck 1997). They also contain naphthoquinones such as chimaphilin, sesquiterpenes, arbutin, and ursolic acid. Extracts are reported to have pain-relieving, anti-inflammatory, and even myocardial circulation enhancement activities (Farnsworth 1999).

Potential: The scientific evidence supports many of the traditional uses. There is potential for the development of this plant both as a medicinal and as an ornamental.

RANUNCULACEAE
(Buttercup Family)

Red Baneberry

Other Names: Chipewyan: *jíé slini* ("bad berry"); Cree: *maskōminānātik*; French: *poison de couleuvre*; Slave: *sa^h dzhī* ("bear berry").

(R. Marles)

Scientific Name: *Actaea rubra* (Ait.) Willd.

Description: An erect perennial with large compound leaves divided two to four times into three parts, with a terminal spray of small white flowers turning into bright red (or white in *A. rubra* forma *neglecta* (Gillman) Robins) berries.

Habitat: Both red- and white-berried (a random mutation) forms are common in rich, shady woodlands and along stream edges across North America.

Medicinal Uses: Red baneberry is known to be poisonous, but the roots have been used with approximately 20 other plants in a decoction drunk to treat bleeding from the nose (D29). The roots of the white-berried plants can be used in a decoction drunk to slow excessive blood flow from menstruation, childbirth, or wounds (M6; Leighton 1985). The root can be mixed with spruce branch tips in a decoction taken to treat stomach problems such as indigestion or constipation, and the whole plant can be used in a purgative tea (M6; Leighton 1985).

Properties: All parts of the plant, especially the roots and berries, are toxic. Protoanemonin is one of several probable toxins in the plant. Symptoms include acute stomach cramps, vomiting, dizziness, headache, delirium, increased pulse, and circulatory failure. Although no fatalities are known for this species, a European species has caused several deaths (Turner and Szczawinski 1991). These properties explain the traditional use as a purgative or emetic, but the extremely irritant nature of the toxin, which if applied to the skin can cause inflammation and blisters (Duke 1986), indicates that the use of this plant is not safe.

Potential: It appears to be too toxic to have any immediate development potential.

ROSACEAE
(Rose Family)

Saskatoon Berry

Other Names: Chipewyan: *kiⁿjíé, k'íⁿhiⁿjíé*; Cree: *misaskatoomena, misaskwatōminātik, msāskwatuwmin, saskwatoomina, saskwatōmin*; English: serviceberry, juneberry; French: *petites poires*; Slave: *kiⁿ dzhīaʰ*.

(R. Marles)

Scientific Name: *Amelanchier alnifolia* (Nutt.) Nutt. ex M. Roemer.

Description: A tall shrub with brown branches, no thorns, simple alternate, oval leaves with teeth at the apex, early-blooming white flowers in sprays at the tips of the branches, and sweet purple fruit (berrylike pomes).

Habitat: Very common along river edges and bluffs and in open woodlands from British Columbia to western Quebec, and midwestern and western USA.

Food Uses: The fruit are eaten fresh, canned, dried (Cree: *pastiwiminisaskwatōmina*), or mixed with dried, powdered meat and lard to make pemmican (C6, C13, C17, C29, C50, D6, M4, M9; Diamant pers. comm.; Morice 1909; Curtis 1928; Lamont 1977; Jarvenpa 1979, 1980; Leighton 1985; Siegfried 1994). Barked and split sticks can be boiled in sturgeon oil to keep the oil fresh during storage (Leighton 1985).

Medicinal Uses: Twelve roots and stems can be boiled and the decoction drunk to treat lung problems including tuberculosis (C29). The root decoction can be drunk to treat lung infections, coughs, chest pain (Leighton 1985), or temporary back "paralysis" due to muscle spasms, pinched nerves, etc.

(Siegfried 1994). A decoction of the roots together with other herbs can be given to children to stop diarrhea (C26) or teething sickness (Leighton 1985). A decoction of the stems with other herbs can be used to treat a fever (Leighton 1985), flu, or bad colds (Welsh, cited in Leighton 1985), and the bud decoction can be drunk to slow diarrhea (C11).

Technological Uses: Stems can be used for making arrows (C29, D9; Richardson, cited in Leighton 1985), bows (Siegfried 1994), sweat lodge frames (M9), walking canes (D29), or birch bark basket rims (Leighton 1985). The berries can be boiled to make a blue dye (C29).

Properties: The fruit (100 g fresh weight, 76% moisture) contains: food energy (90 kcal), protein (0.7 g), fat (1.2 g), total carbohydrate (21.4 g), crude fiber (6.4 g), thiamine (<0.01 mg), riboflavin (<0.01 mg), niacin (0.3 mg), vitamin C (15.7 mg), vitamin A (86 RE), and minerals (ash: 0.7 mg), including Ca (69 mg), P (40 mg), Na (0.6 mg), K (244 mg), Mg (26 mg), Cu (0.4 mg), Zn (0.4 mg), Fe (0.5 mg), and Mn (2.2 mg) (Kuhnlein and Turner 1991). The leaves, bark, and seeds contain cyanogenic glycosides which will release cyanide if crushed, but normal consumption of the fruit with seeds is never a problem and boiling of the leaves or bark will eliminate most or all of the cyanide (Turner and Szczawinski 1991).

Potential: Saskatoon berries have a well-established commercial market.

Wild Strawberry

Other Names: Chipewyan: *ídzíaze* ("little heart"); Cree: *otehiminipukos, otahimin* ("heart berry"), *otehimina, otīhīminah, okdeamena, ow-tiyhiymin, otīhīminipukwah* ("heart berry plant"); French: *fraisier des champs*; Slave: *iⁿdzheah*.

(R. Marles)

Scientific Name: *Fragaria virginiana* Duchesne.

Description: A low-growing herb from scaly rhizomes and runners, with coarsely toothed, broadly egg-shaped, long-stalked leaves, white flowers, and fruit consisting of a juicy red receptacle with tiny achenes on its surface.

Habitat: Common in low spots on prairie and in open woodlands and other moist areas throughout North America.

Food Uses: The very popular fruit is eaten fresh or preserved (C23, C27, D6, D9, D24, M6, M9; Diamant pers. comm.; Mackenzie 1801; Lamont 1977; Jarvenpa 1979; Leighton 1985; Siegfried 1994).

Medicinal Uses: For treating heart conditions the leaves (C23, C27), whole plant (C24, C38), or roots (Siegfried 1994) can be boiled for 45 minutes, then allowed to cool and the decoction can be drunk. The roots, leaves, and runners can be boiled and the liquid drunk as a treatment for diarrhea (M6; Siegfried 1994). Ash made from the roots can be mixed with water to make a paste and applied to open sores to facilitate healing (Lamont 1977).

Properties: The fruit (100 g fresh weight, 85-89% moisture) provides: food energy (54 kcal), protein (0.6-0.7 g), fat (0.6-0.9 g), total carbohydrate (12.5 g), crude fiber (2.1-2.9 g), thiamine (0.03 mg), riboflavin (0.07 mg), niacin (0.6 mg), vitamin C (5.9-23.8 mg), vitamin A (8 RE), and minerals (ash: 0.6-0.7 g), including Ca (43-64 mg), P (25-35 mg), Na (0.6-1.0 mg), K (18-164 mg), Mg

(54 mg), Cu (0.8 mg), Zn (0.2 mg), Fe (0.4-1.0 mg), and Mn (0.8 mg). The leaves (100 g fresh weight) contain vitamin C (229 mg) and riboflavin (3.2 mg) (Kuhnlein and Turner 1991). The leaves of *F. vesca* L. contain ellagitannins, flavonoids including leucoanthocyanins, ascorbic acid, and a small amount of essential oil. Due to the tannin content they can be used as an astringent topically for rashes and internally for diarrhea. Strawberry leaves in teas are considered to be a food additive rather than a drug in Germany (Bisset and Wichtl 1994) and Canada (Blackburn 1993).

Potential: Wild strawberries are not productive enough to compete with commercial hybrid strawberries, but remain a popular item with anyone traveling in the woods. The leaf essential oil is in demand for aromatherapy (Rogers 1997).

Yellow Avens

Other Names: Cree: *kākwīthita-mōwask* ("jealousy plant" because of adhering seeds), *saw-gee-too-wusk* (love root"); French: *benoîte*.

Scientific Name: *Geum aleppicum* Jacq. Also *G. macrophyllum* Willd. var. *perincisum* (Rydb.) Raup.

Description: A coarse erect perennial herb growing up to 1 m tall, hairy all over, with basal leaves divided pinnately into five- to seven-

Geum aleppicum Jacq. in seed (R. Marles)

toothed leaflets of which the terminal one is the largest, with a few very small interspersed leaflets and also leaflike stipules where the leaf stalk joins the stem, stem leaves similar but smaller. The branched inflorescence of bright yellow flowers is up to 2.5 cm in diameter, each developing into a dry fruiting head on which the hooked flower styles persist. Large-leaved yellow avens (*G. macrophyllum*) is very similar to the common yellow avens but has a larger terminal leaf lobe and fuzzy flower styles.

Habitat: Found in wet locations in prairies, meadows, or woods from southern Alaska across Canada, through most of the USA except in the southeast, and Eurasia. Large-leaved yellow avens is found in similar locations, but is not as common nor as widespread, being limited to Canada, western and northern USA, and northern Mexico.

Medicinal Uses: The root decoction can be drunk to treat teething sickness, toothache or sore throat, or to make a person sweat (Leighton 1985). It can be used as a component of compound medicines, but the details are confidential (M9; Leighton 1985).

Properties: *Geum urbanum* L. rhizomes contain 12-28% tannins, especially gallotannins, eugenol as the main constituent of the essential oil, and eugenol glycoside (gein, geoside). It is used in European folk medicine as an astringent gargle for inflammations of the gums, mouth, and throat, and taken internally for diarrhea. There is no professional use of this plant drug (Bisset and Wichtl 1994).

Potential: The astringency of the rhizome would make it effective for the oral uses described above, but there is no market for this plant.

Purple Avens

Other Names: Cree: *kinipagwusk* ("snake root"); English: water avens; French: *benoîte des ruisseaux*.

Scientific Name: *Geum rivale* L.

Description: A tall slender herb with somewhat hairy stems, feathery basal leaves and three-lobed, toothed stem leaves, and large (2 cm wide) nodding flowers with purple to yellowish sepals and flesh-colored to yellowish and purple-veined petals that abruptly narrow at their bases.

Habitat: Found occasionally in stream banks, wet meadows, and marshes across Canada, the mountainous western and northern USA, Iceland, Europe, and western Asia.

Medicinal Uses: The root can be used in a tea drunk to facilitate childbirth (C14, M9). It was used in the past to cause abortions, but is not used this way much anymore (M9).

Properties: Purple avens rhizomes contain up to 17% tannins, some of which are of the pyrogallol type, eugenol, alkaloids, and glycosides (Hetherington and Steck 1997). An extract of the whole plant is reported to have blood coagulant properties, and other species of *Geum* have been reported to have abortion-causing and embryo-damaging effects in pregnant experimental animals (Farnsworth 1999). See also the preceding species.

Potential: No potential at this time except perhaps as an ornamental.

(D. Cahoon)

Shrubby Cinquefoil

Other Names: French: *potentille, quinte feuille*; Slave: *tli^{n}te dedzhine, kothentelī naydī.*

Scientific Name: *Pentaphylloides floribunda* (Pursh) A. Löve, common synonym: *Potentilla fruticosa* L. ssp. *floribunda* (Nutt.) Elk.

(R. Marles)

Description: A freely branched shrub up to 1 m tall, with shredding outer bark, leaves that are short-stalked and pinnate with mostly five (or seven) oblong, hairy leaflets that have smooth curled edges and taper at each end, and flowers that are borne singly or in a small spray, up to 2.5 cm wide, with long yellow petals, developing into hairy hard fruit (achenes).

Habitat: A circumboreal species found on moist to dry plains and in open woods from Alaska across Canada and the western and northern USA, and in Eurasia.

Food Uses: The stems and leaves can be boiled to make a tea (Lamont 1977).

Medicinal Uses: The leaves, stems, and roots can be boiled together and the decoction drunk to treat fever accompanied by body aches and perhaps a cough (Lamont 1977).

Properties: The leaves contain (per 100 g dry weight): crude fiber (9.6 g), Ca (520 mg), and P (190 mg). Snow cinquefoil (*Potentilla nivea* L.) leaves contain 314 mg/100 g dry weight of vitamin C (Kuhnlein and Turner 1991). *Potentilla anserina* L. leaves contain 6-10% ellagic acid-type tannins and some flavonoid glycosides. Because of the tannin content, it is used both externally and internally as an astringent (Bisset and Wichtl 1994). There is so far no scientific evidence to support its use against fever (Dobelis 1986).

Potential: Shrubby cinquefoil is commercially available as an attractive ornamental shrub.

Pin Cherry

Pin cherry in blossom (▲) and fruit (►) (R. Marles)

Other Names: Chipewyan: *jíyëraze* ("little hard berry"); Cree: *pusawemina* ("tart berries"), *pasisāwimin, pāsuwiymayātik*; French: *petit merisier, cerises d'été.*

Scientific Name: *Prunus pensylvanica* L. f.

Description: A small tree 4-8 m high with reddish brown bark, lance-shaped, long-pointed finely round-toothed leaves, small white flowers on long stalks in umbrellalike clusters, and small, sour, bright red cherries.

Habitat: Fairly common in woods, ravines, clearings, and burned areas east of the continental divide across Canada and the northern and eastern USA.

Food Uses: Pin cherries are eaten fresh or cooked to make a jelly (C5, C13, C51, C60, D6, D26, D29, M1; Diamant pers. comm.; Leighton 1985), are mixed with bear grease and powdered meat to make pemmican (M9), or may be used to make wine (D9).

Medicinal Uses: To treat patients delirious with fever, a tea from the bark, berries, leaves, and roots can be given in a dosage of ° cup every hour for 2 or more days (M6). The inner bark infusion can be used as a wash for sore eyes (Leighton 1985). The root decoction can be given to children to treat whooping cough or fever (Siegfried 1994).

Technological Uses: The berries can be boiled to make a red dye (M6).

Properties: The fruit has 30 mg of vitamin C per 100 g fresh weight (Kuhnlein and Turner 1991). See choke cherry for further details.

Potential: There is no significant demand for pin cherries.

Choke Cherry

Other Names: Chipewyan: *jíe yéri* ("berry that is hard"), *jíé Déné yéri*; Cree: *takwahīmināna, takwēhiminān* ("berry that is crushed"), *tākwuhiymin*; French: *cerisier à grappes*.

Scientific Name: *Prunus virginiana* L.

Description: A shrub 1-3 m high with grayish stems, alternate, elliptical, short-pointed leaves with sharply toothed edges, and white flowers in long dense sprays that develop into purplish black fruit (drupes).

Habitat: Very common in thickets, ravines, sand hills, and rocky and open woodlands across most of Canada except for the far north and most of the continental USA except for Alaska and the southeastern states.

Food Uses: Choke cherries can be eaten fresh (C50, Diamant pers. comm.; Lamont 1977; Jarvenpa 1979; Siegfried 1994) or cooked (C5, C6, C51, C61; Leighton 1985; Siegfried 1994). A traditional method of preparation is to crush them between two stones and then warm them up in a pan with lard and sugar or serve them with cream. The crushed fruit can also be frozen for later use (C50), crushed and dried in cakes to be used with pemmican, cooked meat, and stews (M9; Curtis 1928; Leighton 1985), or fermented to make wine (M11).

Choke cherry in fruit (R. Marles)

Medicinal Uses: A tea made from the leaves, stems, bark, and roots can be used for treating colds, fevers, and pneumonia (C29, M9). The tea can also be used to clear the throats of singers and speakers as it loosens phlegm, and it can be good for treating high blood pressure and heart problems (C29). The bark can be boiled to make an emetic drink to relieve a stomachache (C2, C3) or to treat diarrhea (Holmes, cited in Leighton 1985) or colds (Siegfried 1994), or the decoction may be used as a douche (Siegfried 1994). The fruit can be eaten as a laxative (Siegfried 1994). The root can be boiled to make a decoction drunk to treat the flu (Siegfried 1994) or it may be part of a compound medicine for treating diarrhea in children (C26; Welsh, cited in Leighton 1985).

Properties: The fruit (100 g fresh weight, 79% moisture) provides thiamine (0.05 mg) and vitamin C (30 mg). For comparison, the black cherry (*P. serotina* Ehrh., 100 g fresh weight, 90% moisture) provides: food energy (81 kcal), protein (0.8 g), fat (0.4 g), total carbohydrate (8.5 g), crude fiber (2.3 g), thiamine (0.04 mg), riboflavin (0.04 mg), niacin (1.1 mg), vitamin C (18 mg), vitamin A (9 RE), and minerals (ash: 0.3 g), including Ca (40 mg), P (35 mg), and Fe (0.8 mg) (Kuhnlein and Turner 1991). The bark is well known as an ingredient of cough remedies, but scientific testing has shown it to be only slightly effective. The leaves, twigs, bark, and pits contain the cyanogenic glycoside amygdalin (Turner and Szczawinski 1991). When the plant parts are crushed or chewed, an enzyme is liberated from storage cells that splits the glycoside to release cyanide. The highest concentration of cyanide occurs in large succulent leaves on vigorous shoots, but children have been fatally poisoned by swallowing large numbers of the pits when eating the cherries (Turner and Szczawinski 1991). Usually the pits must be chewed or crushed to release the cyanide, and the traditional method of preparation described above would cause maximal release of cyanide as a gas (HCN), which would be driven off by heating the crushed fruit in the pan, leaving it safe to eat. Thorough boiling of bark or leaves should also eliminate all traces of the cyanide.

Potential: Choke cherries have an established market for making jellies and wine, and the bark has a long history of use in cough syrups.

Prickly Rose

Other Names: Chipewyan: *íntsólé;* Cree: *kaminakuse* ("thorn plant"), *okīnīak, okwāminakwasi-āhtik, okinīwapīgwīnīwa, ogimina-kasiatik, ōginīatik, owkiniy* ("rose hip"), *owkāmnekusiy;* French: *églantier;* Slave: *untshu.*

Scientific Name: *Rosa acicularis* Lindl. and related species.

Description: A low bush with stems densely covered by straight, weak bristles, leaves of five to seven hairy leaflets, glandular and hairy stipules, large pink flowers usually borne singly, and oval fruit (a hip) with a constricted neck.

Habitat: Common in woods, fields, and roadsides from northern Alaska, south through the mountains to New Mexico, east from Yukon and Alberta to New Brunswick, and the midwestern and northeastern USA.

Prickly rose hips (R. Marles)

Food Uses: Rose hips are eaten fresh (D3, D9, D12, D24, M5; Diamant pers. comm.; Fidler 1792; Curtis 1928; Lamont 1977; Leighton 1985), but the seeds are always removed first because if swallowed they would irritate the intestinal tract (D24; Leighton 1985: part of a Wisakechak traditional story). Rose hips can be made into a jelly or beverage (D12, D14, M5; Lamont 1977) or syrup (Siegfried 1994). The pink flower petals can be eaten as a treat by young children (C23, C27; Lamont 1977).

Medicinal Uses: Four branches can be boiled to make a decoction drunk to relieve excessive menstruation (C28). The root decoction can be given to children to treat diarrhea (C13, D12) or coughs (Lamont 1977; Leighton 1985), drunk to correct problems of irregularity of menstruation (Siegfried 1994), or used as eye drops to treat soreness such as from snow blindness (C11, D6, D29; Leighton 1985). The roots can be part of a compound medicine for chest colds (Siegfried 1994). Rose hips can be eaten raw to prevent or treat colds and fevers (D12). Rose petals can be used as a heart tonic (D12) or chewed and applied topically to a bee sting (Lamont 1977).

Technological Uses: A toy pipe can be made from a hollowed rose hip for the bowl and a hollow piece of grass, fireweed, or willow twig for a pipestem (D3, D6, D24, D32; Leighton 1985). The hips can also be used as beads for a toy necklace (Leighton 1985).

Properties: Prickly rose fruit (100 g fresh weight, 65% moisture) contains: food energy (55 kcal), protein (2.4 g), fat (0.7 g), total carbohydrate (21.3 g), thiamine (0.12 mg), riboflavin (0.10 mg), niacin (1.1 mg), vitamin C (1481 mg), vitamin A (263 RE), and minerals (ash: 2.0 g). Although the mineral content of the fruit of this species was not listed, the levels for the fruit of related species are: Ca (77-355 mg), P (37-110 mg), Na (1.8 mg), Mg (26 mg), Cu (0.1 mg), Zn (0.2 mg), Fe (0.3 mg-3.9), Mn (0.9-1.5 mg), and Mo (<0.1 mg). Rose flowers provide 350 RE of vitamin A per 100 g fresh weight (Kuhnlein and Turner 1991).

Potential: Rose hips can be a good source of vitamin C, but the actual level in commercial products varies considerably depending on how they are processed (Foster and Tyler 1999). Their flavor is popular in jellies and teas, but it is not likely that the native species can be produced competitively except perhaps for local markets. The red color of the hips comes from rubixanthin, beta-carotene, and lycopene (Bisset and Wichtl 1994), carotenoids of interest for their antioxidant and cancer-fighting properties. The essential oil is in demand for aromatherapy (Rogers 1997). There is also an interest in rose hips for the dried or preserved floral trade (Mater Engineering 1993). Mater Engineering (1993) categorizes prickly rose as a Priority Level 2 product for further development and describes the market in some detail.

Dewberry

Other Names: Chipewyan: *ts'ëlin-adláraze* ("frog's little cloudberry"), *tlh'ogh naⁿdlári* ("grass cloudberry"); Cree: *ōskīsikomin, owsgiysīguwmin* ("eye berries"); English: dwarf raspberry; French: *mûres rouges* (*R. arcticus*), *catherinettes* (*R. pubescens*); Slave: *tsahliʰ kiʰ*.

Rubus articus L. (R. Marles)

Scientific Name: *Rubus arcticus* L. ssp. *acaulis* (Michx.) Focke, common synonym: *R. acaulis* Michx. Also *R. pubescens* Raf. which has the same common names in English and Cree and is believed to hybridize naturally with *R. arcticus* (Boivin 1967; Scoggan 1978-79; Moss and Packer 1994).

Description: *Rubus arcticus* is a low, herbaceous, unarmed perennial with leaves divided into three leaflets, small pink flowers, and red fruit like a raspberry but with fewer drupelets. *Rubus pubescens* is trailing or climbing and more woody, has a pointed rather than rounded middle leaflet, the flowers are produced in groups of two or three instead of singly, with white or pink petals and reflexed sepals, and the red aggregate fruit has only a few drupelets.

Habitat: Both are common locally in moist woods or meadows, bogs, and tundra from northern Alaska, south through British Columbia to Oregon, in the mountains to Colorado, and east through the territories and northern parts of the provinces to Quebec and northern USA. *Rubus arcticus* tends to be in more boggy areas and tundra, *R. pubescens* in wooded areas.

Food Uses: The fruit is quite popular, being eaten fresh (D6, D9, D24, D29; Diamant pers. comm.; Lamont 1977; Leighton 1985; Siegfried 1994) or made into jam (D6; Siegfried 1994). At Île à la Crosse and Lake Athabasca, Saskatchewan, they were abundant enough to be gathered in large quantities (Macoun 1882).

Properties: *Rubus arcticus* fruit has 38.8 mg of vitamin C and 11 RE of vitamin A, while *R. pubescens* fruit has 21 mg of vitamin C per 100 g fresh weight. Dewberry fruit (not identified to species, 100 g fresh weight, 84% moisture) also has protein (0.9 g), fat (0.8 g), total carbohydrate (14 g), and minerals (ash: 0.6 g) including Ca (54 mg) and P (31 mg) (Kuhnlein and Turner 1991). See *R. idaeus* for further details.

Potential: The fruit are not productive enough to have much market potential.

Cloudberry

Other Names: Chipewyan: *nadláre, naⁿdlári*; Cree: *kwakwakacōsimin, mistahīmins*; English: baked-apple berry; French: *mûres blanches, plaquebière, chicouté*; Slave: *tsuīkali*.

Scientific Name: *Rubus chamaemorus* L.

Description: A herbaceous perennial with two or three stalked, round, five- to nine-lobed leaves, large white flowers borne singly, and fruit like a raspberry but golden yellow when ripe.

(R. Marles)

Habitat: Common in bogs and swamps in the boreal forest and moist tundra; circumboreal, in North America from the high arctic to southwestern British Columbia and across the forested regions of Canada to the Maritimes and northeastern USA.

Food Uses: For the Chipewyan this is the second most important fruit after blueberries. The fruit can be eaten fresh or cooked with sugar (D6, D28; Diamant pers. comm.; Mackenzie 1801; Macoun 1882; Birket-Smith 1930; Lamont 1977; Leighton 1985). It is also a favorite fruit of the Inuit who preserve it in seal oil (Porsild and Cody 1980). The leaves are commonly used as a tobacco additive or substitute. Sometimes they are mixed with bearberry leaves and red osier dogwood inner bark (D6, D9). Long ago the leaves were gathered in large quantities and boiled with 10 B plug tobacco. When thoroughly dried, the leaves could be used as a substitute that tasted just as good as the tobacco. Thus one plug was made into many (D29; Munsterhjelm 1953).

Medicinal Uses: The root and stem decoction can be drunk to remedy barrenness in women or to aid a woman in hard labor (Leighton 1985).

Properties: Cloudberries (100 g fresh weight, 84% moisture) have: food energy (50 kcal), protein (2.0 g), fat (1.0 g), total carbohydrate (9.6 g), crude fiber (6.0 g), thiamine (0.05 mg), riboflavin (0.07 mg), niacin (0.9 mg), vitamin C (130 mg), and minerals (ash: 0.5 g), including Ca (17 mg), P (53 mg), Na (0.6 mg), K (231 mg), Mg (40.8 mg), Cu (0.1 mg), Zn (0.7 mg), Fe (0.4 mg), Mn (0.5 mg), and Mo (<0.1 mg) (Kuhnlein and Turner 1991).

Potential: This delicious fruit is quite unknown in Canadian cities, and there might be good potential for value-added fruit products. Local processing will be necessary to reduce the weight and bulk, and to minimize shipping costs and spoilage.

Raspberry

Other Names: Chipewyan: *tthek-álhjíé* ("flat rock berry"), *tthekálé jíé, dakálé jíé;* Cree: *anosh'kanek, ayoos-kunak, ayuwskun, uyooskan, ayōsikan* ("soft berry"), *athōskunatikwah, athōskan;* French: *framboisier;* Slave: *daᶜkali.*

Scientific Name: *Rubus idaeus* L. ssp. *strigosus* (Michx.) Focke.

Description: A large bush with bristly stems, leaves pinnately divided into three to five leaflets, white flowers, and red aggregate fruit.

Habitat: Common in shady woods, burned-over areas, and river banks across Canada, throughout the continental USA except the southeast, in northern Mexico, and in Eurasia.

(R. Marles)

Food Uses: Wild raspberries are a popular fruit for eating fresh or canned (C23, C27, C50, C60, D6, D9, D28, M10; Diamant pers. comm.; Curtis 1928; Lamont 1977; Jarvenpa 1979, 1980; Leighton 1985; Siegfried 1994), as a syrup (Siegfried 1994), or for a home brew (Lamont 1977). You can also peel and eat the very young stems (Cree: *masukah*) (C23, C27; Lamont 1977; Leighton 1985) or boil the older stems and roots to make a beverage (Lamont 1977).

Medicinal Uses: The leaf tea can be given to women giving birth to strengthen them and aid the process (M10). The stems can be dried and then boiled to make a decoction for treating fevers (C44). The roots can be boiled and the cooled decoction used as eye drops to treat soreness such as from snow blindness (D6). A decoction of the cleaned but unpeeled roots and stems together with other plants can be used as a drink given to children to treat diarrhea (C26), stomachache (Lamont 1977), dysentery and cholera infantum (Strath 1903), or teething sickness (Leighton 1985), to help a woman recover after childbirth and to slow menstrual bleeding (Leighton 1985), or as a wash for skin infections (D29). The vapor created by boiling raspberry roots with birch inner (reddish) bark can be inhaled (the steam is trapped with a cloth over the head) to treat asthma (C13). The fruit is believed to be good for the heart (Welsh, cited in Leighton 1985).

Technological Uses: The berries can be boiled to make a red dye (M10).

Properties: Raspberry fruit (100 g fresh weight, 83% moisture) provides: food energy (65 kcal), protein (0.6 g), fat (0.8 g), total carbohydrate (15.8 g), crude fiber (4.5 g), thiamine (0.03 mg), riboflavin (0.09 mg), niacin (0.1 mg), vitamin C (22.3 mg), vitamin A (13 RE), and minerals (ash: 0.5 g), including Ca (36 mg), P (38 mg), Na (0.4 mg), K (152 mg), Mg (18 mg), Cu (0.5 mg), Zn (0.6 mg), Fe (1.0 mg), Mn (2.8 mg), and Mo (<0.1 mg). The peeled shoots of thimbleberry (*R. parviflorus* Nutt.) have the following nutrients (per 100 g fresh weight, 93% moisture): food energy (22 kcal), protein (0.6 g), fat (0.4 g), total carbohydrate (5.5 g), crude fiber (1.0 g), thiamine (0.01 mg), riboflavin (0.09 mg), niacin (0.3 mg), vitamin C (5.9 mg), vitamin A (41 RE), and minerals (ash: 0.6 g), including Ca (24 mg), P (26 mg), Na (1.0 mg), Mg (29 mg), Cu (0.4 mg), Zn (0.4 mg), Fe (0.4 mg), and Mn (0.2 mg) (Kuhnlein and Turner 1991). Raspberry leaves contain gallotannins and ellagitannins, flavonoids, and some vitamin C. Because of its tannin content, the leaf infusion is effective as an astringent gargle for throat or mouth conditions, topically to treat skin conditions (Bisset and Wichtl 1994), and internally to treat diarrhea (Dobelis 1986). The leaf infusion also has proven antispasmodic activity helpful for treating menstrual cramps and as an aid in childbirth (Dobelis 1986).

Potential: The market potential of the fruit is well established, and there may be a market for the leaves for herbal medicine as well.

Mountain Ash

Other Names: Chipewyan: *naidí dechëné* ("medicine stick"); Cree: *maskōminānātik, esniywachiywa(h)tik*; French: *cormier*; Slave: *tsu duga^h, kolo^n dzhī*.

Scientific Name: *Sorbus americana* Marsh. Also *S. scopulina* Greene and *S. decora* (Sarg.) Schneid. Although some texts including Kartesz and Kartesz (1980) distinguish these three species as valid, Boivin (1967) found no botanical justification for separating them.

Description: A shrub or small tree with reddish brown stems, pinnate leaves of 11-13 lance-shaped, tooth-edged leaflets, flat-topped dense clusters of white flowers, and red or orange fruit.

Habitat: Occasionally found in moist woods or on open slopes from Alaska south to California, and east across Canada and central and northern USA.

Food Uses: The twigs can be used to flavor tea (Siegfried 1994).

Medicinal Uses: The Chipewyan name, meaning "medicine stick," indicates its importance in traditional medicine. The stem can be chewed but more often is boiled to make a decoction drunk to treat colds (D6, D9, D22, D29), coughs (D4, D9, D23; Lamont 1977: fruit and root also), hemorrhaging (from tuberculosis? D32), headaches (D6, D9, D22, D29), heart trouble or a sore chest (D6, D9, D22, D29; Lamont 1977; Siegfried 1994), kidney pain

Sorbus scopulina Greene (R. Marles)

(D3, D22), back pain, and rheumatism (Leighton 1985; Welsh, cited in Leighton 1985; Siegfried 1994), or to facilitate labor during birth (D24). The stem and root decoction can be taken to treat tuberculosis (Lamont 1977). The bark decoction can be drunk to treat general pains in the body and can be considered to be good for the bones (C20). For headaches and sore chest the steam from boiling the stems could be inhaled (D6). The root decoction can be drunk to treat back pain or in combination with other herbs as a treatment for diabetes, and mountain ash can be part of a compound medicine to treat cancer (Siegfried 1994).

Properties: European mountain ash or rowan (*S. aucuparia* L.) fruits contain a toxic compound, parasorbic acid, which is neutralized by cooking. The fruits should never be eaten raw (Dobelis 1986). The seeds contain a cyanogenic glycoside and so should not be eaten (Turner and Szczawinski 1991).

Potential: Mountain ash is grown as an ornamental. There is no demand for the fruit here, although it is used commercially in Europe.

RUBIACEAE
(Madder Family)

Northern Bedstraw

Other Names: French: *gaillet.*

Scientific Name: *Galium boreale* L., common synonym: *G. septentrionale* Roemer & J.A. Schultes

Description: An erect perennial herb up to 60 cm tall, with narrow leaves in whorls of four around smooth square stems. Terminal sprays of small white four-lobed flowers with a faint fragrance produce pairs of tiny round nutlets covered with short white hairs.

Habitat: Common in woodland openings and moist meadows or prairies throughout Canada, most of the USA except the southeast, and Greenland, Iceland, and Eurasia.

Technological Uses: The roots can be used to make a red dye for porcupine quills (C29).

(R. Marles)

Properties: Northern bedstraw contains flavonoids and iridoid glycosides. In Scotland, *G. verum* L. is used as a dye (Bisset and Wichtl 1994). *Galium aparine* L. roots have also been used as a source of a red dye (Dobelis 1986). *Galium aparine* also contains phenolic acids, coumarins, and tannins, and is a mild diuretic (Bradley 1992).

Potential: Madder (*Rubia tinctoria* L.), the dye plant used originally to color British soldiers' jackets red, is also in the Rubiaceae. A minor market is possible among weavers who prefer natural dye materials.

SALICACEAE
(Willow Family)

Balsam Poplar

Other Names: Chipewyan: *k'es t'álé* ("poplar which has cracks"); Cree: *metos, mayi metos, mayi-mītos* ("ugly tree"), *maymiytos, māthamītos, osīmisk* ("bud"); English: black poplar; French: *peuplier noir, liard*; Slave: *thlo*[n] *due*[h].

Scientific Name: *Populus balsamifera* L.

Description: A large tree up to 25 m tall, with gray bark becoming deeply furrowed with age, egg-shaped leaves with long-pointed tips, finely toothed edges, dark green above and silver-green underneath, developing from very fragrant buds, and pendulous catkins appearing before the leaves.

(R. Marles)

Habitat: Common along shores, in moist woods and parklands, and spreading into the boreal forest; found across Canada and northern USA.

Food Uses: During the summer the cambium can be scraped off and eaten by hunters, and it is also a starvation food (Lamont 1977).

Medicinal Uses: The sap can be drunk to treat diabetes and high blood pressure. The bark and sap together may be boiled to make a tea given to children to treat asthma. The aromatic spring buds ("balm of Gilead") can be gathered and placed in very hot bathwater, allowed to steep until a layer of extract forms on the surface and the water is cool enough to bathe in, and also rubbed on afflicted areas to treat skin diseases such as eczema or psoriasis (C6, M1). For teething babies the buds can be rubbed directly on the gums and after cooling an infusion can be used to rinse the baby's mouth (D26). The young bud can be held on a sore tooth to treat a toothache. This is a strong medicine that may cause the tooth to break and fall out (C24,

C25, C35, C36, C38, C42, C44, C52). A bud can be placed into the nostril to stop a nosebleed (Leighton 1985). A decoction of two buds can be drunk to treat heart problems (C23, C27). The buds can be boiled for 30 minutes with aspen branch bark and the decoction can be drunk to treat diabetes (C38). The fresh bark from the south side of the tree can be mixed with another plant and the decoction can be given to people who suffer from seizures (C28). A decoction of the inner bark from the base of a sapling can be drunk to treat a stomachache (Lamont 1977). The leaves can be applied to a sore to draw out the infection (Leighton 1985).

Technological Uses: The thick bark can be carved into toy boats (D9) or buttons (Lamont 1977). The wood can be used to make various items such as cradleboards (Leonard pers. comm.) or canoe paddles, but it is not very strong (D29). The buds can be mixed with other ingredients to make a trap lure (Leighton 1985).

Properties: Balsam poplar bark provides 230 kcal of food energy and 1.9 g of protein from 100 g fresh weight (Kuhnlein and Turner 1991). The bud exudate consists of flavonoids (60-74%), predominantly as dihydrochalcones but numerous flavones, flavonols, and flavanones also are present, as well as aromatic acids and esters (9-16%), such as coumaric and cinnamic acids and their esters, terpenoids (11-13%) of which the major compound is bisabolol, arachidonic acid and prostaglandin derivatives of it, and phenolic glycosides including salicin and populin. The bud exudate has proven expectorant, antibacterial, antifungal, and anti-inflammatory activities. It can be used topically to treat skin infections, as a gargle for laryngitis, and has been used internally to treat acute and chronic upper respiratory tract problems (Bradley 1992). The salicin content of the buds relieves pain as well as inflammation when applied topically (Dobelis 1986). Bee propolis is a brown resin that bees obtain from poplar and conifer buds to use to fill gaps or cracks in their hives. Health food stores are promoting propolis as a natural antibiotic. Propolis does

Balsam poplar buds (R. Marles)

have some antibacterial and antifungal activity (weaker than most commercial drugs) due to the presence of substances derived from the source plant – flavonoids, pinocembrin, galangin, pinobanksin, and pinobanksin-3-acetate, plus *p*-coumaric acid benzyl ester and caffeic acid esters (Foster and Tyler 1999).

Potential: There is a strong market among interior decorating firms for tree tops to make natural-looking semiartificial trees (real trunks and branches with silk leaves). Branches are used for baskets, wreaths, bird cages, decorative furniture, and specially preserved leafy branches for decorative purposes (Mater Engineering 1993). "Balm of Gilead" has some potential as a perfume ingredient. Some of the traditional uses are supported by scientific evidence, but the economic potential as a medicine is probably quite limited.

Trembling Aspen

Other Names: Chipewyan: *k'es*;
Cree: *metos, miytos, wapisk-mītos*
("white poplar"), *wasī-mītos* ("bright
poplar"), *mistik* ("wood, stick"),
mītos, mitosinipiah ("aspen leaves");
French: *tremble*; Slave: *dīaʰ*.

Scientific Name: *Populus tremuloides*
Michx.

Description: A slender tree with
grayish white bark, which is smooth
except for furrowing at the base of
the tree. Leaves are broadly egg-
shaped, abruptly pointed, with saw-
toothed margins, each on a flat stalk
that makes the leaves tremble in the
slightest breeze. Catkins produce
small capsules with hairy seeds.

Trembling aspen stand (R. Marles)

Habitat: Very common on moist to
dry soils and burns in the parklands and boreal forest. This is one of the
most widely distributed tree species, being found across North America
except in the southeastern USA.

Food Uses: The outer bark can be stripped off and the inner bark and
cambium (Cree: *mistan, miston*) peeled off with a knife and eaten in the springtime, when it tastes almost like honeydew melon (C23, C27, C38, C52, D6;
Leighton 1985; Holmes, cited in Leighton 1985; Siegfried 1994; Welsh, cited
in Leighton 1985). The sap can be collected for making syrup (C23, C27).
Dry or rotting wood can be used to smoke meat and fish (C57, D27, M8;
Lamont 1977; Leighton 1985). Aspen wood ashes were used as a source of
salt long ago (Lamont 1977).

Medicinal Uses: The leaves can be chewed and applied to bee or wasp stings
to relieve the pain (C21, C22, C24, C25, C39, C45, C52, D6, D27; Leighton
1985). They can also be used for mosquito bites (C24, C25) or cuts (C35, C36,
C44). The bark from a young tree can be cut into squares that can be placed
under the tongue to treat a stomachache or when the patient is spitting up
blood (C44). A strip of bark about the length of the heart, cut from the south

side of a mature tree at heart height, can be chewed and the juice swallowed as a heart medicine (C11). A small strip (2 × 5 cm) of fresh green bark may be chewed and swallowed for relief from food poisoning or diarrhea (M9). An aspen bark (Cree: *wathukisk*) infusion (decoction would be too strong) can be drunk to treat cancer;

Harvesting aspen inner bark for food (N. Tays)

it makes you throw up but helps to flush out of the body whatever is making you sick (C35, C36). The bark infusion can also be drunk to treat diabetes (C20). The bark decoction can be drunk to treat a stomachache (C44), diarrhea (C47), fever (D27), venereal disease (Welsh, cited in Leighton 1985), or coughing (D27; Holmes, cited in Leighton 1985). Aspen branch bark can be boiled for 30 minutes with balsam poplar buds for a decoction drunk to treat diabetes (C38). The inner green bark can be used as a wound dressing to stop bleeding (Welsh, cited in Leighton 1985; Siegfried 1994). The white "dust" on the bark (crustose lichens and dead tree periderm) can be scraped off and applied to cuts and even deep wounds to coagulate the blood and thus stop the bleeding (D26; Leighton 1985) or used in a treatment for venereal disease (Leighton 1985). The bud can be used like balsam poplar buds, applied directly to a toothache (C39). The young seeds can be chewed and swallowed to try to cause an abortion (D6).

Technological Uses: The wood can be used to make canoe paddles (D3), tepee poles, deadfalls (Leighton 1985), snow shovels, temporary snowshoe frames, and plates (Lamont 1977), and knurls can be hollowed out to make bowls (Curtis 1928; Lamont 1977). It is also an important firewood (Lamont 1977). The stems can be used to make whistles (D27; Leighton 1985). Young branches can be stripped of leaves, and split in half to make a cooking stick used to hold meat over the fire for cooking (C37). The rotted wood is burned to smoke hides (Lamont 1977). The ashes can be put into a sack through which boiling water can be poured, and the resulting caustic solution can be boiled with rendered caribou grease to make soap (D6, D24, D29, D30). The ashes can also be rubbed into moose hides during tanning to soften them (D29).

Properties: Aspen bark (100 g fresh weight) provides 1.3 g of protein, 31.7 g of crude fiber, 1.6 g of ash, 684 mg of Ca, 17 mg of P, 1.8 mg of Na, 130 mg of K, 53.1 mg of Mg, 0.5 mg of Cu, 8.3 mg of Zn, 4.4 mg of Fe, and 1.2 mg of Mn (Kuhnlein and Turner 1991). The leaves and bark contain salicylates and thus have pain-relieving, fever-reducing, and anti-inflammatory activities (Dobelis 1986; see *Salix* for further information).

Potential: Interior decorating firms use tree tops to make natural-looking semiartificial trees (real trunks and branches with silk leaves). Branches are used for baskets, wreaths, bird cages, decorative furniture, and specially preserved leafy branches for decorative purposes (Mater Engineering 1993). Aspen is currently an important forest species for pulp and oriented-strand board made from the wood chips. Extraction of salicylates could provide an important secondary product.

Willow

Other Names: Chipewyan: *k'ái*; Cree: *nepise, nepiseatik, wekope* (grey willow), *atikwupamuk* ("deer or birch willow"), *nīpīsīs, nīpīsī, nīpīsīah, nīpīsīgībī* ("willow root"), *nīpīstakwah* ("willow rotted wood"); French: *saule*; Slave: *ka kelī, ka daʰ, ka thule, ka tha* (different groups of willow species).

Scientific Name: *Salix bebbiana* Sarg. Also *S. myrtillifolia* Anderss., *S. planifolia* Pursh, *S. pyrifolia* Anderss., and other species.

Description: Shrubs with alternate, narrow to elliptical leaves, male and female flowers in catkins on separate plants, and fruit consisting of a capsule that splits open along two sides to release hairy seeds.

Habitat: Willows are common along shores, forest openings, and even in the tundra throughout the northern hemisphere in temperate to arctic zones.

Food Uses: The wood can be burned to smoke meat, and the branches can be boiled, the first water discarded, then boiled again to add flavor to home brew (Lamont 1977).

Medicinal Uses: For medicinal use you peel and discard the outer bark. To treat diarrhea and stomachaches young willow branches (in the "pussy-willow" or flowering stage; Chipewyan: *k'áí lhiⁿaze* = "willow puppy") can be cut, the outer bark removed, and the inner green bark decocted alone or mixed with another plant (C24, C25, C35, C36; Leighton 1985). To treat constipation you peel the inner bark towards yourself, tie it in four knots, boil it and drink the decoction. To treat diarrhea, you peel the inner bark away from yourself, tie it in four knots, and drink the decoction (C10). The branch

Willow catkins (R. Marles)

Salix bebbiana Sarg. (N. Tays)

decoction can also be taken to treat a toothache (C23, C27) or cough (Lamont 1977). The bark can also be peeled, boiled, and used as a poultice applied hot to treat back "paralysis" (probably a slipped disk: Siegfried 1994). The root can be peeled and boiled, and the decoction drunk to relieve fatigue and provide strength (C38). The peeled root can also be applied directly to an aching tooth (C23, C24, C25, C27), and the chewed inner root bark can be applied to deep cuts to stop the bleeding and promote healing without infection (Leighton 1985). Mackenzie (1801) mentioned that the Dene people burned and powdered willow bark and placed it on infected wounds and ulcers.

Technological Uses: The wood is used to make pipe stems (D32), bows (D9; Curtis 1928; Leighton 1985), canoe ribs (D6), emergency snowshoes (D6; Petitot 1868), wooden nails (D11), whistles (D6, D29; Leonard pers. comm.; Racette pers. comm.; Birket-Smith 1930; Leighton 1985), drum sticks (Saddle Lake, Alberta, Museum display), birch bark basket rims (Leighton 1985), wicker baskets (D29; Elford and Elford 1981), bead weaving looms (Leighton 1985), sweat lodge frames (M9), and frames for hide stretching and ptarmigan snares (Birket-Smith 1930). A willow stem is bent and tied into a circle to make the frame for a dream-catcher charm (C39). Twelve willow branches can be used to make the frame for a sweat lodge (C24, C25). The rotted wood can be used for smoking hides (C24, C25, C44). Green willow branches may be burned to smoke meat (M8). Rope, twine, and fish nets (Chipewyan:

tabí"lh) can be made by twisting together wet strands of
inner bark fibers and gluing
them with spruce gum (D6,
D9, D23, D24; Morice 1910;
Curtis 1928; Birket-Smith
1930; Breynat 1948; Leechman 1948; Smith GW 1973;
Lamont 1977; Leighton 1985;
Welsh, cited in Leighton
1985). Willow bark can also

Willow root being prepared as a medicine (N. Tays)

be wrapped around rawhide nooses to protect them from the weather (Morice
1910). A tube of willow bark can be used as a drinking straw (Lamont 1977).
Short lengths of forked willow branches can be debarked and heated, then
twisted into the hair to make a simple curling iron (D24, D29, D30).

Ritual Uses: When a man killed a bear he would weave 21 willow twigs into
an offering (Cree: *niyptāskwan*) to thank the bear's spirit for giving up its life
in order that the man and his family might live and not go hungry. The
offering was taken into the bush, willow fungus (*Trametes suaveolens* (L. ex
Fries) Fries, Coriolaceae) was burned as part of the ceremony, and red material was tied to a nearby bush (Siegfried 1994).

Properties: Willow bark is famous for its content of at least 12 different
salicylates (1.5% to >11% dry weight), especially salicin and its esters:
salicortin, tremulacin, and 2'-O-acetylsalicortin, as well as aromatic alde-
hydes (e.g., vanillin), flavonoids, and tannins. The constituents vary by species and by season (Bradley 1992). The salicylates were the original starting
material for the synthesis of acetylsalicylic acid (ASA). When willow bark
extract is consumed the salicylates are gradually broken down by gastric
juices and intestinal microorganisms into sugars and salicyl alcohol, which
is readily absorbed (>86%), providing a constant blood plasma level for
several hours. Enzymes in the blood and liver convert salicyl alcohol into
salicylic acid, which has the pain-relieving, fever-reducing, and anti-
inflammatory effects that we associate with ASA. Due to the slow, prolonged
absorption of the natural salicylates, willow bark is less effective in treating
acute headache than ASA pills, but more effective where prolonged therapy
is required, and it is less likely to cause stomach upset or hypersensitivity,
although these side effects are possible in some individuals (Bisset and Wichtl
1994). Salicylic acid has been reported to differ from ASA in having fewer

side effects and no action on platelet function (Bradley 1992). Bisset and Wichtl (1994) suggest that since salicin, salicortin, and salicylic acid, unlike ASA, may not inhibit thrombocytes irreversibly, there should be no increased interaction with blood coagulants and hence no danger of hemorrhage during the final months of pregnancy. However, some of the evidence for this comes from laboratory tests that need to be confirmed by clinical trials. The tannins provide astringency which would contribute to the medicinal effects, such as when applied topically to cuts or sores (Dobelis 1986).

Potential: Willow bark is in demand by herbalists; this market could increase if the therapeutic benefits over ASA could be clinically confirmed. However, studies to determine appropriate local species are needed, because salicylate levels are quite variable. Willow withes are used for wickerwork, and willow charcoal is used in artists' charcoal pencils (Dobelis 1986). Diamond willow (*S. bebbiana*) wood is very decorative and a market exists for it (Mater Engineering 1993).

SANTALACEAE
(Sandalwood Family)

Northern Comandra

Other Names: Chipewyan: *sas jíé* ("bear berry"); English: false or bastard toadflax; French: *comandre*; Slave: *nothe dzhī* ("marten berry").

Scientific Name: *Geocaulon lividum* (Richards.) Fern., common synonym: *Comandra livida* Richards.

Description: A small, slender, erect herb with oval leaves and one or a few green to reddish flowers in the leaf axils that produce a red fleshy fruit (a drupe).

(R. Marles)

Habitat: Found occasionally in moist coniferous forests and sphagnum bogs where it parasitizes the roots of strawberries, cranberries, and other plants. Its distribution spans most of Canada and northern USA.

Food Uses: The fruit are considered edible but not delicious (Lamont 1977; Siegfried 1994).

Medicinal Uses: A few drupes can be swallowed once a year for persistent chest trouble (possibly tuberculosis) (D9). The roots are also believed to have medicinal value due to their peculiar odor (Siegfried 1994).

Properties: The seeds have been reported to have red blood cell clumping activity (Farnsworth 1999). The closely related bastard toadflax (*Comandra umbellata* (L.) Nutt.) may accumulate toxic levels of selenium in its fruit (Underhill 1974).

Potential: Since the fruit is not delicious and could contain selenium if grown on selenium-rich soil, eating it is not recommended.

SARRACENIACEAE
(Pitcher Plant Family)

Pitcher Plant

Other Names: Chipewyan: *ts'ĕli tili* ("frog pail"); Cree: *ayekitas, ayikitās, ayīkicās* ("little frog pants"), *athīkacās*; French: *sabot, cochon de pelé, herbe-crapaud.*

Scientific Name: *Sarracenia purpurea* L.

Description: A bog plant with distinctive, hollow pitcher-shaped leaves with purple veins and hoodlike tops, half full of water and trapped insects. The large purple flowers grow singly on a tall stalk.

Habitat: Occasionally found in peat bogs and muskeg from northeastern British Columbia and the western Northwest Territories to the Maritimes, and in the eastern half of the USA, with an apparently disjunct population in California.

Medicinal Uses: The leaf can be used, generally mixed with other medicinal plants, for a wide variety of health problems including chronic chest

trouble (tuberculosis?), coughs (D4, D9, D23), back pain (Leighton 1985), difficulty urinating, fever, headaches (Siegfried 1994), and "women's ailments" (C49, D29), including sickness associated with absence of the menstrual period (Leighton 1985). It can also be part of a compound medicinal tea taken to ease childbirth (C14). The root can be used as a poultice on cuts (C47) or boiled and the decoction drunk to prevent sickness after childbirth, to help expulsion of the afterbirth, or to treat venereal disease (Leighton 1985).

Technological Uses: The leaf is used by children as a toy kettle (Leighton 1985).

Pitcher plant in bloom (R. Marles)

Pitcher plant's insect-trapping leaves (R. Marles)

Properties: The leaves have been found to have a complex mixture of flavonoids (including quercetin, rhamnetin, and hyperoside), benzenoids, and triterpenes (betulin, amyrins, lupeol). They also tested positive for the presence of alkaloids. There have been some positive results for related species in experiments in treating leukemia models in animals (Farnsworth 1999).

Potential: There is a strong market in the floral trade for pitcher plants. Mater Engineering (1993) categorizes pitcher plant as a Priority Level 3 product for further development, recommends seed collection from the wild to cultivate it, and describes the market in some detail. Barl et al. (1996) provide information on sourcing, cultivation, and possible buyers.

SAXIFRAGACEAE
(Saxifrage Family)

Alum-Root

Other Names: Cree: *pithīkōcīpihk.*

Scientific Name: *Heuchera richardsonii* R. Br.

Description: A perennial herb growing from a stout, scaly rhizome, with basal heart-shaped, broadly lobed and toothed leaves 6 cm in diameter, bristly hairs on the stem and leaf lower surfaces, flowering stalks up to 50 cm tall with some glandular hairs and papery bracts but no stem leaves, and a narrow inflorescence of flowers each about 1 cm long, with asymmetrical, fuzzy sepals and spatula-shaped, fuzzy purple petals only slightly longer than the sepals. The oval seeds develop in a small capsule.

(J.D. Johnson)

Habitat: Common in moist prairies, on open sandy ground, and on rocky slopes or shores into the southern fringe of the boreal forest; distributed from the Northwest Territories south to central USA, and from British Columbia to western Ontario.

Medicinal Uses: The chewed root or its decoction can be taken to treat diarrhea or used as a wash for sore eyes (Leighton 1985) or poultice for wounds and sores (Richardson, cited in Leighton 1985).

Properties: Alum-root gets its name from its astringency, a property that may explain many of the traditional uses. The plant contains a wide variety of flavonoids, including derivatives of kaempferol, myricetin, quercetin, and rhamnetin, which may contribute to the pharmacological effects (Farnsworth 1999).

Potential: There may be a market in the herbal medicine trade.

Mitrewort

Other Names: Cree: *amiskōcawak-ayipak, ōcawakāyipak*; English: bishop's-cap; French: *mitrelle*; Slave: *nde(k)eto^n* ("mud plant").

Scientific Name: *Mitella nuda* L.

Description: A low-growing, slender perennial herb with scaly rhizomes, leaves that are long stalked, mostly basal, heart shaped with shallow lobes, blunt teeth, and sparse hairs, up to 5 cm in diameter. The slender, fuzzy, leafless or one-leafed flower stalk up to 20 cm tall bears a narrow column of flowers with four short greenish sepals and five yellowish white petals that are very finely divided, almost like a feather, and 10

(J.D. Johnson)

stamens. The flowers produce a few black, smooth, shiny seeds.

Habitat: Fairly common in cold, wet woodlands across Canada, northern USA, and Eurasia.

Medicinal Uses: The leaf can be crushed, wrapped in a cloth, and inserted into the ear to treat an ear ache (Leighton 1985).

Properties: Derivatives of the flavonoids kaempferol, quercetin, and isorhamnetin have been identified in this plant (Hetherington and Steck 1997). A Japanese species has been reported to have antimutagenic activity, of possible significance to cancer and toxicology research (Farnsworth 1999).

Potential: There is not enough information about the medicinal properties of this species to make a judgement, although there appears to be some potential. The flower is small, but it has an unusual shape that might interest the floral trade if it can be cultivated.

SCROPHULARIACEAE
(Foxglove Family)

Red Paintbrush

Other Names: English: Indian paint-brush, painted-cup.

Scientific Name: *Castilleja miniata* Dougl. ex Hook.

Description: A perennial with smooth or slightly hairy stems up to 60 cm tall, with alternate stalkless, narrow leaves and an unusual inflorescence consisting of a terminal spike of bright red bracts from which project tubular flowers with two lips, the upper one arched, which are green with red margins. It is partially parasitic on the roots of neighboring plants.

Habitat: Found in open woods (especially pine) and meadows on the southern edge of the boreal forest in western Canada and western USA.

(C. Clavelle)

Medicinal Uses: The flower heads can be dried and added to wild chamomile (perhaps a *Matricaria* species, Asteraceae) flowers to make a tea to cure headaches and relax nerves (M6).

Properties: The flowers and leaves of this species and other paintbrushes have been reported to contain pyrrolizidine alkaloids, quinolizidine alkaloids, monoterpene alkaloids, the lignan acteoside, and numerous monoterpenes, including aucubin (Farnsworth 1999). The presence of pyrrolizidine alkaloids suggests that paintbrush should probably not be taken internally due to the risk of liver damage.

Potential: Although paintbrush definitely has pharmacologically active compounds of potential significance, it is too toxic to recommend for development as a medicinal herb. It is an attractive ornamental, but would require cultivation of a suitable host plant.

Lousewort

Other Names: English: arctic rattle; Slave: *saʰ tīleʰ*.

Scientific Name: *Pedicularis langsdorfii* Fisch. ex Stev. ssp. *arctica* (R.Br.) Pennell, common synonym: *P. arctica* R.Br. Also *P. kanei* Dur., common synonym: *P. lanata* Cham. & Schlecht.

Description: Arctic rattle (*P. langsdorfii*) is a small perennial herb with a stout stem up to 15 cm high, long narrow leaves divided almost to the middle into oblong lobes with bumpy edges, and a terminal spike of deep pink flowers that have fuzzy sepals, petals in two lips, the upper lip (galea) flattened from the sides, arched, and bearing a slender tooth on each side below the tip, the lower

Pedicularis labradorica Wirsing (R. Marles)

lip shorter and three-lobed; they develop into a flattened seed capsule with smooth brown seeds. Woolly lousewort (*P. kanei*) resembles arctic rattle, but has a lemon yellow rather than a pale yellow taproot, a densely hairy inflorescence, a galea that is not arched and has no teeth, a longer lower lip, and seeds with a gray honeycombed coat.

Habitat: Both species are found on moist alpine slopes of the north, from Siberia and Greenland to Alaska, British Columbia, Alberta, Yukon, and the Northwest Territories

Food Uses: In times of starvation the roots of arctic rattle can be eaten raw (Lamont 1977).

Medicinal Uses: Small pieces of sun-dried roots of woolly lousewort can be mixed with tobacco and smoked in a pipe to relieve headaches (Lamont 1977).

Technological Uses: Woolly lousewort fresh or dried roots can be used to make a yellow dye for moose hides (Lamont 1977).

Properties: Willard (1992) describes a variety of medicinal uses for louseworts, but Johnson et al. (1995) caution that they contain poisonous glycosides. Duke (1985) lists the genus as toxic but provides no details. Turner and Szczawinski (1991) and Mulligan and Munro (1990) do not list it. According to Farnsworth (1999), acute toxicity tests conducted in mice by intraperitoneal injection of alcoholic extracts of different lousewort species in amounts up to 1 g of extract per kilogram body weight showed no lethality, and the median lethal dose of extract administered orally was 8 g/ kg, so lousewort is in fact not very toxic. Louseworts have been found to contain glycosides of iridoids (e.g., aucubin) and other monoterpenoids, lignans, and phenylpropanoids, plus triterpenoids, flavonoids, and alkaloids in the monoterpene, indole, and quinolizidine classes. Intravenous injections of a lousewort (*P. comosa* L.) aqueous infusion in cats and dogs were reported to lower blood pressure and cause central nervous system depression (respectively).

Potential: Scientific evidence that perhaps is relevant to the traditional use suggests that lousewort is worthy of further investigation as a possible source for new medicines.

URTICACEAE
(Stinging Nettle Family)

Stinging Nettle

Other Names: Chipewyan: *bek'-áílhts'ii*; Cree: *masān, musān, musan-usk, assan, masānah* ("itchy weed"); French: *ortie*; Slave: *kotsī*.

Scientific Name: *Urtica dioica* L.

Description: A perennial herb growing up to 2 m tall from an extensive network of rhizomes, with square stems, opposite, oval to lance-shaped, coarsely toothed leaves bearing stinging hairs, and greenish flowers borne in clusters at the junction of the stem and leaf stalk.

Habitat: Very common around sloughs, stream banks, and waste places, and in moist shady woods across North and South America, Greenland, Iceland, and Eurasia.

(R. Marles)

Food Uses: Young leaves can be boiled and eaten (D27; Siegfried 1994).

Medicinal Uses: The leaf decoction can be used as a face wash to treat acne (C41) and can be drunk to treat diarrhea or intestinal worms (D27). The stem decoction is taken specifically by men who have trouble urinating (Siegfried 1994). The root decoction can be used as a wash to relieve the itching and inflammation caused by touching the stinging leaves (C20) and can be drunk as a blood purifier, to stop internal bleeding, to correct menstrual flow (D27), to keep blood flowing after childbirth (Leighton 1985), to clear phlegm from the lungs and throat (D27), or to treat difficulty with urination (Siegfried 1994). To treat asthma the root can be boiled and the steam inhaled using a blanket draped over the head to collect the vapors (C13). The roots are part of a compound medicine for treating fevers or severe back pain (a pinched nerve? Siegfried 1994).

Technological Uses: Nettle stems have been used by several northern cultures as a source of fiber for cordage (Moerman 1998).

Properties: Stinging nettle greens contain the following nutrients (per 100 g fresh weight, 89% moisture): food energy (38 kcal), protein (1.8-2.3 g), fat (0.6 g), total carbohydrate (7.9 g), crude fiber (1.4 g), ash (1.2-1.9 g), thiamine (0.01 mg), riboflavin (0.22 mg), niacin (0.2 mg), vitamin C (75-90 mg), vitamin A (2 248 RE), Ca (236-263 mg), P (59-73 mg), Na (0.8-12 mg), K (321 mg), Mg (24-63 mg), Cu (0.1-1.9 mg), Fe (1.0-3.0 mg), Mn (0.7-2.3 mg), and Cl (55 mg) (Kuhnlein and Turner 1991). The leaves also contain a number of flavonoids, triterpenes, sterols, and a number of amines in the stinging hairs, including histamine, serotonin, choline, etc. The mild diuretic effect is well established, so it can be used for irrigation in inflammation of the urinary tract and for the prevention and treatment of kidney gravel. The root contains tannins, sterols, phenylpropanoids, lignans, lectins, numerous polyphenols, and several monoterpene diols. The root can be used as an astringent topically or as a gargle, and is currently under investigation for use as a treatment for the congestion and associated difficulties in urination during the early stages of benign prostate hyperplasia. Nettle root extracts have a demonstrated effect on human prostate tissue, and several of the constituents of nettle root show promising relevant pharmacological activities (Bisset and Wichtl 1994). The leaves have also been demonstrated to help stop bleeding, and are helpful as a diuretic to treat edema from either myocardial or chronic venous insufficiency (Bradley 1992).

Potential: The nutritious quality of stinging nettle leaves as a food and their efficacy as a diuretic tea are well established. The leaf and seed are currently available in various products sold in health food stores. Barl et al. (1996) provide information on plant or seed sourcing and possible buyers. The root shows considerably more promise and will have a major market if its activity against prostate problems is confirmed. Mater Engineering (1993) categorizes stinging nettle as a Priority Level 1 product for further development and describes the market in some detail.

VALERIANACEAE
(Valerian Family)

Northern Valerian

Other Names: Cree: *upistagiwasus, apiscisakōwaskwos, apiscakāwaskwos* ("small strong smell"), *apisichīsakwasōsak, apischīsakwaskōsuk, apischisakowasosuk, apiscīsakwīwaskwos, āpisagiywuskos* ("little love plant"); French: *valériane.*

Scientific Name: *Valeriana dioica* L.

Description: A perennial herb with a strongly scented rhizome and erect stems up to 70 cm tall, with a basal rosette of long-petioled, spatula-shaped leaves and two to four pairs of opposite stem leaves which are pinnately divided, and terminal dense clusters of white flowers each about 3 mm across, with bristly in-rolled sepals and petals fused into a five-lobed tube.

Valerian (*Valeriana officinalis* L.) cultivated for medicinal purposes (R. Marles)

Habitat: Fairly common in wet meadows and bogs throughout the boreal forest from British Columbia to Labrador, at higher elevations further south into western USA, and in Europe and southwest Asia.

Medicinal Uses: The leaves can be boiled for 45 minutes until the water turns green, and then the decoction can be given to a child who has lost weight to help the child gain weight (C38). The stems and leaves from two plants can be cleaned and boiled with another plant and then drunk to treat a cold (C23, C27, C37, C43) or fever (C37, C43). The dried plant can be boiled and the decoction drunk to treat a sore aching body, colds, chills, and congestion, helping clear the air passages (C38, C39). Two cups of the dried-leaf decoction can be given to a pregnant woman to help prevent a miscarriage or ease labor pains (it is considered to be a medicine for the unborn baby) (C24, C37). The dried leaves can be crushed, mixed with beaver fat, and applied as an ointment to facial rashes (C43). A decoction of the roots from a valerian plant that has not flowered is considered to be a very powerful tonic to be taken when someone feels bad. It can also be abused by being used in love medicines (C47, C57; Leighton 1985) or by being given to a racehorse to make it run fast. When abused it will make the user (or horse) very sick, but if used properly it can be safe and effective (C47, C57). A root can also be held in the mouth or chewed to treat severe heart trouble (C33, M9), chewed and wrapped in a cloth as a compress for an earache, headache, or seizures in babies (Leighton 1985), and can help to prevent aging and wrinkles and keep you active (C20). The root can be used in many compound medicines, such as for treating pneumonia (Leighton 1985), to make them work better or faster (C47, C57, M9; Leighton 1985).

Ritual Uses: The whole dried plant can be crushed, passed through willow fungus (*Trametes suaveolens* (L. ex Fries) Fries, Coriolaceae) smoke while prayers are said, and then carried in a pouch over the heart (e.g., in a breast pocket) as a good luck charm, perhaps for bingo playing (Siegfried 1994).

Properties: Valerian root (*V. officinalis* L.) is chemically highly variable. The roots contain up to 0.7% dry weight of volatile oil, of which bornyl acetate and several other bornyl derivatives are the main constituents, along with other monoterpenes, sesquiterpenes, and phenylpropanoids; valeric acid, formic acid, acetic acid, and several alkaloids, including chanitine, actinidine, valerine, and valerianine, are also present (Duke 1985). If the roots are dried below 40°C they will contain 0.5-2% valepotriates, which are bicyclic iridoid monoterpenes. The sedative effect of the roots in treating restlessness and nervous disturbance of sleep is well established, but the identity of the active ingredients is not established. Most likely it involves combined effects of the degradation products of the valepotriates (baldrinals) rather than the valepotriates themselves, and effects of the essential oil constituents, for example, some of the sesquiterpenes have antispasm or muscle-relaxant activity or inhibit the breakdown of the brain neurotransmitter gamma-aminobutyric acid (GABA). Valerian root also has applications to treat nervous tension and nervous gastrointestinal cramps. A mixture of pure unsaturated valepotriates prepared from other species of *Valeriana* has tranquilizing activity useful in treating psychomotor and psychosomatic problems, loss of concentration, and stress and anxiety states (Bisset and Wichtl 1994). The root extract has also been reported to have blood-pressure-lowering activity (Bradley 1992).

Potential: Valerian has a strong potential as a medicinal herb, particularly as a sleep aid. However, because local populations are so variable, chemical assays of the constituents are needed before undertaking agronomic and therapeutic studies. Careful attention must be paid to processing and storage to have reliable levels of the baldrinals and other active ingredients. Barl et al. (1996) provide an overview of valerian cultivation, harvesting, and currently available products. Mater Engineering (1993) categorizes valerian as a Priority Level 1 product for further development and describes the market in some detail.

LILIOPSIDA

ACORACEAE
(Sweet Flag Family)

Sweet Flag

Other Names: Chipewyan: *dzën ni* ("muskrat food"); Cree: *wachusko-mechiwin* ("muskrat food"), *wachus-kowmiytsuwin, wacaskōmīcowin, wacaskwatapih* ("muskrat root"), *wiy(h)kiyuw, wihkes, wīkīs, wihkis*; English: ratroot, calamus; French: *belle-Angélique*.

Scientific Name: *Acorus americanus* (Raf.) Raf. The most commonly cited name is *A. calamus* L., but its use can be restricted to other genotypes not found in Canada's boreal forest region.

Description: An aquatic perennial herb growing from an aromatic rhizome, with long, narrow, sword-shaped leaves and a leaflike flower-ing stalk that produces a dense

(R. Marles)

cylindrical spike of tiny yellowish flowers jutting out to one side and then continues upward as a green bract.

Habitat: In scattered locations in swamps and along water courses in the boreal forest, possibly introduced into some locations by Aboriginal people. There are several genotypes characteristic of particular parts of its range across the northern hemisphere.

Medicinal Uses: "Ratroot," as it is commonly referred to by Aboriginal people, is one of the most widely known and used of all their traditional me-dicinal plants. Many people chew the rhizome and swallow the juice to treat colds, coughs including whooping cough, sore throat, dry mouth, upset stomach, toothache, teething pain, headache, rheumatism, muscle pain, pounding heart, or intestinal worms (C11, C12, C13, C15, C20, C22, C32,

C39, C44, C47, C57, D3, D9, D14, D22, D23, D28, D29, D32, M6, M9; Smith GW 1973; Lamont 1977; Jarvenpa 1982; Leighton 1985; Siegfried 1994). To treat diabetes a bit of the rhizome can be chewed constantly (C13, D14). The rhizome may also be chewed to relieve fatigue on a long hike (D26). If the rhizome is

Sweet flag rhizomes for medicine (C. Clavelle)

held in the mouth for an extended period it will "get rid of the tonsils by burning them off" (C23, C27). The rhizome may be boiled and the liquid drunk as an expectorant (C57) or to treat a sore throat or cold (C24, C35; Leighton 1985), tonsillitis (C35, C36), sinus congestion (C39), pneumonia (C30, C39), diabetes (C20), whooping cough, coughing up of blood, stabbing pains in the chest, lower back pain, teething sickness, stomachache, facial paralysis, venereal diseases (Leighton 1985), diarrhea, high blood pressure (Siegfried 1994), or menstrual cramps (Strath 1903). The steam from boiling the rhizome can be trapped with a towel over the head and inhaled to relieve congestion (C39, C42) or headaches (C35, C36). To treat an earache, crushed or chopped rhizomes can be mixed with hot water and dropped on a hot flat rock, and the resulting steam can be trapped with a towel over the head (C23, C27), or a small piece can be softened in warm water and inserted into the ear (C8, M6), or the ground rhizome can be boiled and mixed with flour to make a batter which is poured onto a cloth, and this compress is then placed over the affected ear (C39). The rhizome may also be smoked to treat a cough (D32, M6) or boiled to make a wash for sore eyes (D13). Dried and ground rhizome or fresh grated rhizome can be chewed and used as a poultice to treat painful joints from arthritis (C20, C55), and headaches (C20) or sores (Lamont 1977). To treat muscle cramps, such as leg cramps, the rhizome can be chopped, soaked in water, and then rubbed on the sore area (C23, C27). To treat arthritis the rhizome can be chopped and dropped into boiling water, and then flour is added to make a paste which is applied as hot as can be tolerated to the affected area; the area is then wrapped up with warm towels or a cloth, which are left on overnight (C39).

Some of the decoction can also be drunk to aid the healing (C39, C42). It is one component of many compound medicines, for example, taken internally to treat venereal disease (M6), heart trouble (C54), headaches, and fever (C20, C54), or as a poultice to treat headaches (C20, C54; Leighton 1985), infected wounds (C54; Leighton 1985), or foot or other local pain in muscles or joints including rheumatism (C20; Leighton 1985).

Ritual Uses: The rhizome can be part of a love charm (M6) or a good luck charm, perhaps to be kept in the car or taken to bingo games (Siegfried 1994).

Properties: The rhizome is rich in essential oils consisting of sesquiterpenes and phenylpropanoids. The main active constituents of *A. americanus* are acorone and related bitter sesquiterpene diketones with antispasm activity suitable for treating gastrointestinal upset and cramps. The North American species may be completely free of two of the main constituents of the Asian and European species (*A. calamus*): beta-asarone and eugenol methyl ether. Beta-asarone has carcinogenic and mutagenic (chromosome damaging) properties, so its absence from our material would make it a safer remedy than the Old World species (Bisset and Wichtl 1994). The chemistry of the European and Asian material is quite well known (Duke 1985), but more work is needed on *A. americanus*.

Potential: If more extensive testing confirms that the toxins are absent from Canadian sweet flag rhizome in general, and not just from the few local populations already tested, there could be a strong market for this material as a crude drug for export in competition with the less desirable material coming from India, the former USSR, and Yugoslavia that currently dominates the market (Bisset and Wichtl 1994). The essential oil (asarone-free) is in demand for aromatherapy (Rogers 1997). There is also a strong demand for the rhizome among North American Aboriginal people. The potential for breeding asarone-free material should be examined; the plant propagates readily from rhizomes and could be developed as an aquacultural product by modifying wild rice production methods. There is also limited scope for sustainable harvest from wild populations (Morgan 1999). See Barl et al. (1996) for further production and marketing information.

ALISMATACEAE
(Water Plantain Family)

Water Plantain

Other Names: Cree: *mitīhīmaskīhkīh.*

Scientific Name: *Alisma triviale* Pursh, common synonym: *A. plantago-aquatica* L. var. *americanum* J.A. Schultes.

Description: A perennial aquatic plant growing from a corm, with oval, parallel-veined, long-stalked leaves up to 18 cm long,

(R. Marles)

and an open spray up to 30 cm tall of small flowers with three green sepals and three white petals.

Habitat: Common in marshes, ponds, and ditches across the northern hemisphere, South America, and North Africa.

Medicinal Uses: The stem base can be eaten or ground, mixed with water and drunk to treat heart troubles, heart burn, stomachache, stomach flu, cramps, and constipation, and to prevent fainting during childbirth (Leighton 1985).

Properties: The rhizome contains triterpene alisol derivatives, sesquiterpene alismol derivatives, and gave positive screening results for alkaloids and saponins. The rhizome of *A. orientale* (Sam.) Juz. in Kom. is used in Oriental medicine to treat liver disease, high blood cholesterol, and high blood sugar, but tests to verify its activity were all done on multicomponent prescriptions (Farnsworth 1999).

Potential: Not enough is known about this species to make a judgment at this time.

Arrowhead

Other Names: English and Algonkian: wapato; French: *flèche d'eau*; Slave: *kodzelī (aʰ) naydī* ("sore heart medicine"), *tsale thoneʰ*.

Scientific Name: *Sagittaria cuneata* Sheldon.

Description: A perennial marsh plant with distinctive leaves shaped like arrowheads growing from rhizomes that produce small

(R. Marles)

edible tubers and waxy white three-petaled flowers borne in whorls of three around the stem.

Habitat: Very common in shallow water, along muddy shores, and in marshes across Canada and continental USA except the southeast.

Food Uses: Although the tubers are edible and mentioned in many edible plant and outdoor survival books (e.g., Willard 1992; Duke 1992c), none of the Chipewyan elders considered it a food source. Our efforts to harvest the tubers in northern Saskatchewan indicated it is not productive enough to be worth the trouble.

Medicinal Uses: The fresh leaf can be washed and applied as a poultice to inflamed patches of skin which are associated with scrofula (tuberculous lymphadenitis: an infection of the lymph glands by tuberculosis bacteria). The leaf can be left on until it falls off by itself, and then the treatment must be repeated, several times (C11). The root decoction can be taken for a "sore heart" (heartburn? Lamont 1977).

Properties: Broadleaf arrowhead (*S. latifolia* Willd.) tubers have the following food value per 100 g fresh weight (68% moisture): food energy (103 kcal), protein (4.7 g), fat (0.2 g), total carbohydrate (20 g), crude fiber (0.8 g), thiamine (1.60 mg), riboflavin (0.25 mg), niacin (1.4 mg), vitamin C (5.0 mg), and minerals (ash: 1.5 g), including Ca (12 mg), P (165 mg), Na (22 mg), K (922 mg), Mg (51 mg), Zn (0.7 mg), and Fe (6.6 mg) (Kuhnlein and Turner 1991).

Potential: The tubers would be best left as a food source for waterfowl, for which it does play a role.

ARACEAE
(Arum-Lily Family)

Water Calla

Other Names: Chipewyan: *tlh'ogh chëné slini* ("grass stem which is bad [poisonous]"); Cree: *ōcicākokātask*; English: water arum; French: *choucalle*

Scientific Name: *Calla palustris* L.

Description: A fleshy marsh plant growing from creeping rhizomes, with broad heart-shaped leaves and a

(R. Marles)

distinctive inflorescence consisting of a thick green flower spike (spadix) that develops bright red berries, half-surrounded by an oval white sheath (spathe).

Habitat: Fairly common in marshes, swamps, and shallow water throughout the boreal forest east of the Rockies, from Alaska and Yukon east to Newfoundland and northeastern USA, and in northern Eurasia.

Medicinal Uses: Elders consider the rhizome to be poisonous (C22, D7, D9, D23; Leighton 1985) so it is only rarely used internally, in small amounts in combination with other plants. It can be used alone topically to treat leg sores (D23; Leighton 1985).

Properties: The leaves and roots contain irritating crystals of calcium oxalate which, if the plant is consumed, pierce the tender tissues of the mouth, tongue, and throat, causing intense burning pain and inflammation. If severe enough, this could cause choking due to the swelling. Several protein-dissolving enzymes in the plant also contribute to the irritation by triggering the release of histamines and kinins by the body. Because of the immediate discomfort, people rarely consume enough to seriously harm themselves, although the plant is potentially fatally toxic. The leaves and roots can also cause skin irritation on contact (Turner and Szczawinski 1991).

Potential: The strongly irritant nature of this plant suggests that there will not be any potential for development as a medicinal. It does make a very attractive aquatic ornamental.

CYPERACEAE
(Sedge Family)

Sedge

Other Names: Chipewyan: *tlh'ogh tsëné* ("grass which smells"), French: *laîche*; Slave: *tlho^h dathe tsho, nezhi tlho^h* ("moose brain grass").

Scientific Name: *Carex aquatilis* Wahl.

Description: An aquatic plant growing up to 80 cm high, with three rows of long, narrow, sharp-edged leaves folded around each other at their bases giving the impression of a triangular stem. The sedge produces thick spikes of tiny female flowers that produce hard achenes and thinner spikes of tiny male flowers higher up the stalk.

(R. Marles)

Habitat: Common along the edges of sloughs and in marshes and wet meadows across Canada, northern USA, Greenland, and Eurasia.

Medicinal Uses: The fragrant roots can be used in a medicine to induce a delayed menstrual period or as part of a compound tea for intestinal problems (D29).

Technological Uses: A dye for porcupine quills can be made from sedges (Lamont 1977). Food can be wrapped in sedge leaves before being cooked next to the fire (Lamont 1977). The leaves can be used to sieve moose brains for making a tanning solution (Lamont 1977).

Properties: Although this species of sedge does not appear to have been studied scientifically, other species have been shown to contain flavonoids including luteolin derivatives, phenylpropanoids, benzenoids, and indole alkaloids. Pharmacological activities shown for other species include antitumor, antibacterial including antimycobacterial, antifungal including antiyeast, and sedative effects (Farnsworth 1999). Luteolin has anti-inflammatory and antibacterial properties (Harborne and Baxter 1993).

Potential: Sedges are very common plants which, given the traditional uses and what is known about the chemistry and pharmacology of the genus, should be investigated further.

Cotton Grass

Other Names: French: *linaigrette.*

Scientific Name: *Eriophorum* sp.

Description: Perennial tufted grass-like plants with long, narrow, tubular leaves and a dense terminal spike of achenes covered with long white silky bristles, looking like a tuft of cotton.

(R. Marles)

Habitat: Common in boggy areas throughout the boreal forest and tundra of the northern hemisphere.

Food Uses: The leaves can be eaten, especially the tender white base (M9).

Properties: The carbohydrates galactose and xylose and the flavonoids cyanidin, kaempferol, and quercetin have been isolated from the leaves of cotton grass.

Potential: This plant might make an attractive semiaquatic ornamental, with its straight narrow leaves and terminal tufts of white hairs.

Bulrush

Other Names: Chipewyan: *tlh'ogh chogh* ("big grass"); Cree: *kichekumewusk, kiychiykāmiyuwusk, ōkīhcīkamīwask* ("ocean plant"), *wechahkamewuskwa* ("straight stem plant"), *mwaskosīwan*; English: tule; French: *grand jonc*; Slave: *tlhoʰ gathoⁿ*.

Scientific Name: *Schoenoplectus acutus* (Muhl. ex Bigelow) A. & D. Löve, common synonyms: *Scirpus acutus* Muhl. ex Bigelow, *S. lacustris* L. in part, and some botanists include *S. validus* Vahl in this complex. The features used to distinguish these species are variable and inconsistently interpreted in the various floras.

(R. Marles)

Description: A very tall (up to 3 m) plant growing from stout, extensively creeping rhizomes, with a leafless cylindrical green stem producing a branched spray of brown spikelets near the top, with a stemlike erect bract continuing to form the tip of the plant.

Habitat: Very common, often forming extensive borders around sloughs and along lakeshores across much of North America and Eurasia.

Food Uses: Edible parts include the young shoots and leaf bases in the springtime (D6, D13, D29, M6; Curtis 1928; Jarvenpa 1979; Leighton 1985; Welsh, cited in Leighton 1985), the inner stem after the tough outer part has been peeled off, and the roots (Siegfried 1994).

Medicinal Uses: The stems can be boiled to make a medicine for coughs and fevers (M6). The stem pith can be used as a wound dressing to stop bleeding (Welsh, cited in Leighton 1985).

Technological Uses: Fresh green bulrushes can be woven into mats, mattresses, and baskets (M6).

Properties: Bulrush shoots provide 42 kcal of food energy and 0.9 g of minerals (ash) per 100 g fresh weight (Kuhnlein and Turner 1991).

Potential: Bulrushes could be cultivated for their edible shoots and as a basketry material.

JUNCAGINACEAE
(Arrow-Grass Family)

Seaside Arrow-Grass

Other Names: Cree: *minahikos* ("little spruce"); French: *herbe soelting, faux jonc.*

Scientific Name: *Triglochin maritimum* L.

Description: A perennial herb growing from a short rootstock, with a basal tuft of long, narrow, half-cylindrical leaves up to 30 cm long and 3 mm wide, whose bases are usually covered by old leaf sheaths. The flowering stems are up to 80 cm tall with a long narrow spikelike inflorescence of small greenish flowers with a whorl of three sepals and a whorl of three similar petals, six stamens and six feathery stigmas on the pistil. The fruit is a dry capsule that splits along one side.

(J.D. Johnson)

Habitat: Common in brackish marshes, sloughs, and other wet places across Canada, western and northern USA, Mexico, Iceland, Eurasia, North Africa, and Patagonia.

Medicinal Uses: The whole plant can be boiled and the decoction drunk to relieve diarrhea that has blood in the stool (C41).

Properties: Arrow-grass contains cyanogenic glycosides that have caused cyanide poisoning in livestock (Turner and Szczawinski 1991). Boiling thoroughly would eliminate most or all of the cyanide.

Potential: There is no apparent market potential.

LILIACEAE
(Lily Family)

Note: The Lily Family is treated here conservatively to follow the majority of published references. However, recent genetic studies at the Royal Botanic Gardens, Kew, UK, have shown that *Allium* should be placed in the Alliaceae (onion family), *Disporum, Maianthemum,* and *Streptopus* in the Convallariaceae (lily-of-the-valley family), and *Veratrum* and *Zigadenus* in the Melanthiaceae (bunchflower family). This leaves *Lilium* and *Fritillaria* as the only genera in this text still belonging to the more narrowly defined lily family (Royal Botanic Gardens 1999).

Wild Onions and Chives

Other Names: Chipewyan: *tlh'ogh ts'íaze* ("little beaver grass"); Cree: *pikwacīwīcikaskosī, wechekuskose* ("stinking grass"); French: *oignon sauvage*; Slave: *tlho[h] dzhīo[n]*.

Scientific Name: *Allium textile* Nels. & Macbr., *A. cernuum* Roth, *A. stellatum* Fraser, *A. schoenoprasum* L.

Description: Perennials growing from a small aromatic bulb, with many long,

Wild onion (*Allium acuminatum* Hook.) (R. Marles)

narrow, cylindrical leaves and a flowering stalk that terminates in an umbel of white or pink flowers, each with one six-membered whorl of similar sepals and petals with a red midvein. Nodding onion (*A. cernuum*) has a slender bulb and nodding inflorescence. Pink-flowered onion (*A. stellatum*) has dark pink flowers and a membranous bulb coat. Prairie onion (*A. textile*) has white or pale pink flowers and a fibrous, netted bulb coat. Wild chives (*A. schoenoprasum*) is the largest and has hollow leaves (the others have solid leaves) and a membranous bulb coat.

Habitat: Wild chives is the species found in the northern boreal forest, where it occurs infrequently in wet meadows and on stream banks and lake shores.

Its distribution spans Canada, northern USA, and Eurasia. Pink-flowered onion is found fairly commonly in wooded areas of the parklands of Saskatchewan, Manitoba, Ontario, and south to Texas. Nodding onion is found occasionally in parkland, grassy openings, open slopes, and rock slides across North America. Prairie onion is common in dry prairies and grassy areas of the parklands in the Prairie provinces and south to New Mexico.

Allium schoenoprasum L. (R. Marles)

Food Uses: Wild chive or onion leaves were used as a flavoring for soups and stews (C57), and the bulbs can be eaten raw (Lamont 1977) or boiled (D3, D6, D9, D13, D20, D24, D29, D32, M9; Lamont 1977).

Properties: Wild onion (*A. drummondii* Regel, common synonym: *A. nuttallii* S. Watts) bulbs were found to contain (per 100 g fresh weight, 64% moisture): protein (2.8 g), fat (0.2 g), niacin (0.5 mg), vitamin C (15 mg), and minerals (ash: 1.0 g), including Ca (29 mg), P (202 mg), Na (19 mg), K (529 mg), and Fe (1.5 mg) (Kuhnlein and Turner 1991). Wild chive leaves have (per 100 g fresh weight): food energy (27 kcal), protein (2.7 g), fat (0.6 mg), thiamine (0.10 mg), riboflavin (0.06 mg), niacin (0.5 mg), vitamin C (32 mg), Ca (83 mg), P (41 mg), and Fe (0.8 mg) (Kuhnlein and Turner 1991). Wild onions have been known to cause digestive upset if consumed in excess (Turner and Szczawinski 1991). Members of the onion family owe their pungency to sulfur-containing amino acid derivatives such as alliin, which is converted into the strong-smelling thiosulfinate allicin by the enzyme alliinase, which is released when the bulb is crushed. Drying or processing cause changes to allicin resulting in the production of varying amounts of other sulfur compounds (Bradley 1992). There is scientific evidence that garlic and onion as a frequent dietary component or supplement can help to reduce blood levels of cholesterol, fat, and glucose (Dobelis 1986). There is also scientific evidence that garlic reduces high blood pressure, stimulates the immune system, inhibits the growth of some types of cancer cells (e.g., stomach cancer), and inhibits aggregation of blood platelets, which may be helpful in conditions of atherosclerosis, coronary thrombosis, and stroke, but these effects are generally seen only at very high doses of garlic in the diet (e.g., 5-20 cloves/day) (Foster and Tyler 1999).

Potential: Although we have seen wild onion and garlic species from the forest sold on roadsides in the Gatineau area of western Quebec, this practice is not sustainable because wild populations are low. There might be some potential for cultivation of wild species as a specialty food, particularly if they can be brought fresh to market. If wild species can be shown to have special health benefits comparable to or superior to those of garlic, this would provide an important marketing advantage.

Fairybells

Other Names: None known.

Scientific Name: *Disporum trachy-carpum* (S. Wats.) Benth. & Hook. f.

Description: A branched perennial herb up to 80 cm tall with parallel-veined heart-shaped leaves and white bell-shaped flowers that occur singly or in pairs at the tips of the branches. The fruit are orange to red berries.

Habitat: Moist woods and thickets throughout the southern boreal forest and parklands from central British Columbia to Ontario, and south in the mountainous western and midwestern states.

(R. Marles)

Medicinal Uses: The whole plant can be mixed with another herb and drunk as a spring tonic (M6).

Properties: This species has been tested for antibacterial and antifungal activity, without success. Other species were inactive in anticancer tests. There is no information on the presence of bioactive compounds in *Disporum* (Farnsworth 1999).

Potential: This very pretty flower has ornamental potential, but probably little medicinal value.

Western Wood Lily

Other Names: Cree: *wapayoominusk, wākican, wākiychān*; English: tiger lily.

Scientific Name: *Lilium philadelphicum* L.

Description: A herb growing from a thick-scaled white bulb, with a stem up to 80 cm tall producing narrow leaves alternately on the lower stem and then in one or two whorls on the upper stem, and one to three

(R. Marles)

large showy flowers with three sepals and three petals similarly narrow at their base, 5-6 cm long, and red or orange-red with purplish black spots on the inner lower surface.

Habitat: Found in moist meadows, open woodlands, and prairies from eastern British Columbia to western Quebec, and in central and eastern USA, but becoming scarcer with settlement and overpicking.

Food Uses: Attached to the roots are numerous tubers only a little larger than a grain of rice, which can be eaten fresh or dried (Leighton 1985; Welsh, cited in Leighton 1985; Siegfried 1994).

Medicinal Uses: The root can be part of a compound medicine for treating heart problems (D26). A dried tuber can be placed in a tooth cavity and then crushed to relieve the toothache (Siegfried 1994). To treat appendicitis the tubers can be boiled and the resulting soup eaten (Siegfried 1994).

Properties: Although no information could be found regarding western wood lily, the food value of the ricelike bulbs of riceroot lily (*Fritillaria camschatcensis* (L.) Ker Gawl.) per 100 g fresh weight (74% moisture) is as follows: food energy (98 kcal), protein (2.9 g), fat (0.3 g), total carbohydrate (21.8 g), crude fiber (1.9 g), thiamine (0.04 mg), riboflavin (0.04), niacin (0.2 mg), vitamin C (29 mg), and minerals (ash: 1.0 g), including Ca (10 mg), P (61 mg), Na (18 mg), Mg (23 mg), Cu (0.2 mg), Zn (0.7 mg), Fe (2.2 mg), and Mn (0.4 mg) (Kuhnlein and Turner 1991). Although Willard (1992) and Foster and Duke (1990) mention other traditional medicinal uses, no scientific information is available on the medicinal properties of this lily.

Potential: It seems wasteful to eat the roots of this beautiful flower, which is Saskatchewan's provincial floral emblem.

Wild Lily-of-the-Valley

Other Names: Cree: *sōsō-wīpukōsak, sosowipukwa, so-soskīpukosah, sosokopukasi, sōskōpukwah, sōskōpukwagōh*; French: *petit muguet*; Slave: *tsaʰli dzhī* ("frog berry").

Scientific Name: *Maian-themum canadense* Desf.

Description: A small herb spreading by stolons, with numerous solitary, sterile, heart-shaped leaves with

(R. Marles)

parallel veins up to 15 cm tall, and less numerous stems bearing two (some-times three) oval leaves and a terminal narrow inflorescence of small white flowers that are unusual for a lily in having only two sepals and two similar petals. The fruit is a berry that is brownish green speckled with red, gradu-ally maturing to pale red.

Habitat: Common in moist woods across Canada and midwestern and east-ern USA.

Food Uses: The fruit can be eaten (Lamont 1977). Two other lilies, three-leaved Solomon's seal (*Maianthemum trifolium* (L.) Sloboda, common syno-nym: *Smilacina trifolia* (L.) Desf.) and twisted stalk (*Streptopus amplexifolius* (L.) DC.), have similar habitats, lance-shaped parallel-veined leaves, and red berries. They were not distinguished by different Slave names and the fruits of all were considered edible (Lamont 1977).

Star-flowered Solomon's seal (*Maianthemum stellatum* (L.) Link) (R. Marles)

Medicinal Uses: To promote heal-ing and prevent infection the leaf can be cleaned and applied directly to a cut which is then bandaged (C21, C22, C23, C24, C25, C27, C38, C39), or the dried leaf can be boiled and the decoction cooled and then used to soak a cut. The leaf poultice can also be used to treat swellings of the limbs. The leaves are picked early in the summer and dried quickly to prevent spoiling, which happens easily (C24, C25, C38).

Properties: The fruit of false Solomon's seal (*Maianthemum racemosum* (L.) Link, common synonym: *Smilacina racemosa* (L.) Desf., 100 g fresh weight, 76% moisture) contains: food energy (88 kcal), protein (2.3 g), fat (0.6 g), total carbohydrate (20.7 g), crude fiber (1.5 g), vitamin C (122 mg), and minerals (ash: 0.5 g), including Ca (39 mg), Mg (13.7 mg), Zn (0.3 mg), and Fe (0.8 mg) (Kuhnlein and Turner 1991). *Maianthemum racemosum* contains a small amount of diosgenin (Hetherington and Steck 1997), a steroid once used as a starting material for birth control hormone synthesis.

False Solomon's seal in fruit (*Maianthemum racemosum* (L.) Link) (C. Clavelle)

Potential: These lilies are not abundant enough, and the fruit are not delicious enough, for any economic potential.

False Hellebore

False hellebore flowers (R. Marles)

False hellebore growing beside a trail (R. Marles)

Other Names: English: Indian poke; French: *tabac du diable*; Slave: *nda^h dzeku* ("throw-up root").

Scientific Name: *Veratrum viride* Ait. ssp. *eschscholtzii* (Gray) Löve and Löve, common synonym: *V. eschscholtzii* (R. & S.) A. Gray.

Description: A coarse herb up to 2 m tall, growing from a thick rhizome, with a stout stem that is leafy to the top and somewhat hairy, leaves that clasp the stem, elliptical with pointed tips, up to 30 cm long, strongly parallel-veined and often plaited, and flowers that are numerous in a large open terminal spray, with six yellowish green, pointed sepals and petals up to 1 cm long, developing into an oval seed capsule containing many large flat seeds.

Habitat: Moist forests and open slopes from south-central Alaska, central Yukon, and the southwestern Northwest Territories, through British Columbia and western Alberta, south to the Pacific Northwest in the USA, in the Rockies, and in the east from the Canadian Maritimes south through eastern USA.

Medicinal Uses: A small piece of the fresh or dried root can be taken to induce vomiting to clear the stomach, but only by adults as it is considered too strong for children (Lamont 1977).

Properties: All parts of the plant (especially the rhizome) are poisonous due to their content of alkaloids, including veratridine, veratrosine, veratramine, germidine, and germitrine. Vomiting is one of the symptoms of intoxication, and other symptoms are burning in the mouth and throat and pain in the upper abdomen, followed by watering of the mouth, diarrhea, sweating, blurred vision, hallucinations, headache, general paralysis, spasms, and, in severe cases, shallow breathing, slow or irregular pulse, lower body temperature, convulsions, and death. The *Veratrum* alkaloids protoveratrine A and B are used in modern pharmacology as hypotensives to lower blood pressure. The crude drug green veratrum used to be used for this purpose but natural variability in the plant's alkaloid content made standardization difficult, resulting in an unacceptably high incidence of adverse effects. Although other Aboriginal peoples have used this plant as a purgative, all healers have clearly stated their awareness of the danger of improper use of this drug (Dobelis 1986; Turner and Szczawinski 1991).

Potential: The toxicity of this plant has led to its abandonment as a crude drug, and there would seem to be little demand for it except perhaps as a source of pure alkaloids, for which suppliers are already well established.

Mountain Death Camas

Other Names: Cree: *maskēkwaskisīy* ("muskeg wild onion"); English: white camas, smooth camas, alkaligrass; Slave: *naydī dakalī tloʰ* ("medicine of white grass").

Scientific Name: *Zigadenus elegans* Pursh. Also spelled *Zygadenus*.

Description: An onionlike herb growing from a bulb, with long, linear, keeled, and somewhat flattened basal leaves and a flowering stalk

(R. Marles)

growing up to 60 cm tall with a terminal, open cylindrical inflorescence consisting of grayish, greenish, or yellowish white flowers with very similar sepals and petals that have a short and narrow base and a dark gland just where the sepal and petal expands, six stamens, and a pistil with three pronounced lobes that develops into a capsule.

Habitat: Very common in damp or saline meadows or prairies, open woods, shores, and bogs from the coast of Alaska, south across Canada and the northern USA, and in the mountains south to northern Mexico in the west and to Georgia in the east.

Medicinal Uses: A very small piece of the fresh or dried bulb can be boiled and one teaspoonful of the decoction taken, and/or applied externally, to treat a "sore heart" (heartburn? Lamont 1977).

Ritual Uses: The bulb may be used in a love medicine (C57).

Properties: The toxicity of this plant is due to the alkaloids zygacine, zygadenine, isogermidine, neogermidine, and protoveratrine, present in all parts of the plant. Symptoms of poisoning are similar to those described for *Veratrum*, including lowered blood pressure and slow, irregular heartbeat. Thus it will act as a medicine that affects the heart but it is very dangerous (Turner and Szczawinski 1991). The plant has caused poisoning of livestock (Moss and Packer 1994).

Potential: This poisonous plant has attractive flowers, but because of the bulb's resemblance to edible wild onions and camas (*Camassia* spp., Liliaceae/Hyacinthaceae), development does not seem to be a good idea.

ORCHIDACEAE
(Orchid Family)

Sparrow's-Egg Lady's Slipper

Other Names: English: northern lady's slipper; French: *sabot de la Vierge.*

Scientific Name: *Cypripedium passerinum* Richardson.

Description: A perennial herb growing up to 25 cm tall from a thick root, with fuzzy stems, oval to lance-shaped, parallel-veined leaves up to 15 cm long, and a few showy

Small white lady's slipper (*Cypripedium candidum* Muhl. ex Willd.) (R. Marles)

flowers with three green rounded sepals and white petals 1.5 cm long, the lower two of which form a slipperlike lip with some purple spots inside.

Habitat: A rare and protected species; found in moist coniferous woods and stream banks from British Columbia to Quebec, Alaska, and central Yukon, and south to Montana.

Ritual Uses: As a "girl medicine" love charm, a single strand of a girl's hair was tied about the stem and it was carried next to the man's heart (Lamont 1977).

Yellow lady's slipper (*Cypripedium calceolus* L.) (R. Marles)

Properties: There is scientific evidence that the root of yellow lady's slipper (*C. calceolus* L.) is probably effective as a sedative and for spasm relief (Dobelis 1986).

Potential: Lady's slipper orchids are very attractive and would be popular ornamentals. Although there is also some demand for stemless lady's slipper

(*C. acaule* Ait.) as a herbal medicine, these orchids could never withstand harvest from the wild. Efforts are currently under way to establish techniques for mass propagation and cultivation of several native Canadian orchids, primarily for ornamental purposes (Oliver pers. comm.; Mater Engineering 1993; Barl et al. 1996). Mater Engineering (1993) categorizes stemless lady's slipper as a Priority Level 3 product for further development if propagation becomes successful, and describes the market in some detail.

POACEAE
(Grass Family)

Marsh Reedgrass

Other Names: Cree: *maskosī*; English: bluejoint; French: *foin bleu*; Slave: *tlhoʰga dītlī* ("grass which is blue").

Scientific Name: *Calamagrostis canadensis* (Michx.) Beauv. Also *C. purpurascens* R. Br.

Description: A tufted grass growing up to 1.5 m tall from creeping rhizomes, with few or no basal leaves, smooth leaf sheaths, flat and rather lax leaf blades up to 10 mm wide, and a prominent flap of tissue (ligule) up to 6 mm long where the leaf blade joins the sheath. The inflorescence is up to 20 cm long, broad and either open or dense, somewhat nodding, with the seed spikelet lower bracts (glumes) up to 4 mm long, pointed and rough textured, and upper bracts (lemmas) with a straight, slender needle (awn) attached just below their middle. Purple reedgrass (*C. purpurascens*) is shorter (up to 60 cm) with rough sheaths and blades which are narrower (4 mm), a narrower but dense inflorescence with a purplish color, and bent awns projecting from near the base of the lemmas.

Calamagrostis canadensis (Michx.) Beauv. (R. Marles)

Habitat: Marsh reedgrass is common in marshes, lakeshores, meadows, and moist woods around the northern hemisphere; in North America its range extends from northern Alaska throughout Canada to northern Mexico, but not southeastern USA. Purple reedgrass is also widespread in woodlands and open slopes of Canada and western USA.

Technological Uses: Marsh reedgrass can be used as a mattress stuffing or lining for food storage pits (Leighton 1985). The hollow stems of purple reedgrass can be used as drinking straws (Lamont 1977).

Properties: The traditional uses depend on physical characteristics.

Potential: Reedgrasses are best left where they are, protecting wetlands and their associated wildlife. Marsh grasses in general play an important role in filtering runoff as it seeps into the marshes and streams, helping to maintain water quality.

Sweet-grass

Other Names: Chipe-wyan: *tlh'otsën* ("grass that smells"); Cree: *weh-kuskwa, wekus*; French: *foin d'odeur, herbe sainte*; Slave: *hleko^n* ("sweet").

Scientific Name: *Hierochloe odorata* (L.) Beauv.

Description: A perennial sweet-smelling grass growing up to 60 cm tall from long rhi-

Braid of sweet-grass (R. Marles)

zomes, often with a single culm bearing just a few leaves and only a few sterile leafy shoots. The leaf sheaths are smooth, the blades are lance-shaped and up to 6 mm wide, seldom more than 5 cm long on the culm, with a ligule 1-2 mm long at the base of the blade. The inflorescence is a pyramidal panicle (spray) up to 7 cm wide at the base and 10-15 cm long, with spreading branches. The three-flowered spikelets are bronze-colored, maturing to a lustrous golden yellow, about 6 mm long, with thin, shiny, oval glumes, fuzzy boat-shaped lemmas without awns, and single-nerved paleas.

Habitat: Found in meadows, wet ground, and shores across central and northern North America, Greenland, Iceland, and Eurasia.

Medicinal Uses: Four sweet-grass braids can be boiled and the decoction given to a young girl in a difficult labor to facilitate childbirth (C28).

Ritual Uses: Sweet-grass is picked, braided, and dried for use as an incense. One end of the braid is lit and allowed to smolder. The smoke is swept with cupped hands over the head, arms, torso, and legs for purification. The smoke purifies the body and air of evil spirits and carries prayers up to the Creator. It is used to bless food at the beginning of a feast and to bless people at the beginning of a meeting or ceremony (C32, M9, M10).

Properties: The sweet smell is due to the presence of coumarins (Hetherington and Steck 1997).

Potential: There is a well-established demand among Aboriginal peoples. The essential oil is in demand for aromatherapy (Rogers 1997).

Foxtail Barley

Other Names: Chipewyan: *tlh'ogh k'á* ("arrow grass"), *tlh'ogh ena* ("enemy grass"); Cree: *iskwesikan, iskwasisekan* ("like a woman's hair"); English: squirrel-tail grass; French: *queue d'écureuil*; Slave: *tli*^{n} *tse* ("dog tail").

(R. Marles)

Scientific Name: *Hordeum jubatum* L.

Description: A densely tufted perennial grass with stems up to 1 m tall, roughly fuzzy leaves with flat blades 2-9 mm wide, and a long (up to 12 cm) nodding seed head, slender when young but spreading widely at maturity, bearing very long awns (bristles) that are purplish green when young, turning creamy white when mature.

Habitat: Very common in wetlands, salty soils, waste areas, and roadsides throughout most of North America, some areas of South America, and Eurasia. Patches are easily spotted by the creamy color of the mature seed head.

Food Uses: The young shoots can be eaten in early summer (D19).

Technological Uses: During the hard times of the Depression in the 1930s, the mature seed heads were used as a mattress stuffing, but this was not a cultural practice (D19). The long sharp "seeds" can be mixed with meat as a way of killing stray dogs that might interfere with the caribou hunt (D6, D7, D9, D23, D24, D29).

Properties: Although no nutritional information on the shoots of this species was found, an analysis of the greens of northern manna grass (*Glyceria borealis* (Nash) Batch., 100 g fresh weight), a common boreal forest species, found that they had 0.6 g of protein, 3.0 g of crude fiber, and 1.1 g of minerals (ash), including Ca (40 mg) and P (16 mg). Foxtail barley seeds (100 g fresh weight) have 3.8 g of protein, 39 g of crude fiber, and 16.9 g of minerals (ash) (Kuhnlein and Turner 1991). The sharply awned florets of foxtail barley have been reported to cause choking when they became lodged in the throats of animals and people (Turner and Szczawinski 1991).

Potential: There is no established use for this common weedy species, other than perhaps as an indicator of poor soils.

Reed

Other Names: Chipewyan: *tlh'ogh elghá^n nachel ghi^nla* ("grass which is connected together," i.e., large nodes); French: *roseau commun.*

Scientific Name: *Phragmites australis* (Cav.) Trin. ex Steud., common synonym: *P. communis* Trin.

Description: A giant grass growing up to 4 m tall, with prominent nodes, growing from stout, long rhizomes, with flat leaf blades 1-3 cm wide and a large tawny spray of silky seed heads.

Habitat: Common around sloughs, marshes, and lakes across North America and Eurasia.

(R. Marles)

Food Uses: The young spring shoots can be eaten (D3, D4, D23).

Technological Uses: Sections of the hollow stem have been used as pipe stems (D29).

Properties: The shoots (100 g dry weight, 5% moisture) contain: protein (5.2 g), fat (0.9 mg), total carbohydrate (89 g), crude fiber (32 g), and minerals (ash: 5.8 g) (Kuhnlein and Turner 1991).

Potential: Reeds grow abundantly around sloughs and could be developed as a cultivated fresh vegetable similar to bamboo shoots, and as a basketry material.

Fowl Bluegrass

Other Names: Chipewyan: *tlh'ogh* ("grass"); English: swamp meadowgrass; French: *pâturin*.

Scientific Name: *Poa palustris* L.

Description: A loosely tufted perennial grass growing up to 100 cm high, with purplish stem bases, narrow leaves that are flat or loosely folded, and seed heads in an open, pyramid-shaped spray (panicle).

Habitat: Fairly common in moist woods and meadows and along river or lake shorelines. It was introduced from Eurasia and is now found throughout central and northern North America.

(R. Marles)

Medicinal Uses: The seed heads can be boiled to make a rinse which women use on their hair after washing it, to make the hair grow thicker and longer (D6).

Properties: Although information on bluegrass seed heads was not found, for comparison we provide below the nutrients of 100 g fresh weight (10% moisture content) of the seeds of some other common grasses: quackgrass or couchgrass (*Elytrigia repens* (L.) Desv. ex B.D. Jackson, common synonyms *Agropyron repens* (L.) Beauv. and *Elymus repens* (L.) Gould) has 18.5 g of protein, 1.8 g of fat, 16.7 g of crude fiber, and 5.3 g of minerals (ash); downy brome (*Bromus tectorum* L.) has 7.32 g of protein, 72.7 g of total carbohydrate including 19.1 g of crude fiber, and 5.5 g of minerals (ash); wild rye (*Elymus canadensis* L.) has 24.2 g of protein, 2.6 g of fat, and 2.0 g of minerals (ash); green foxtail (*Setaria viridis* (L.) Beauv.) has 14.5 g of protein, 5.9 g of fat, 64.7 g of total carbohydrate including 10.9 g of crude fiber, and 7.3 g of minerals (ash) including Ca (270 mg), P (324 mg), Na (6.7 mg), K (536 mg), Mg (252 mg), Cu (0.1 mg), Zn (7.5 mg), Fe (59.3) and Mn (5.6 mg). Vitamins are also present: for example, common barnyard grass (*Echinochloa crusgalli* (L.) Beauv.) seeds contain (per 100 g fresh weight) thiamine (0.33 mg), riboflavin (0.10 mg), and niacin (4.0 mg) (Kuhnlein and Turner

1991). Flowers of quackgrass and many other genera and species are listed in the German Commission E monographs for use in a hot bath to alleviate pain in the treatment of "degenerative rheumatic conditions." It is believed that grass flower extracts applied topically may increase local blood circulation and the coumarins present in many grasses may have a mild effect on the nerves (Bisset and Wichtl 1994). Quackgrass essential oil consists mainly of carvacrol, anethole, carvone, thymol, menthol, menthane, and *p*-cymene (Hetherington and Steck 1997).

Potential: From the chemical (protein, mineral, vitamin, coumarin) and pharmacological properties of the plant, there appear to be slight effects in relieving irritation and promoting blood circulation and a healthy scalp, thus benefiting hair growth. There is certainly an established demand for herbal shampoos, so grass inflorescences could be examined for this potential market.

TYPHACEAE
(Cattail Family)

Cattail

Other Names: Chipewyan: *tlh'ogh k'a* ("grass fat" refers to shoots), *tlh'ochok'ághe, káláchuzé* (refers to fluffy seed spikes), *k'élachuze*; Cree: *otawuskwa, ōtawaskwa* ("water-edge plant"), *ā(h)towusk, wahōtāhuk, pāsīhkan* (refers to flower spike); French: *massette, quenouille*; Slave: *nathīta*[h] *tlho*[h].

Scientific Name: *Typha latifolia* L.

Description: A marsh plant growing up to 3 m high from extensive creeping rhizomes. The leaves are long and slender (3 cm), and the tiny flowers are in a terminal spike divided into a lower, thick, dark-brown female part and an upper, narrow male part. The spike falls apart to release fluffy seeds in autumn.

(R. Marles)

Habitat: Very common along the margins of sloughs and marshes and along lakeshores and river banks across North America, Eurasia, and North Africa.

Food Uses: The young rhizomes and shoots can be eaten fresh in the spring (D9, D29, M5, M6; Leighton 1985; Welsh, cited in Leighton 1985), the young inner stem can be eaten (Siegfried 1994), and the mature rhizomes can be peeled, cooked (roasted or fried), and eaten (C47, M5; Curtis 1928; Lamont 1977; Leighton 1985) or dried and ground to make a flour (M1, M5; Curtis 1928; Leighton 1985).

Medicinal Uses: The mature, fluffy seed head can be cut when fresh, allowed to dry, and used as a poultice for burns. It forms a flexible cushion and promotes healing without scars (C11, C57, C58, M9; Siegfried 1994: mixed with lard).

Technological Uses: The fluffy seeds can be used as insulation in clothing, blankets, or bedding (C23, C27, D9, D24, M6) or mixed with peat moss in diapers to make them warmer and more comfortable (the seed fluff is not absorbent) (C20, D3, M6; Lamont 1977). Sections of the dried stems are used in games by the Chipewyan (Curtis 1928).

Properties: Dried cattail rhizomes (9% moisture) have the following nutrients per 100 g: protein (7.7 g), fat (4.9 g), total carbohydrate (79.1 g), and minerals (ash: 2.5 g). The flour from the rhizomes (100 g, 8% moisture) has 5.7-7.5 g of protein, 2.8-3.7 g of fat, 79.7-83.8 g of total carbohydrate, and 2.4-2.7 g of minerals (ash). The greens (100 g fresh weight, 90% moisture) provide: protein (0.6 g), Ca (51 mg), P (10 mg), Na (16 mg), K (59 mg), Mg (44 mg), Cu (0.1 mg), Zn (0.3 mg), Fe (0.7 mg), Mn (1.7 mg), and Cl (88 mg). The shoots (100 g fresh weight, 83% moisture) contain: food energy (68 kcal), protein (1.7 g), fat (0.7 g), crude fiber (5.7 g), riboflavin (0.13 mg), and minerals (ash: 1.0 g), including Ca (133 mg), P (11 mg), Na (118 mg), K (367 mg), and Mg (31 mg). The peeled stems provide 0.13 mg of riboflavin and 21 RE of vitamin A per 100 g fresh weight (Kuhnlein and Turner 1991).

Potential: There is significant demand for cattail in dried flower arrangements. A market could be developed for the edible shoots or for foods with a certain percentage of cattail rhizome flour.

Appendix A:
List of Contributors

⁊ə

Code	Gender	Culture	Location	Interviewed
C1	female	Cree	Shoal Lake, SK	1995
C2	male	Cree	Shoal Lake, SK	1995
C3	female	Cree	Shoal Lake, SK	1995
C4	male	Cree	Shoal Lake, SK	1995
C5	female	Cree	Athabasca River region, AB	1994
C6	female	Cree	Athabasca River region, AB	1994
C7	female	Cree	Athabasca River region, AB	1994
C8	male	Cree	Athabasca River region, AB	1994
C9	female	Cree	James Smith 100 Reserve, SK	1994
C10	female	Cree	James Smith 100 Reserve, SK	1994
C11	male	Cree	James Smith 100 Reserve, SK	1994
C12	female	Cree	James Smith 100 Reserve, SK	1994
C13	female	Cree	Athabasca River region, AB	1994
C14	female	Cree	Northwestern Alberta region, AB	1994
C15	male	Cree	Northwestern Alberta region, AB	1994
C16	female	Cree	Athabasca River region, AB	1994
C17	male	Cree	Pelican Bay, Moose Lake, AB	1994
C18	male	Cree	Athabasca River region, AB	1994
C19	male	Cree	Athabasca River region, AB	1994
C20	female	Cree	Shoal Lake, SK	1995
C21	female	Cree	Nelson House, MB	1994, 1995
C22	male	Cree	Nelson House, MB	1994, 1995
C23	female	Cree	Nelson House, MB	1994, 1995
C24	female	Cree	Nelson House, MB	1994, 1995
C25	male	Cree	Nelson House, MB	1994, 1995
C26	female	Cree	James Smith 100 Reserve, SK	1994
C27	female	Cree	Nelson House, MB	1994, 1995
C28	male	Cree	Chitek Lake, SK	1994
C29	male	Cree	East-central Alberta region, AB	1994
C30	female	Cree	Shoal Lake, SK	1995
C31	male	Cree	Northwestern Alberta region, AB	1994, 1995
C32	male	Cree	Northwestern Alberta region, AB	1994, 1995
C33	female	Cree	Shoal Lake, SK	1995
C34	male	Cree	Nelson House, MB	1994, 1995
C35	male	Cree	Nelson House, MB	1994, 1995
C36	female	Cree	Nelson House, MB	1994, 1995
C37	female	Cree	Nelson House, MB	1994, 1995
C38	male	Cree	Nelson House, MB	1994, 1995

Code	Gender	Culture	Location	Interviewed
C39	female	Cree	Nelson House, MB	1994, 1995
C40	male	Cree	Nelson House, MB	1994, 1995
C41	female	Cree	Chitek Lake, SK	1994
C42	male	Cree	Nelson House, MB	1994, 1995
C43	female	Cree	Nelson House, MB	1994, 1995
C44	female	Cree	Nelson House, MB	1994, 1995
C45	male	Cree	Nelson House, MB	1994, 1995
C46	male	Cree	Nelson House, MB	1994, 1995
C47	male	Cree	James Smith 100 Reserve, SK	1994
C48	male	Cree	Northwestern Alberta region, AB	1994, 1995
C49	female	Cree	Northwestern Alberta region, AB	1994, 1995
C50	female	Cree	James Smith 100 Reserve, SK	1994
C51	female	Cree	Athabasca River region, AB	1994
C52	female	Cree	Nelson House, MB	1994, 1995
C53	female	Cree	Northwestern Alberta region, AB	1994, 1995
C54	female	Cree	Shoal Lake, SK	1995
C55	male	Cree	James Smith 100 Reserve, SK	1994
C56	female	Cree	James Smith 100 Reserve, SK	1994
C57	male	Cree	James Smith 100 Reserve, SK	1994
C58	female	Cree	James Smith 100 Reserve, SK	1994
C59	female	Cree	Northwestern Alberta region, AB	1994, 1995
C60	male	Cree	Athabasca River region, AB	1994
C61	female	Cree	Athabasca River region, AB	1994
C62	female	Cree	Northwestern Alberta region, AB	1994, 1995
C63	female	Cree	The Pas, MB	1994
C64	female	Cree	Nelson House, MB	1994, 1995
D1	male	Dene	Black Lake, SK	1980-82
D2	male	Dene	Cold Lake, AB	1994
D3	male	Dene	Stony Rapids, SK	1980-82
D4	male	Dene	Fond du Lac, SK	1980-82
D5	female	Dene	Black Lake, SK	1980-82
D6	female	Dene	Stony Rapids, SK	1980-82
D7	male	Dene	Black Lake, SK	1980-82
D8	male	Dene	Fond du Lac, SK	1980-82
D9	male	Dene	Fond du Lac, SK	1980-82
D10	female	Dene	Black Lake, SK	1980-82
D11	male	Dene	Black Lake, SK	1980-82
D12	male	Dene	Northwestern Alberta region, AB	1994, 1995
D13	male	Dene	Fond du Lac, SK	1980-82
D14	female	Dene	Fort Chipewyan, AB	1994
D15	male	Dene	Cold Lake, AB	1994
D16	male	Dene	Stony Rapids, SK	1980-82
D17	female	Dene	Stony Rapids, SK	1980-82
D18	male	Dene	Fond du Lac, SK	1980-82
D19	female	Dene	Cold Lake, AB	1994
D20	male	Dene	Fond du Lac, SK	1980-82
D21	male	Dene	Stony Rapids, SK	1980-82

Code	Gender	Culture	Location	Interviewed
D22	male	Dene	Black Lake, SK	1980-82
D23	male	Dene	Fond du Lac, SK	1980-82
D24	male	Dene	Stony Rapids, SK	1980-82
D25	male	Dene	Stony Rapids, SK	1980-82
D26	male	Dene	Janvier Reserve, AB	1994
D27	female	Dene	Cold Lake, AB	1994
D28	female	Dene	Stony Rapids, SK	1980-82
D29	male	Dene	Black Lake, SK	1980-82
D30	female	Dene	Fond du Lac, SK	1980-82
D31	male	Dene	Fond du Lac, SK	1980-82
D32	male	Dene	Fond du Lac, SK	1980-82
D33	male	Dene	Stony Rapids, SK	1980-82
D34	female	Dene	Stony Lake, SK	1980-82
M1	male	Métis	Athabasca River region, AB	1994
M2	male	Métis	Elizabeth Métis Settlement, AB	1994
M3	male	Métis	Athabasca River region, AB	1994
M4	male	Métis	Athabasca River region, AB	1994
M5	male	Métis	Northwestern Alberta region, AB	1994, 1995
M6	male	Métis	Elizabeth Métis Settlement, AB	1994
M7	female	Métis	Northwestern Alberta region, AB	1994, 1995
M8	male	Métis	Northwestern Alberta region, AB	1994, 1995
M9	male	Métis	Sucker Creek First Nation, AB	1994, 1995
M10	female	Métis	Bonnyville, AB	1994
M11	male	Métis	Fort McMurray, AB	1994

Appendix B:
Voucher Specimens

৪৯

Listed below, in the same taxonomic order as in the text, are the voucher specimen numbers for the plants collected during our original ethnobotanical fieldwork. A voucher specimen is a pressed, dried sample of the plant mounted on high-quality white cardboard and labeled with the plant's scientific and common names and a brief description of where, when, why, and by whom it was collected. Because common plant names vary from one location to another and are unreliable as a basis for storing and collating information, voucher specimens can be used to identify positively each plant and can serve as a permanent record of the collection. In this book, voucher specimen numbers are not cited where the plant's use was obtained from the literature and thus the plant was not collected by the authors' research team. Most of those literature sources do cite their own voucher specimen collections.

Multiple voucher specimens were collected during our research. For those plants collected in Alberta (collectors Monteleone, Rudiak, and Paquette), a set of voucher specimens has been accessioned in the University of Alberta Vascular Plant Herbarium; for those collected in Saskatchewan (Clavelle and Marles), a set has been accessioned in the University of Saskatchewan's W.P. Fraser Herbarium. A full set of voucher specimens for the collections from Manitoba (Miles and Spence [maiden name of N. Tays]), Saskatchewan, and Alberta is accessioned in the Brandon University Herbarium. Please note that the following voucher specimen numbers are our collection numbers rather than herbarium accession numbers. The voucher specimens can be found in folders with other specimens of the same species, arranged in herbarium cabinets in taxonomic order. Each specimen bears a label that clearly identifies it as a voucher specimen for our Boreal ethnobotany project, with the collection number to connect an individual specimen to the data in this book. For further information on the voucher specimens, readers are invited to contact the first author.

Organism	*Voucher #*
FUNGI	
Basidiomycota	
Amanitaceae	
Amanita muscaria Fr.	Marles 134
Coriolaceae (Polyporaceae)	
Fomes fomentarius (L. ex Fries)	Marles 92, Paquette D-19-94,
J. Kickx f.	Spence 56
Trametes suaveolens (L. ex Fries) Fries	Rudiak C-18-94, Monteleone L-9-94
Hymenochaetaceae	
Inonotus obliquus (Ach. ex Pers.) Pil.	Marles 90, Spence 3 and 33
Lycoperdaceae	
Bovista pila B. & C.	Spence 53
Lycoperdon gemmatum Batsch.	Spence 54
Lycoperdon perlatum Pers.	Marles 89
Lycoperdon pyriforme Pers.	Marles 88
Lycoperdon umbrinum Pers.	Spence 55
LICHENS	
Parmeliaceae	
Parmelia sulcata Taylor	Monteleone L-18-94
Umbilicariaceae	
Actinogyra muhlenbergii (Ach.) Schol.	Marles 96
Usneaceae	
Evernia mesomorpha Nyl.	Marles 95
Usnea hirta (L.) F.H. Wigg.	Paquette D-44-94, Spence 65
NONVASCULAR PLANTS	
Bryophyta	
Dicranaceae	
Dicranum groenlandicum Brid.	Marles 159
Hylocomiaceae, Hypnaceae, Brachytheciaceae	
Pleurozium schreberi (Willd. ex Brid.)	Monteleone L-14-94,
Mitt., Hylocomiaceae; *Ptilium*	Rudiak C-39-94
crista-castrensis (Hedw.) De Not.,	(mixed collections)
Hypnaceae; *Tomentypnum nitens*	
(Hedw.) Loeske, Brachytheciaceae	
Sphagnaceae	
Sphagnum fuscum (Schimp.) Klinggr.	Marles 98
Sphagnum nemoreum Scop.	Marles 99
VASCULAR SPORE-PRODUCING PLANTS	
Equisetophyta	
Equisetaceae	
Equisetum arvense L.	Paquette D-26-94, Rudiak C-40-94
Equisetum sylvaticum L.	Marles 124

▶

Organism	*Voucher #*
Polypodiophyta	
Dryopteridaceae	
Dryopteris carthusiana (Vill.) H.P. Fuchs	Marles 32
Matteuccia struthiopteris (L.) Todaro	Marles 93, Monteleone L-16-95
GYMNOSPERMS	
Pinophyta	
Cupressaceae	
Juniperus communis L.	Marles 72, Paquette D-62-94, Spence 8 and 34
Juniperus horizontalis Moench	Paquette D-61-94, Rudiak C-45-94
Thuja occidentalis L.	Clavelle 95-31a
Pinaceae	
Abies balsamea (L.) P. Mill.	Rudiak C-1-94, Spence 20
Larix laricina (Du Roi) K. Koch	Marles 14 and 120, Rudiak C-38-94, Spence 4
Picea glauca (Moench) Voss	Clavelle 95-44b, Marles 50
Picea mariana (P. Mill.) B.S.P.	Marles 15, Spence 1 and 19
Pinus banksiana Lamb.	Marles 9, Rudiak C-9-94
ANGIOSPERMS	
Magnoliophyta: Magnoliopsida	
Aceraceae	
Acer negundo L.	Clavelle 94-41b
Apiaceae	
Heracleum maximum Bartr.	Clavelle 95-3a and 95-3b, Paquette D-4-94, Rudiak C-25-94, Spence 31, 32, and 56
Apocynaceae	
Apocynum androsaemifolium L.	Paquette D-60-94
Araliaceae	
Aralia nudicaulis L.	Marles 30, Monteleone L-6-94, Spence 24
Asteraceae	
Achillea millefolium L.	Clavelle 94-10a, Marles 17 and 170, Monteleone L-4-94, Paquette D-7-94, Rudiak C-12-94, Spence 14, 15, and 21
Achillea sibirica Ledeb.	Clavelle 95-46b
Artemisia campestris L.	Marles 35
Artemisia frigida Willd.	Monteleone L-21-95, Paquette D-47-94
Artemisia ludoviciana Nutt.	Paquette D-39-94
Aster ciliolatus Lindl.	Monteleone L-15-95, Paquette D-42-94
Aster laevis L.	Paquette D-65-94
Aster puniceus L.	Marles 31 and 155, Rudiak C-13-94, Spence 7 and 25

▶

Organism	*Voucher #*
Chrysanthemum leucanthemum L.	Paquette D-58-94
Cirsium arvense (L.) Scop.	Paquette D-28-94
Grindelia squarrosa (Pursh) Dunal.	Monteleone L-12-95
Helenium autumnale L. var. *montanum* (Nutt.) Fern.	Clavelle 95-36b
Matricaria discoidea DC.	Marles 177, Paquette D-59-94
Petasites sagittatus (Banks ex Pursh) A. Gray	Monteleone L-11-95
Solidago canadensis L.	Paquette D-31-94, Monteleone L-17-95
Tanacetum bipinnatum (L.) Schultz-Bip. ssp. *huronense* (Nutt.) Breitung	Marles 34
Taraxacum officinale G.H. Weber ex Wiggers	Paquette D-43-94, Spence 48
Betulaceae	
Alnus viridis (Vill.) Lam. & DC. ssp. *crispa* (Ait.) Turrill	Marles 11, Spence 23
Betula neoalaskana Sarg.	Marles 12 and 122, Paquette D-38-94, Rudiak C-2-94
Betula papyrifera Marsh.	Spence 9
Betula x sargentii Dugle	Marles 3, Marles 114
Corylus cornuta Marsh.	Clavelle 94-29b, Paquette D-14-94
Campanulaceae	
Campanula rotundifolia L.	Marles 24, Paquette D-20-94
Caprifoliaceae	
Lonicera dioica L.	Clavelle 95-33b, Marles 98-1, Spence 36, 37, and 38
Lonicera involucrata (Richards.) Banks.	Paquette D-25-94
Symphoricarpos albus (L.) Blake	Paquette D-29-94
Symphoricarpos occidentalis Hook.	Clavelle 95-16a, Paquette D-34-94
Viburnum edule (Michx.) Raf.	Marles 28, Paquette D-45-94, Rudiak C-29-94, Rudiak C-30-94, Spence 52
Viburnum opulus L. var. *americanum* (Mill.) Ait.	Clavelle 94-12a, Paquette D-46-94, Rudiak C-30-94
Chenopodiaceae	
Chenopodium album L.	Rudiak C-22-94
Chenopodium capitatum (L.) Asch.	Monteleone L-7-94
Salicornia rubra A. Nels.	Clavelle 95-37b
Cornaceae	
Cornus canadensis L.	Marles 20 and 166, Paquette D-30-94, Spence 27
Cornus sericea L.	Clavelle 94-27a, Marles 65, Monteleone L-5-94, Paquette D-6-94, Rudiak C-37-94, Spence 28, 29

▶

Organism	*Voucher #*
Elaeagnaceae	
Shepherdia canadensis (L.) Nutt.	Clavelle 95-39a, Marles 60, Paquette D-57-94, Rudiak C-31-94
Empetraceae	
Empetrum nigrum L.	Marles 73
Ericaceae	
Arctostaphylos alpina (L.) Spreng.	Marles 310
Arctostaphylos rubra (Rehd. & Wilson) Fern.	Spence 57
Arctostaphylos uva-ursi (L.) Spreng.	Marles 51 and 156, Paquette D-22-94
Kalmia polifolia Wangenh.	Marles 2 and 119
Ledum groenlandicum Oeder	Clavelle 94-6b, Marles 1, Monteleone L-13-94, Paquette D-1-94, Rudiak C-28-94, Spence 13 and 35
Vaccinium myrtilloides Michx.	Clavelle 94-22a, Marles 45, Paquette D-21-94, Spence 50
Vaccinium oxycoccos L.	Marles 76 and 158
Vaccinium vitis-idaea L. ssp. *minus* (Lodd.) Hultén	Clavelle 95-23a, Marles 19 and 156, Paquette D-16-94, Rudiak C-19-94, Spence 51
Vaccinium uliginosum L.	Marles 4 and 165
Fabaceae	
Medicago sativa L.	Clavelle 95-34b
Melilotus albus Medik.	Clavelle 94-21a
Trifolium hybridum L.	Paquette D-41-94, Rudiak C-21-94
Grossulariaceae	
Ribes americanum P. Mill.	Rudiak C-26-94
Ribes glandulosum Grauer	Marles 115
Ribes hirtellum Michx.	Paquette D-52-94
Ribes hudsonianum Richards.	Marles 58
Ribes lacustre (Pers.) Poir.	Paquette D-53-94
Ribes oxyacanthoides L.	Marles 57
Ribes triste Pall.	Marles 130
Lamiaceae	
Agastache foeniculum (Pursh) Ktze.	Clavelle 94-9a, Paquette D-23-94
Galeopsis tetrahit L.	Paquette D-8-94
Mentha arvensis L.	Clavelle 94-2a, Marles 115, Miles 17, Monteleone L-2-95, Rudiak C-16-94, Spence 6 and 41
Monarda fistulosa L.	Clavelle 94-8b
Scutellaria galericulata L.	Clavelle 94-13a, Monteleone L-3-95, Rudiak C-6-94
Nymphaeaceae	
Nuphar lutea (L.) Sm. ssp. *variegata* (Dur.) E.O. Beal	Marles 75, Monteleone L-20-95, Spence 42

▶

Organism	*Voucher #*
Onagraceae	
Epilobium angustifolium L.	Marles 23 and 161, Monteleone L-8-94, Paquette D-27-94, Rudiak C-24-94, Spence 16, 18, and 30
Plantaginaceae	
Plantago major L.	Clavelle 95-35a, Paquette D-54-94, Rudiak C-23-94
Polygalaceae	
Polygala senega L.	Clavelle 95-30a, Monteleone L-22-95
Polygonaceae	
Rumex aquaticus L. ssp. *occidentalis* (S. Wats.) Hult.	Rudiak C-5-94
Rumex salicifolius Weinm.	Paquette D-48-94
Pyrolaceae	
Orthilia secunda (L.) House	Marles 29
Pyrola asarifolia Michx.	Marles 64, Paquette D-9-94
Ranunculaceae	
Actaea rubra (Ait.) Willd.	Marles 68, Paquette D-64-94
Rosaceae	
Amelanchier alnifolia (Nutt.) Nutt. ex M. Roemer	Clavelle 94-26b, Marles 66, Paquette D-13-94, Rudiak C-34-94
Fragaria virginiana Duchesne	Marles 26, Spence 10 and 11
Geum aleppicum Jacq.	Monteleone L-24-95
Prunus pensylvanica L.f.	Marles 46, Paquette D-5-94, Rudiak C-27-94
Prunus virginiana L.	Clavelle 94-24b, Marles 186, Paquette D-12-94, Rudiak C-33-94
Rosa acicularis Lindl.	Clavelle 94-17b, Marles 27 and 121, Paquette D-2-94, Spence 45
Rubus arcticus L. ssp. *acaulis* (Michx.) Focke	Marles 16 and 155
Rubus chamaemorus L.	Marles 71 and 150
Rubus idaeus L. ssp. *strigosus* (Michx.) Focke	Clavelle 94-25a, Marles 25 and 172, Paquette D-11-94, Rudiak C-32-94, Spence 46
Sorbus scopulina Greene	Marles 33
Rubiaceae	
Galium boreale L.	Paquette D-17-94
Salicaceae	
Populus balsamifera L.	Clavelle 94-18b, Marles 59 and 157, Paquette D-18-94, Rudiak C-42-94, Spence 43

►

Organism	Voucher #
Populus tremuloides Michx.	Clavelle 94-19b, Marles 13, Paquette D-32-94, Rudiak C-46-94, Spence 44
Salix bebbiana Sarg.	Marles 6, Spence 2 and 47
Salix myrtillifolia Anderss.	Marles 8
Salix planifolia Pursh	Marles 7
Salix pyrifolia Anderss.	Marles 5
Santalaceae	
Geocaulon lividum (Richards.) Fern.	Marles 69
Sarraceniaceae	
Sarracenia purpurea L.	Marles 94
Urticaceae	
Urtica dioica L.	Clavelle 94-14a, Paquette D-10-94, Spence 49
Valerianaceae	
Valeriana dioica L.	Clavelle 94-5b, Monteleone L-10-94, Spence 5

Magnoliophyta: Liliopsida

Acoraceae	
Acorus americanus (Raf.) Raf.	Clavelle 94-1b, Marles 36, Monteleone L-23-95, Rudiak C-47-94, Spence 21
Alismataceae	
Sagittaria cuneata Sheldon	Marles 52
Araceae	
Calla palustris L.	Marles 132, Spence 26
Cyperaceae	
Carex aquatilis Wahl.	Marles 83
Schoenoplectus acutus (Muhl. ex Bigelow) A. & D. Löve	Marles 77, Paquette D-3-94
Juncaginaceae	
Triglochin maritimum L.	Clavelle 94-11a
Liliaceae	
Disporum trachycarpum (S. Wats.) Benth. & Hook. f.	Paquette D-63-94
Maianthemum canadense Desf.	Spence 12, 39, and 40
Zigadenus elegans Pursh	Clavelle 94-7a
Poaceae	
Hierochloe odorata (L.) Beauv.	Monteleone L-1-94, Paquette D-15-94
Hordeum jubatum L.	Marles 210, Paquette D-24-94
Phragmites australis (Cav.) Trin. ex Steud.	Marles 81
Poa palustris L.	Marles 63
Typhaceae	
Typha latifolia L.	Clavelle 94-28b, Marles 55 and 153

Glossary

֍

achene	A small, hard, dry fruit, such as a sunflower "seed," in which the single seed inside is attached to the wall of the fruit at only one point.
alkaloid	A class of fairly common plant chemicals characterized by a carbon skeleton with a nitrogen atom inserted, usually as part of a ring, usually basic in chemical nature, and usually derived from an amino acid. There are many different subclasses, such as pyrrolizidine, indole, aporphine, etc., based on different types of carbon skeletons and the position of the nitrogen(s). They are important as plant self-defense compounds that affect animals that eat the plants by mimicking the animals' nerve signal transmitters.
anthocyanidin	A type of flavonoid pigment responsible for the red, purple, or blue color of many flowers such as roses, geraniums, violets, and cornflowers. It is usually bound to a sugar in which case it is called an anthocyanin.
anthraquinone	A type of plant chemical consisting of three six-carbon aromatic rings attached side by side, the middle ring bearing two (opposite) double-bonded oxygen substituents. Various other hydrocarbon or oxygenated substituents may be attached to the rings. There are several different metabolic pathways by which plants may make anthraquinones. They are usually colored but serve physiological and chemical defense roles in the plant. Several (e.g., cascaroside, sennoside) are in commercial laxatives.
antispasmodic	A medicinal agent that prevents or relieves muscular spasms by having a sedative effect on the nervous system.
antitumor	A medicinal agent that stops the growth of tumors in experimental animals and may therefore be useful for cancer treatment in humans.
astringent	A medicinal agent that causes tissues to contract or shrink, decreasing the release of blood, mucus, and other fluids.
awn	A slender bristle at the tip of a grass floret (from the glume and/or lemma).
axil	The angle between an organ and its axis, such as the angle between a leaf stalk and the stem.

benzenoid	A type of plant chemical consisting of a six-carbon aromatic ring with simple hydrocarbon or oxygenated substituents, such as benzoic acid.
bipinnate	A leaf divided into segments like a feather, each segment being again divided into featherlike segments.
calyx	A collective term for the sepals of a flower.
carcinogenic	Causing a cancer to arise.
carotenoid	A plant chemical consisting of eight linked isoprene units, such as beta-carotene, which makes carrots and canteloupe orange and which the body converts into vitamin A. Carotenoids are important antioxidants.
chemotype	A race of plants within one species that is chemically different from other members of the same species due to genetic differences. Selection of the correct chemotype (e.g., of tansy) is very important for commercial development of medicinal plants that have the desired activity and potency and minimal toxicity. Often plants of different chemotypes look the same, so scientific testing is necessary to distinguish them.
circumboreal	Found all the way around the world in boreal regions.
condensed tannin	A type of tannin composed of flavonoid (catechin, proanthocyanidin) units linked together in a complex web. If treated with acid it does not dissolve but condenses into a sticky dark red material, so it is nonhydrolyzable.
corm	A thickened, vertical, solid underground stem, as in a crocus or gladiolus.
corolla	A collective term for the petals of a flower.
coumarin	A type of plant chemical derived from an oxygenated phenylpropanoid, mainly responsible for the scent of new-mown hay.
culm	The stem of a grass or sedge.
cytotoxic	A medicinal agent that kills cells. This may relate to anticancer activity, but unfortunately many cytotoxins kill all cells, although cancer cells (and hair follicle and stomach lining cells) may be more susceptible due to their rapid rate of growth.
decoction	Extract made by boiling the plant material in water (like a soup).
demulcent	A medicinal agent that soothes irritated mucous membranes.
diterpene	A plant chemical consisting of four linked isoprene units, such as grayanotoxin I, which makes bog laurel poisonous (see also terpene).
diuretic	Agent that stimulates the production of urine.
drupe	A fleshy fruit with one large, hard-walled seed, such as a cherry.

edema | Abnormal bodily fluid accumulation.

ellagitannin | A type of tannin composed of several molecules of hexahy-droxydiphenic acid attached by ester bonds to a central molecule of sugar. It breaks down and dissolves in acid, releasing ellagic acid, so it is hydrolyzable.

emetic | A medicinal agent that stimulates vomiting.

enzyme | A type of protein found in all organisms that facilitates particular reactions in the chemistry of life.

essential oil | Also known as volatile oil, it can be distinguished from fixed oils (such as a cooking oil) by the fact that it is aromatic and if spotted on a piece of paper will volatilize without leaving a greasy mark. Chemically, essential oils are complex mixtures of terpenoids (monoterpenes and sesquiterpenes, perhaps with a few resinous diterpenes or triterpenes), phenylpropanoids, and benzenoids; occasionally other compounds may be present, such as isothiocyanates in mustard essential oil.

expectorant | A medicinal agent that promotes the loosening and expulsion of mucus from the lungs and throat.

flavonoid | A class of very common plant chemicals characterized by two rings of six carbons joined together by a three-carbon chain, with attached alcohol groups (hence a type of phenolic or polyphenolic compound). There are several subclasses including flavones, flavanones, flavonols, isoflavones, aurones, chalcones, catechins, and anthocyanidins. Many are important as antioxidants but they have many other physiological functions and effects.

floret | A small flower that is part of a complex inflorescence, such as the yellow, tubular, central disk florets and the white, strap-shaped ray florets of a daisy flower head.

gallotannin | A type of tannin composed of several molecules of gallic acid attached by ester bonds to a central molecule of sugar. It breaks down and dissolves in acid, so it is called a hydrolyzable tannin.

glume | A sterile bract at the base of a grass spikelet.

glycoside | A type of plant chemical that has one or more sugar molecules attached, thus making it more water-soluble so the plant can transport it easily from where it is made to where it is needed. Medicinally, glycosides are an efficient way to deliver drugs orally. Once in the digestive tract the sugars are usually digested off and the remaining part of the glycoside (aglycone) enters the blood stream to cause its therapeutic or toxic effect.

hydroquinone | A type of simple phenolic plant chemical consisting of a six-carbon aromatic ring with two oxygen substituents at opposite sides of the ring. They have antibacterial, anticancer, blood-pressure-raising, and antioxidant activities.

inflorescence | The flowering part of a plant or cluster of flowers.

infusion	Extract made by adding plant material to water after it has stopped boiling (like tea).
internode	The length of stem between one node and the next.
iridoid	A type of bitter-tasting plant chemical derived from a mono-terpene, found in more advanced families of flowering plants where they serve to deter herbivores and bacterial infections.
lemma	The outer of the two bracts that encloses a grass floret.
lignan	A type of plant chemical consisting of two phenylpropanoids linked together by their side chains. They are the main active constituents of the medicinal plants mayapple and milk-thistle.
lignin	A type of plant chemical consisting of a long chain of phenyl-propanoid units linked head to tail. Lignin is deposited inside the walls of plant veins and fibers to give them strength. Wood is lignified xylem cells.
monoterpene	A type of plant chemical consisting of two isoprene units linked together, such as menthol (peppermint flavor) (see also terpene).
mutagenic	Chromosome damaging.
naphthoquinone	A type of plant chemical consisting of two six-carbon aromatic rings attached side by side, the second ring bearing two (opposite) double-bonded oxygen substituents plus any of various other hydrocarbon or oxygenated substituents. There are several different metabolic pathways by which plants may make naphtho-quinones. They are usually colored but serve physiological and chemical defense roles in the plant.
node	A stem joint from which buds develop into shoots or flowers.
oleoresin	A resin rich in essential oils.
oxalate	A salt of oxalic acid, a two-carbon organic acid also known as ethanedioic, usually found in plants as the free acid (provides the tartness of rhubarb and sorrels), soluble potassium salt (in spinach), or insoluble crystalline calcium salt (in water calla). The crystals or solution are irritating to the skin and mucous membranes, and the soluble form binds to calcium in the blood and acts as a nerve poison if consumed in excessive doses.
palea	The inner of the two bracts that encloses a grass floret.
palmate	An arrangement of leaf segments in a divided leaf or veins in a leaf similar to the arrangement of fingers radiating from the palm of the hand.
petiole	The stalk of a leaf.
phenolic	The largest group of organic compounds produced by plant secondary metabolism. Some are derived from the acetate metabolic pathway, some from the shikimic acid pathway, and some from

both, so they have different origins within the plant and may occur in many different forms and combinations. Common classes of phenolics include simple phenolics, flavonoids, anthocyanidins, tannins, coumarins, lignans, lignins, anthraquinones, and naphthoquinones. They are important as medicinals, antioxidants, and sources of colors, flavors, and aromas.

phenylpropanoid A type of plant chemical consisting of a six-carbon ring with a three-carbon side-chain, mainly responsible for the flavors of cinnamon, cloves, and anise. Flavonoids, tannins, coumarins, lignans, lignins, and benzenoids such as vanillin are phenolics derived from phenylpropanoids.

phloroglucinol A type of simple phenolic compound (six-carbon aromatic ring with alcohols attached) usually linked together in chains of two, three, or four phenols.

photosensitize To make susceptible to biological damage, usually involving rashes, burns, blisters, or abnormal pigmentation, caused by a reaction between the plant chemical present in or on the skin and exposure to sunlight.

phytosterol A steroid type of plant chemical (derived from a triterpene) such as sitosterol, stigmasterol, and campesterol. These three are found in all plants as structural components of cell membranes (like cholesterol in animals), but other sterols have physiological roles.

pinnate Like a feather, e.g., a single leaf split on both sides all the way to the central vein, so that it has fine segments and looks like a feather.

pinnatifid A leaf divided almost like a feather except that the splits do not go all the way to the central vein.

polyacetylene A type of plant chemical consisting of a long chain of carbons, some of which are linked by triple bonds. Most common in the daisy family, these compounds are derived from fatty acids and serve as plant chemical defenses against herbivores.

pome A fleshy fruit derived mostly from the floral tube rather than the ovary wall, such as an apple.

purgative A medicinal agent that causes purgation, also known as a cathartic. Like a laxative but stronger, it causes rapid evacuation of the bowels.

resin A sticky, viscous exudate produced in special resin ducts, as opposed to sap, which is watery, contains dissolved sugars and minerals, and is transported in the veins (xylem and phloem) of the plant. Resin is a mixture of alcohols, phenols, esters, and resenes (see also oleoresin).

rhizome An underground horizontal stem that can be distinguished from a root by the presence of scale-leaves, green leaves, and/or roots at its nodes.

saponin	A type of plant chemical that creates a soapy froth if shaken in water. There are two main types: triterpene saponins (e.g., ginsenosides in ginseng) and steroid saponins (e.g., digitonin from foxglove).
sepals	The outermost ring of flower parts, which may be colored like the petals (e.g., in a tulip) or green and leaflike (e.g., in a rose).
sesquiterpene	A type of plant chemical consisting of three linked isoprene units, such as cadinene, a constituent of conifer leaf oils used in perfumery (see also terpene).
sesquiterpene lactone	Type of plant chemical derived from a sesquiterpene, such as achillin from a yarrow. They cause the bitter taste of many daisy family plants.
stigma	The tip of the flower's pistil, which is usually either feathery or sticky to catch pollen.
stilbene	A type of plant phenolic related to flavonoids but having two rings joined by a two-carbon chain instead of a three-carbon chain. Some are antifungal.
stipe	The stalk of a leaf (especially of a fern) or mushroom.
stipule	An appendage on each side of the base of the leaf stalk.
style	In the flower, the neck of the pistil or female part.
tannin	A type of phenolic plant constituent that tans leather by precipitating proteins so that bacteria cannot break them down. When a tannin-containing plant extract is applied to a wound, it tans the tissues, which helps to stop bleeding and to prevent infection, but excessive consumption (e.g., of strong tea) can damage the throat and other gastrointestinal linings.
terpene	A very common class of plant chemicals derived from the plant's mevalonic acid biosynthetic pathway. The plant constructs terpenes by joining together five-carbon units called isoprene. Isoprene itself is a volatile compound released by many plants, especially trees. Chains of increasing numbers of isoprene units create monoterpenes, sesquiterpenes, diterpenes, triterpenes, carotenoids, and rubber.
triterpene	A type of plant chemical consisting of six linked isoprene units. Often sugars are attached as well to create a triterpene glycoside (saponin) such as glycyrrhizin (licorice flavor).
tuber	A fleshy, short, usually underground storage stem with many buds, such as a potato.
umbel	An upside-down umbrellalike arrangement of the flowers in a complex inflorescence, as in cow parsnip or dill plants.
volatile oil	See essential oil.

References

Abler TS, Sanders DE, Weaver SM. 1974. A Canadian Indian bibliography 1960-1970. University of Toronto Press, Toronto, ON.

Abou-Zaid M. 1996. Historical knowledge of medicinal plants used by Northern Ontario First Nations People as a guide to the identification of new bioactive natural products. Northern Ontario Development Agreement Progress Report (1995-96), Project Agreement No. 4559, Natural Resources Canada, Canadian Forest Service, Sault Ste. Marie, ON.

Adney ET, Chapelle HI. 1964. The bark canoes and skin boats of North America. Smithsonian Institution, Washington, DC.

Ager TA, Ager LP. 1980. Ethnobotany of the Eskimos of Nelson Island, Alaska. Arctic Anth. 17(1):27-48.

Ainsworth GC, Sparrow FK, Sussman AS. 1973. The fungi: An advanced treatise. Academic Press, New York, NY.

Akerele O, Heywood V, Synge H (eds.). 1991. The conservation of medicinal plants. Cambridge University Press, Cambridge.

Anderson A. 1980. Some native herbal remedies. Friends of the Devonian Botanic Garden Publication No. 8A: rev. ed.

Anderson A. 1982. Herbs of long ago. Cree Productions, Edmonton, AB.

Anderson JP. 1939. Plants used by the Eskimo of the northern Bering Sea and arctic regions of Alaska. Am. J. Bot. 26(9):714-716.

Angier B. 1978. Field guide to medicinal wild plants. Stackpole Books, Harrisburg, PA.

Annis RC (ed.). 1985. Abstracts of Native studies, vol. 2. Abstracts of Native Studies Press, Brandon, MB.

Arnason T, Hebda RJ, Johns T. 1981. Use of plants for food and medicine by native peoples of eastern Canada. Can. J. Bot. 59:2189-2325.

Barl B, Loewen D, Svendsen E. 1996. Saskatchewan herb database. Department of Horticulture Science, University of Saskatchewan, Saskatoon, SK.

Beardsley G. 1942. Notes on Cree medicines, based on a collection made by I. Cowie in 1892. Pap. Mich. Acad. Sci. Arts Lett. 27:483-496.

Berkes F, Farkas CS. 1978. Eastern James Bay Cree Indians: Changing patterns of wild food use and nutrition. Ecol. Food Nutr. 7:155-172.

Birket-Smith K. 1930. Contributions to Chipewyan ethnology. Report of the 5th Thule Expedition, 1921-1924. AMS Press (1976 ed.), New York. Vol. 6(2).

Birket-Smith K, de Laguna F. 1938. The Eyak Indians of the Copper River Delta, Alaska. Det Kgl. Danske Videnskabernes Selskab., Levin & Munksgaard, Copenhagen, Denmark.

Bisset NG, Wichtl M. 1994. Herbal drugs and phytopharmaceuticals: A handbook for practice on a scientific basis. Medpharm Scientific Publishers, Stuttgart, Germany, and CRC Press, Boca Raton, FL.

Black MJ. 1978. Plant dispersal by Native North Americans in the Canadian subarctic. *In* Ford, RI (ed.), The nature and status of ethnobotany. Anthropological Papers No. 67, Museum of Anthropology, University of Michigan, Ann Arbor, MI.:255-262.

Black MJ. 1980. Algonquin ethnobotany: An interpretation of Aboriginal adaptation in Southwestern Quebec. Canadian Ethnology Service Paper No. 65, National Museum of Man, Mercury Series, National Museums of Canada, Ottawa, ON.

Blackburn JL, chairman. 1993. Second report of the Expert Advisory Committee on Herbs and Botanical Preparations. Health Canada, Ottawa, ON.

Blanchet GH. 1925. Notes on Indian life in the country (of Great Slave Lake and Lake Athabasca). Typed manuscript with appended response to queries by Diamond Jenness. Dep. with National Museum of Man, Canadian Ethnology Service, Ottawa, ON.

Blanchet GH. 1928. Untitled manuscript on the Athapaskan Indians of northern Canada. Dep. with National Museum of Man, Canadian Ethnology Service, Ottawa, ON.

Blanchet GH. 1946. Emporium of the north. Beaver 276:32-35.

Blumenthal M, Busse WR, Goldberg A, Gruenwald J, Hall T, Riggins CW, Rister RS (eds.). 1998. The complete German Commission E monographs. Therapeutic guide to herbal medicines. American Botanical Council, Austin, TX.

Bodeker G, Bhat KKS, Burley J, Vantomme P. 1997. Medicinal plants for forest conservation and health care. Non-Wood Forest Products Series No. 11, Global Initiative for Traditional Systems (GIFTS) of Health, Food and Agriculture Organization of the United Nations, Rome, Italy.

Boivin B. 1967-1981. Flora of the Prairie provinces. Mémoires de l'Herbier Louis-Marie, Faculté d'Agriculture, Université Laval, Québec, Provancheria No. 2 (1967), 3 (1968-1969), 4 (1972), and 5 (1981).

Bompas WC. 1890. Words of the Chipewyan Indians of Athabasca and vocabulary of the language of the Tinne Indians of McKenzie River. Bureau of American Ethnology, National Anthropology Archives, Smithsonian Institution, Washington, DC.

Bompas WC. 1894. On the Indians of the Mackenzie and Yukon Rivers, Canada. Report of the 63rd Meeting of the British Association for the Advancement of Science, 1893. John Murray, London. pp. 901-902.

Bondartsev AS. 1953. The Polyporaceae of the European USSR and Caucasia. Academy of Sciences of the USSR, Komarov Botanical Institute. Translated (1971) from Russian by the Israel Program for Scientific Translations, Jerusalem.

Boon H, Smith M. 1998. Pharmacist training program in botanical medicine. Canadian College of Naturopathic Medicine, Toronto, ON.

Bradley PR (ed.). 1992. British herbal compendium, Vol. 1: A handbook of scientific information on widely used plant drugs. (Companion to Vol. 1 of the British Herbal Pharmacopoeia.) British Herbal Medicine Association, Bournemouth, UK.

Brandson LE. 1981. From tundra to forest: A Chipewyan resource manual. Manitoba Museum of Man and Nature, Winnipeg, MB.

Breynat G. 1948. Cinquante ans au pays des neiges. I: Chez les mangeurs de Caribous. 2nd ed. Fides, Montreal, QC.

Brown B. 1965. The end-of-the-earth people. North 12(6):16-21.

Brumbach HJ, Jarvenpa R, Buell C. 1982. An ethnoarchaeological approach to Chipewyan adaptations in the late fur trade period. Arctic Anth. 19(1):1-49.

Budd AC, Looman J, Best KF. 1987. Budd's flora of the Canadian Prairie provinces. Research Branch, Agriculture Canada, Ottawa, ON. Publication 1662.

Carrier Linguistic Committee. 1973. Hanúyeh Ghun 'Útni-i: Plants of Carrier Country. Central Carrier Language. Carrier Linguistic Committee, Fort St. James, BC.

Castleman M. 1991. The healing herbs. Rodale Press, Emmaus, PA.

Chandler RF, Freeman L, Hooper SN. 1979. Herbal remedies of the Maritime Indians. J. Ethnopharmacol. 1(1):49-68.

Chandler RF, Hooper SN. 1979. Herbal remedies of the Maritime Indians: A preliminary screening. Can. J. Pharm. Sci. 14(4):103-106.

Churchill L. 1981. Personal communication (March 24, 1981) on Chipewyan artifacts of plant origin in the Museum collection. Curatorial Assistant, Ethnology Department, Glenbow Museum, Calgary, AB.

Clark AM. 1974. The Athapaskans: Strangers of the north. National Museum of Man, National Museums of Canada, Ottawa, ON.

Clavelle CM. 1997. Ethnobotany of two Cree communities in the southern boreal forest of Saskatchewan. MA thesis, Department of Anthropology and Archaeology, University of Saskatchewan, Saskatoon, SK.

Clément D. 1990. L'Ethnobotanique Montagnaise de Mingan. Collection Nordicana No. 53, Centre d'études nordiques, Université Laval, Québec, QC.

Colegate SM, Molyneux RJ, eds. 1993. Bioactive natural products: Detection, isolation, and structure determination. CRC Press, Boca Raton, FL.

Compton BD. 1999. Personal communication (February 8, 1999) on Carrier ethnobotanical research. Department of Botany, University of British Columbia, Vancouver, BC.

Compton BD, Rigsby B, Tarpent M-L (eds.). 1997. Ethnobotany of the Gitksan Indians of British Columbia by Harlan I. Smith. Mercury Series Paper 132, Canadian Ethnology Service, Canadian Museum of Civilization, Hull, QC.

Coon N. 1979. Using plants for healing: An American herbal. Rodale Press, Emmaus, PA.

Cooper JM. 1938. Snares, deadfalls, and other traps of the northern Algonquians and northern Athapaskans. Catholic University of America, Anthropological Series No. 5, Catholic University of America Press, Washington, DC.

Cowen DL. 1984. The impact of the materia medica of the North American Indians on professional practice. *In* Hein W-H (ed.), Botanical drugs of the Americas in the Old and New Worlds. Wissenschaftliche Verlagsgesellschaft, Stuttgart, Germany. pp. 51-63.

Crowe KJ. 1974. A history of the original people of northern Canada. Arctic Institute of North America. McGill-Queen's University Press, Montreal, QC.

Crucible Group. 1994. People, plants, and patents: The impact of intellectual property on biodiversity, conservation, trade, and rural society. International Development Research Centre, Ottawa, ON.

Cunningham AB. 1996. Ethics, biodiversity, and new natural products development. World Wildlife Fund International Publication, Gland, Switzerland.

Curtis ES. 1928. The North American Indian. Reprinted 1970 by Johnson Reprint Corporation, New York, NY. Vol. 18:1-253.

Davidson DS. 1937. Snowshoes. Mem. Am. Phil. Soc. 6:1-159.

Densmore F. 1928. Uses of plants by the Chippewa Indians. *In* 44th annual report 1926-1927, Bureau of American Ethnology, Smithsonian Institution, pp. 275-397. Republished 1974 as "How Indians use wild plants for food, medicine and crafts." Dover Publications, New York, NY.

Diamant RMF. 1995. Personal communication (July 27, 1995) regarding food plants of the Cross Lake Cree people. Associate Professor, Department of Foods and Nutrition, Faculty of Human Ecology, University of Manitoba, Winnipeg, MB.

Dobelis IN (ed.). 1986. Magic and medicine of plants. Reader's Digest Association, Pleasantville, NY.

Dodge JR. 1871. Food products of the North American Indians. *In* Report of the Commissioner of Agriculture 1870. Government Printing Office, Washington, DC. pp. 404-428.

Draper HH. 1977. The Aboriginal Eskimo diet in modern perspective. Am. Anth. 79:309-316.

Driver HE. 1969. Indians of North America, 2nd ed. University of Chicago Press, Chicago, IL.

Duchaussois P. 1928. Au glaces polaires: Indiens et Esquimaux. Editions SPES, Paris, France.

Duke JA. 1985. CRC handbook of medicinal herbs. CRC Press, Boca Raton, FL.

Duke JA. 1986. Handbook of northeastern Indian medicinal plants. Quarterman Publications, Lincoln, MA.

Duke JA. 1992a. Handbook of biologically active phytochemicals and their activities. CRC Press, Boca Raton, FL.

Duke JA. 1992b. Handbook of phytochemical constituents of GRAS herbs and other economic plants. CRC Press, Boca Raton, FL.

Duke JA. 1997. The green pharmacy. Rodale Press, Emmaus, PA.

Ebner Fr. 1982. Personal communication (February 23, 1982) on Chipewyan artifacts in their museum collection. Director, Northern Life Museum and National Exhibition Centre, Fort Smith, NWT.

Elford LW, Elford M. 1981. English-Chipewyan dictionary. Northern Canada Evangelical Mission, Prince Albert, SK.

Emmons GT. 1911. The Tahltan Indians. University of Pennsylvania, The Museum, Anthropological Publications 4(1):1-120.

Erichsen-Brown C. 1979. Use of plants for the past 500 years. Breezy Creeks Press, Aurora, ON.

Farnsworth NR (ed.). 1999. NAPRALERT: Natural Products Alert Database. Program for Collaborative Research in the Pharmaceutical Sciences, Department of Medicinal Chemistry and Pharmacognosy, College of Pharmacy, University of Illinois at Chicago, IL.

Fidler P. 1792. A journal of a journey with the Chepawyans or northern Indians, to the Slave Lake, and to the east and west of the Slave River, in 1791 and 1792. *In* Tyrrell JB (ed.), Journals of Samuel Hearne and Philip Turnor. Pub. Champlain Soc. (1934) 21:493-555.

Flexon C. 1898. Some medicines of the Swampee Cree Indians of the north. Can. Pharm. J. 31:126-129.

Ford RI. 1981. Ethnobotany in North America: An historical phytogeographic perspective. Can. J. Bot. 59:2178-2188.

Ford RI (ed.). 1985. Prehistoric food production in North America. Anthropological Papers No. 75, Museum of Anthropology, University of Michigan, Ann Arbor, MI.

Ford RI (ed.). 1986. An ethnobiology source book: The use of plants and animals by American Indians. Garland Publishing, New York, NY.

Foster S. 1993. Herbal renaissance. Gibbs-Smith, Salt Lake City, UT.

Foster S. 1995. Forest pharmacy: Medicinal plants in American forests. Forest History Society, Durham, NC.

Foster S, Duke JA. 1990. A field guide to medicinal plants: eastern and central North America. Houghton Mifflin, Boston, MA.

Foster S, Tyler VE. 1999. Tyler's honest herbal: A sensible guide to the use of herbs and related remedies, 4th ed. Haworth Herbal Press, New York, NY.

Franklin J. 1823. Narrative of a journey to the polar sea, in the years 1819, 20, 21, and 22. JM Dent and Sons, Ltd., London.

Freeman MMR, Carbyn LN (eds.). 1988. Traditional knowledge and renewable resource management in northern regions. Occasional Publication No. 23, IUCN Commission on Ecology and the Boreal Institute for Northern Studies, Edmonton, AB.

French DH. 1981. Neglected aspects of North American ethnobotany. Can. J. Bot. 59:2326-2330.

Fulda S, Jeremias I, Steiner HH, Pietsch T, Debatin KM. 1999. Betulinic acid: a new cytotoxic agent against malignant brain-tumor cells. Int. J. Cancer 82(3):435-441.

Fytokem Products. 1999. The science of nature. World Wide Web address: http://www.fytokem.com

Gamache CE. 1970. Raven heads: The Indian fellow-citizen. Unpublished manuscript in the collection of R. Marles, Brandon University, Brandon, MB.

Gaudiel R. 1997. Research and development of aromatic crops. *In* Proceedings of the Prairie Medicinal and Aromatic Plants '97 Conference, Brandon, MB. p. 43-44.

Gillespie BC. 1976. Changes in territory and technology of the Chipewyan. Arctic Anth. 13(1):6-11.

Gilman AG, Goodman LS, Gilman A. 1980. Goodman and Gilman's The pharmacological basis of therapeutics, 6th ed. MacMillan, New York, NY.

Gilmore MR. 1931. Dispersal by Indians a factor in the extension of discontinuous distribution of certain species of native plants. Pap. Mich. Acad. Sci. Arts Lett. 13:89-94.

Goddard PE. 1912. Chipewyan texts. Anth. Pap. Am. Mus. Nat. Hist. 10(1):1-65.

Gordon BC. 1977. Prehistoric Chipewyan harvesting at a barrenland caribou water crossing. W. Can. J. Anth. 7(1):69-83.

Gordon BC. 1981. Man-environment relationships in barrenland prehistory. Musk-Ox 28:1-19.

Graham A. 1775. Observations on Hudsons Bay. *In* Rich EE (ed.) (1949). James Isham's Observations on Hudsons Bay, 1743. The Champlain Society, Toronto, ON.

Grand Council of Treaty 8 First Nations. 1993. Great Bear environmental health study, Year One Report. Grand Council of Treaty 8 First Nations Environment Committee report submitted to Health and Welfare Canada, Ottawa, ON.

Groves JW. 1979. Edible and poisonous mushrooms of Canada. Research Branch Publication 1112, Agriculture Canada, Ottawa, ON.

Gruenwald J, Brendler T, Jaenicke C, Mehta M, Fleming T, Deutsch M, Hamid M, Nathan J, Pareddy K, Rodgers K, Troncone-Liebfried M (eds.). 1998. PDR for herbal medicines, 1st ed. Medical Economics Company, Montvale, NJ.

Hall J. 1981. Personal communication (April 6, 1981) and catalogue of Chipewyan artifacts of plant origin in the museum collection. Cataloguer, Canadian Ethnology Service, National Museum of Man, Ottawa, ON.

Hammond P. 1990. Personal communication (January 3, 1990) regarding research projects on antidiabetic medicines. Division of Endocrinology, Glaxo Research Laboratories, Research Triangle Park, NC.

Hara HS. 1980. The Hare Indians and their world. Canadian Ethnology Service Paper No. 63, National Museum of Man, Mercury Series, National Museums of Canada, Ottawa, ON.

Harborne JB, Baxter H (eds.). 1993. Phytochemical dictionary: A handbook of bioactive compounds from plants. Taylor & Francis, London, UK.

Harms VL. 1997. Personal communication (June 27, 1997) regarding the westward spread of white cedar. Curator, W.P. Fraser Herbarium, University of Saskatchewan, Saskatoon, SK.

Harper F. 1931. Some plants of the Athabasca and Great Slave Lake region. Can. Field-Nat. 45(3):97-107.

Hawkins WW (ed.). 1983. Recommended nutrient intakes for Canadians. Health and Welfare Canada, Ottawa, ON.

Hawksworth DL, Kirk PM, Sutton BC, Pegler DN. 1995. Ainsworth and Bisby's dictionary of the fungi, 8th ed. CAB International, New York, NY.

Health Canada. 1995a. Drugs Directorate guideline: Traditional herbal medicines. Health Protection Branch, Ottawa, ON.

Health Canada. 1995b. Drugs Directorate policy: Medicinal herbs in traditional herbal medicine. Health Protection Branch, Ottawa, ON.

Health Canada. 1996. Labelling standard: Chamomile. Drugs Directorate, Ottawa, ON.

Health Canada. 1997. Functional foods and nutraceuticals: discussion document. Consultation Workshop, Food Directorate and Drugs/Medical Devices Programme, Ottawa, ON.

Hearne, S. 1795. A journey from Prince of Wales's Fort in Hudson's Bay to the Northern Ocean 1769, 1770, 1771, 1772. Glover R (ed.) (1958). MacMillan Canada, Toronto, ON.

Heffley S. 1981. The relationship between northern Athapaskan settlement patterns and resource distribution: An application of Horn's Model. *In* Winterhalder B, Smith EA (eds.). Hunter-gatherer foraging strategies: Ethnographic and archaeological analyses. University of Chicago Press, Chicago, IL. pp. 126-147.

Heller CA, Scott EM. 1967. The Alaska dietary survey, 1956-1961. US Department of Health, Education, and Welfare, Public Health Service, Nutrition and Metabolic Disease Section, Arctic Health Research Center, Anchorage, AK. Environmental Health Series, Arctic Health, Public Health Service Publication No. 999-AH-2. US Government Printing Office, Washington, DC.

Hellson JC, Gadd M. 1974. Ethnobotany of the Blackfoot Indians. Canadian Ethnology Service Paper No. 19, National Museum of Man, Mercury Series, National Museums of Canada, Ottawa, ON.

Helm J. 1973. Subarctic Athapaskan bibliography. Department of Anthropology, University of Iowa, Iowa City, IA.

Helm J. 1976. The Indians of the subarctic: A critical bibliography. Indiana University Press, Bloomington, IN.

Helm J, Lurie NO. 1961. The subsistence economy of the Dogrib Indians of Lac La Martre in the Mackenzie District of the NWT. Publication No. NCRC 61-3, Department of Northern Affairs and National Resources, Northern Coordination and Research Centre.

Henriksen G. 1973. Hunters in the barrens: The Naskapi on the edge of the white man's world. Institute of Social and Economic Research, Memorial University of Newfoundland. Newfoundland Social and Economic Studies No. 12, St. John's, NF.

Hetherington M, Steck W. 1997. Natural chemicals from northern prairie plants: The phytochemical constituents of one thousand North American species. Fytokem Products, Saskatoon, SK.

Hippler AE, Wood JR. 1974. The subarctic Athabascans: A selected annotated bibliography. Institute of Social, Economic and Government Research, University of Alaska, Fairbanks, AK.

319

Hoffman D. 1976. Inuit land use on the barren grounds: Supplementary notes and analysis. *In* Freeman MMR (ed.). Report: Inuit Land Use and Occupancy Project 2: supporting studies. Department of Indian and Northern Affairs, Ottawa, ON. pp. 69-84.

Honigmann JJ. 1946. Ethnography and acculturation of the Fort Nelson Slave. Yale University Publications in Anthropology No. 33, Yale University Press, New Haven, CT.

Honigmann JJ. 1948. Foodways in a muskeg community: An anthropological report on the Attawapiskat Indians. Northern Coordination and Research Centre, Department of Northern Affairs and National Resources, Ottawa, ON. Reprinted 1961.

Hooper SN, Chandler RF. 1981. Herbal remedies of the Maritime Indians: A preliminary screening, Part II. Can. J. Pharm. Sci. 16(1):56-59.

Hopwood VG. 1971. David Thompson: Travels in western North America 1784-1812. MacMillan, Toronto, ON.

Hrapko JO. 1978. Botany reference list: Ethnobotany in North America. Unpublished manuscript. Alberta Culture, Heritage Resources, Provincial Museum of Alberta, Edmonton, AB.

Hrapko JO. 1981. Personal communication (March 18, 1981) regarding Chipewyan artifacts in their collection. Curator of Botany, Provincial Museum of Alberta, Edmonton, AB.

Hutchens AR, Tretchikoff NG, Tretchikoff NK. 1973. Indian herbology of North America. Merco, Windsor, ON.

Idiens D. 1979. A catalogue of northern Athapaskan Indian artefacts in the collection of the Royal Scottish Museum, Edinburgh. Royal Scottish Museum Information Series, Art & Archaeology 3.

Indian and Northern Affairs. 1978a. Nutrition in the north: A look at what Inuit eat. Inuktitut, Summer/Fall 1978. Indian and Northern Affairs Publication No. 8182-010-HE. pp. 26-35.

Indian and Northern Affairs. 1978b. Northern foods: Excellent food value. Inuktitut, Summer/Fall 1978. Indian and Northern Affairs Publication No. 8182-010-HE. pp. 36-38.

Inkpen T. 1999. Healthy people, healthy world: Preserving aspects of traditional knowledge and improving its application to environmental assessment. Master of Natural Resources Management, Natural Resources Institute, University of Manitoba, Winnipeg, MB.

International Organization for Plant Information. 1999. Global Plant Checklist. http://www.bgbm.fu-berlin.de/IOPI/GPC/query.htm

Irimoto T. 1981. Chipewyan ecology: Group structure and caribou hunting system. Senri Ethnological Studies No. 8, National Museum of Ethnology, Osaka, Japan.

Isham J. 1743. Observations on Hudsons Bay. *In* Rich EE (ed.) (1949). James Isham's observations on Hudsons Bay, 1743. The Champlain Society, Toronto, ON. pp. 138,178.

Jarvenpa R. 1979. Recent ethnographic research: Upper Churchill River drainage, Saskatchewan, Canada. Arctic 32(4):355-365.

Jarvenpa R. 1980. The trappers of Patuanak: Toward a spatial ecology of modern hunters. Canadian Ethnology Service Paper No. 67, National Museum of Man, Mercury Series, National Museums of Canada, Ottawa, ON.

Jarvenpa R. 1982. Personal communication (March 9, 1982) regarding the use of plants by the Chipewyan people of the Patuanak, Saskatchewan, area. Assistant Professor of Anthropology, State University of New York at Albany, NY.

Jenness D. 1963. The Indians of Canada, 6th ed. National Museum of Canada Bulletin 65, Anthropological Series 15:385-388.

Johnson D, Kershaw L, MacKinnon A, Pojar J. 1995. Plants of the western boreal forest and aspen parkland. Lone Pine, Edmonton, AB.

Johnson LM. 1997. Health, wholeness, and the land: Gitksan traditional plant use and healing. PhD dissertation, Anthropology Department, University of Alberta, Edmonton, AB.

Johnson M (ed.). 1992. Lore: Capturing traditional environmental information. Déné Cultural Institute/International Development Research Centre, Ottawa, ON.

Johnson-Gottesfeld LM. 1992a. The importance of bark products in the Aboriginal economies of northwestern British Columbia, Canada. Econ. Bot. 46(2):148-157.

Johnson-Gottesfeld LM. 1992b. Use of cinder conk (*Inonotus obliquus*) by the Gitksan of northwestern British Columbia, Canada. J. Ethnobiol. 12(1):153-156.

Johnson-Gottesfeld LM. 1993. Plants, land and people: A study of Wet'suwet'en ethnobotany. MA thesis, Department of Anthropology, University of Alberta, Edmonton, AB.

Johnson-Gottesfeld LM. 1994a. Conservation, territory, and traditional beliefs: An analysis of Gitksan and Wet'suwet'an subsistence, northwest British Columbia, Canada. Hum. Ecol. 22(4):443-465.

Johnson-Gottesfeld LM. 1994b. Wet'suwet'en ethnobotany: Traditional plant uses. J. Ethnobiol. 14(2):185-210.

Johnson-Gottesfeld LM. 1995. The role of plant foods in traditional Wet'suwet'en nutrition. Ecol. Food Nutr. 34:149-169.

Johnson-Gottesfeld LM, Anderson B. 1988. Gitksan traditional medicine: Herbs and healing. J. Ethnobiol. 8(1):13-33.

Johnson-Gottesfeld LM, Hargus S. 1998. Classification and nomenclature in Witsuwit'en ethnobotany: A preliminary examination. J. Ethnobiol. 18(1):69-101.

Johnston A. 1987. Plants and the Blackfoot. Occasional Papers No. 15, Lethbridge Historical Society, Historical Society of Alberta, Lethbridge, AB.

Jones A. 1983. Nauriat Niginaqtuat: Plants that we eat. Maniilaq Association, Kotzebue, AK.

Jones S. 1867. Notes on the Tinneh or Chepewyan Indians of British and Russian America. *In* Gibbs G (ed.) Annual report. Board of Regents, Smithsonian Institution, 1866. Government Printing Office, Washington, DC. pp. 302-327.

Kari PR. 1995. Tanaina plantlore: Dena'ina K'et'una, 4th ed. An ethnobotany of the Dena'ina Indians of southcentral Alaska. Alaska Native Language Center, Fairbanks, AK, Alaska Natural History Association, Anchorage, AK, and the National Park Service, US Department of the Interior, Washington, DC.

Kartesz JT, Kartesz R. 1980. A synonymized checklist of the vascular flora of the United States, Canada, and Greenland. Vol. II: The biota of North America. University of North Carolina Press, Chapel Hill, NC.

Kelsall JP. 1968. The migratory Barren-Ground Caribou of Canada. Queen's Printer, Ottawa, ON.

Kerik J. 1985. Living with the land: Use of plants by the Native people of Alberta. Alberta Culture Circulating Exhibits Program, National Museums of Canada Fund, Provincial Museum of Alberta, Edmonton, AB.

Kobaisy M, Abramowski Z, Lermer L, Saxena G, Hancock REW, Towers GHN. 1997. Antimycobacterial polyynes of devil's club (*Oplopanax horridus*), a North American Native medicinal plant. J. Nat. Prod. 60(11):1210-1213.

Kuhnlein HV, Turner NJ. 1991. Traditional plant foods of Canadian indigenous peoples: Nutrition, botany, and use. Gordon and Breach Science Publishers, Philadelphia, PA.

Lamont SM. 1977. The Fisherman Lake Slave and their environment: A story of floral and faunal resources. MSc thesis, Department of Plant Ecology, University of Saskatchewan, Saskatoon, SK.

Lantis M. 1959. Folk medicine and hygiene: Lower Kuskokwim and Nunivak-Nelson Island areas. Anth. Pap. Univ. Alaska (8)1:5-63.

Leach, F. O.M.I. 1973. 55 years with Indians and settlers on Lake Winnipeg. Self-published, Winnipeg, MB.

Leechman D. 1948. The pointed skins. Beaver 278:14-18.

Leechman D. 1954. The Vanta Kutchin. Anthropological Series No. 33, Bulletin No. 130. Department of Northern Affairs and Natural Resources, National Parks Branch, National Museum of Canada, Ottawa, ON.

Leighton AL. 1982. Ethnobotany of the Nihithawak, Saskatchewan Woods Cree of the "Th" (d) dialect. MSc thesis, Department of Biology, University of Saskatchewan, Saskatoon, SK.

Leighton AL. 1985. Wild plant use by the Woods Cree (Nihithawak) of east-central Saskatchewan. Canadian Ethnology Service Paper No. 101, National Museum of Man, Mercury Series, National Museums of Canada, Ottawa, ON.

Leonard D. 1981. Personal communication (June 18, 1981) regarding Chipewyan artifacts in their collection. Assistant Curator Native Studies, Manitoba Museum of Man and Nature, Winnipeg, MB.

Leung AY, Foster S. 1996. Encyclopedia of common natural ingredients used in food, drugs, and cosmetics, 2nd ed. J. Wiley, New York, NY.

Lewis HT. 1977. Maskuta: the ecology of Indian fires in northern Alberta. W. Can. J. Anth. 7(1):15-52.

Li F-K. 1964. A Chipewyan ethnological text. Int. J. Am. Linguist. 30(2/1):132-136.

List PH, Schmidt PC. 1989. Phytopharmaceutical technology. CRC Press, Boca Raton, FL.

Llano GA. 1951. Economic uses of lichens. *In* Annual report, Board of Regents, Smithsonian Institution, 1950. Government Printing Office, Washington, DC. pp. 385-422.

Lowie RH. 1909. An ethnological trip to Lake Athabasca. Am. Mus. J. 9:10-15.

Lowie RH. 1912. Chipewyan tales. Anth. Pap. Am. Mus. Nat. Hist. 10(3):171-200.

Lynas L. 1972. Medicinal and food plants of the North American Indians: A bibliography. Library of the New York Botanical Garden, Bronx, NY.

McCutcheon AR, Ellis SM, Hancock REW, Towers GHN. 1992. Antibiotic screening of medicinal plants of the British Columbian native peoples. J. Ethnopharmacol. 37(3):213-223.

McCutcheon AR, Ellis SM, Hancock REW, Towers GHN. 1994. Antifungal screening of medicinal plants of British Columbian native peoples. J. Ethnopharmacol. 44(3):157-169.

McCutcheon AR, Roberts TE, Gibbons E, Ellis SM, Babiuk LA, Hancock REW, Towers GHN. 1995. Antiviral screening of British Columbian medicinal plants. J. Ethnopharmacol. 49 (2):101-110.

Macdonell J. circa 1760. The Chipweans. Jenness D (ed.) (1956). The Research Centre for Amerindian Anthropology, University of Ottawa. Anthropologica (1st series) 3:15-33.

McGee JT. 1961. Cultural stability and change among the Montagnais Indians of the Lake Melville region of Labrador. Catholic University of America Anthropological Series No. 19, Catholic University of America Press, Washington, DC.

McGhee R. 1978. Canadian Arctic prehistory. Van Nostrand Reinhold, Toronto, ON.

McKennan RA. 1959. The Upper Tanana Indians. Yale University Publications in Anthropology No. 55, Yale University Press, New Haven, CT.

McKennan RA. 1965. The Chandalar Kutchin. Arct. Inst. North Am. Tech. Pap. No. 17.

Mackenzie A. 1801. Voyages from Montreal on the River St. Lawrence through the continent of North America to the frozen and Pacific Oceans in the years 1789 and 1793, with a preliminary account of the rise, progress, and present state of the fur trade of that country. T Cadell, Jr. and W Davies, Strand, London, UK.

Macoun J. 1882. Manitoba and the great North-West: The field for investment: The home of the emigrant, being a full and complete history of the country ... World Publishing Company, Guelph, ON.

Marie-Victorin Fr, Rouleau E. 1964. Flore Laurentienne. Les Presses de l'Université de Montréal, Montreal, QC.

Marles RJ. 1984. The ethnobotany of the Chipewyan of Northern Saskatchewan. MSc thesis, Department of Biology, University of Saskatchewan, Saskatoon, SK.

Marles RJ, Farnsworth NR. 1995. Antidiabetic plants and their active constituents. Phytomedicine 2:137-189.

Mason JA. 1913. Notes on the Indians of the Great Slave Lake area. Yale University Publications in Anthropology No. 34 (1946 ed.), Yale University Press, New Haven, CT.

Mater Engineering. 1993. Special forest products market analysis for Saskatchewan Timberlands Division, Weyerhaeuser Canada. Natural Resources Canada, Canadian Forest Service, and Saskatchewan Environment and Resource Management, Forestry Branch. Canada-Saskatchewan Partnership Agreement in Forestry Project No. 3017.

Mathiassen T. 1928. Material culture of the Iglulik Eskimos. Report of the 5th Thule Expedition 1921-1924. Gyldendalske Boghandel, Nordisk Forlag, Copenhagen, Denmark. Vol. 6(1): 1-242.

Mazza G (ed.). 1998. Functional foods: Biochemical and processing aspects. Technomic Publishing, Lancaster, PA.

Miller RA. 1997. Dried herbs and spices for the floral trade. Proceedings of the Prairie Medicinal and Aromatic Plants Conference '97, Brandon, MB. pp. 105-114.

Millspaugh CF. 1892. American medicinal plants. Dover Publications (1974), New York, NY.

Minni SJ. 1976. The prehistoric occupations of Black Lake, Northern Saskatchewan. Archaeological Survey of Canada Paper No. 53, National Museum of Man, Mercury Series, Ottawa, ON.

Missouri Botanical Garden 1999. W3TROPICOS: Vascular Tropicos nomenclatural database and associated authority files. http://mobot.mobot.org/Pick/Search/pick.html

Moerman DE. 1979. Symbols and selectivity: A statistical analysis of Native American medical ethnobotany. J. Ethnopharm. 1(2):111-119.

Moerman DE. 1986. Medicinal plants of Native America. Technical Reports No. 19, Vol. 1 & 2, Museum of Anthropology, University of Michigan, Ann Arbor, MI.

Moerman DE. 1998. Native American ethnobotany. Timber Press, Portland, OR.

Moerman DE. 1999. Native American Ethnobotany Database. World Wide Web address: http://www.umd.umich.edu/cgi-bin/herb/

Moes J. 1997. What's new: Manitoba. Proceedings of the Prairie Medicinal and Aromatic Plants Conference '97, Brandon, MB. pp. 7-9.

Morgan S. 1999. Monitoring programs for the sustainable harvest of the non-timber boreal forest products *Acorus americanus* and *Vaccinium angustifolium*. M.Sc. thesis, Department of Botany, University of Manitoba, Winnipeg, MB.

Morice AG. 1906-1910. The great Déné race. Anthropos 1:229-277, 483-509, 695-730; 2:1-34, 181-196; 4:582-606; 5:113-142, 419-443, 643-653, 969-990.

Morris MW. 1972. Great Bear Lake Indians: A historical demography and human ecology. Part I: The situation prior to European contact. Musk-Ox 11:3-27.

Moseley EL. 1931. Some plants that were probably brought to northern Ohio from the west by Indians. Pap. Mich. Acad. Sci. Arts Lett. 13:169-172.

Moss EH, Packer JG. 1994. Flora of Alberta, 2nd ed. University of Toronto Press, Toronto, ON.

Mulligan GA, Munro DB. 1990. Poisonous plants of Canada. Publication 1842/E, Agriculture Canada, Ottawa, ON.

Munsterhjelm E. 1953. The wind and the Caribou. MacMillan, Toronto, ON.

Murdock GP. 1960. Ethnographic bibliography of North America, 3rd ed. Human Relations Area Files, New Haven, CT.

Nash RJ. 1975. Archaeological investigations in the Transitional Forest Zone: Northern Manitoba, Southern Keewatin, NWT. Manitoba Museum of Man and Nature, Winnipeg, MB.

Natural Resources Canada. 1996. The state of Canada's forests 1995-96. Natural Resources Canada, Canadian Forest Service, Ottawa, ON.

Nelson RK. 1973. Hunters of the northern forest: Designs for survival among the Alaskan Kutchin. University of Chicago Press, Chicago, IL.

Newall CA, Anderson LA, Phillipson JD. 1996. Herbal medicines: A guide for health-care professionals. Pharmaceutical Press, London, UK.

Nicholson BA. 1996. Late prehistoric and protohistoric settlement and subsistence in southern Manitoba. *In* Welsted J, Everitt J, Stadel C (eds.). The geography of Manitoba: Its land and its people. University of Manitoba Press, Winnipeg, MB. pp. 65-78.

Nickerson NH, Rowe NH, Richter EA. 1973. Native plants in the diets of North Alaskan Eskimos. *In* Smith CE Jr (ed.). Man and his foods. Studies in the ethnobotany of nutrition: Contemporary, primitive, and prehistoric non-European diets. University of Alabama Press, University, AL. pp. 3-27.

Nigg HN, Seigler D (eds.). 1992. Phytochemical resources for medicine and agriculture. Plenum Press, New York, NY.

Oliver G. 1997. Personal communication (January 6, 1997) regarding in vitro propagation of orchids native to Manitoba. Spirit Sands Wildflowers, Carberry, MB.

Osgood C. 1933. The ethnography of the Great Bear Lake Indians. *In* Annual Report for 1931. National Museum of Canada, Ottawa, ON. pp. 31-97.

Osgood C. 1936. The distribution of the Northern Athapaskan Indians. Yale University Publications in Anthropology No. 7, Yale University Press, New Haven.

Osgood C. 1937. The ethnography of the Tanaina. Yale University Publications in Anthropology No. 16. Reprinted (1966) by Human Relations Area Files Press, Yale University Press, New Haven, CT.

Osgood C. 1940. Ingalik material culture. Yale University Publications in Anthropology No. 22, Yale University Press, New Haven, CT.

Osgood C. 1971. The Han Indians. Yale University Publications in Anthropology No. 74, Yale University Press, New Haven, CT.

Oswalt WH. 1957. A western Eskimo ethnobotany. Anth. Pap. Univ. Alaska 6 (1):17-36.

Oswalt WH. 1966. This land was theirs: A study of the North American Indian. J Wiley, New York, NY.

Oswalt WH. 1967. Alaskan Eskimos. Chandler Publishing, San Francisco, CA.

Overfield T, Epstein WW, Gaudioso LA. 1980. Eskimo uses of *Artemisia tilesii* (Compositae). Econ. Bot. 34(2):97-100.

Overholts LO. 1967. The Polyporaceae of the United States, Alaska and Canada. University of Michigan Press, Ann Arbor MI.

Pan American Health Organization. 1996. Biodiversity, biotechnology, and sustainable development in health and agriculture: Emerging connections. Scientific Publication No. 560, Pan American Health Organization, Washington, DC.

People of 'Ksan. 1980. Gathering what the Great Nature provided: Food traditions of the Gitksan. Douglas & McIntyre, Vancouver, BC.

Petitot E. 1868. Étude sur la Nation Montagnaise. Les Missions Catholiques vol. 1:135-216, vol. 2:7-64.

Pikios P, Winter BJ. 1981. Personal communication (December 1, 1981) regarding Chipewyan artifacts in their collection and information on Chipewyan plant use. P. Pikios, Archival Assistant, and B.J. Winter, Curator of Collections, Prince of Wales Northern Heritage Centre, Yellowknife, NWT.

Pisha E, Chai H, Lee IS, Chagwedera TE, Farnsworth NR, Cordell GA, Beecher CWW, Fong HHS, Kinghorn AD, Brown DM, Wani MC, Wall ME, Hieken TJ, DasGupta TK, Pezzuto JM. 1995. Discovery of betulinic acid as a selective inhibitor of human melanoma that functions by induction of apoptosis. Nat. Med. 1(10):1046-1051.

Poppe R. 1971. Kutchin bibliography: An annotated bibliography of northern Yukon Kutchin Indians. Canadian Wildlife Service, Edmonton, AB.

Porsild AE. 1953. Edible plants of the Arctic. Arctic 6 (1):15-34.

Porsild AE, Cody WJ. 1980. Vascular plants of continental Northwest Territories, Canada. National Museum of Natural Sciences, National Museums of Canada, Ottawa, ON.

Posey DA, Dutfield G. 1996. Beyond intellectual property: Toward traditional resource rights for indigenous peoples and local communities. International Development Research Centre, Ottawa, ON.

Provencher P, La Rocque G. 1976. Provencher: Last of the coureurs de bois. Burns & MacEachern Ltd., Don Mills, ON.

Racette L. 1982. Personal communication (January 21, 1982) including a list and description of Chipewyan artifacts in their collection. Assistant Registrar, McCord Museum, Montreal, QC.

Reid WV, Laird SA, Meyer CA, Gámez R, Sittenfeld A, Janzen DH, Gollin MA, Juma C. 1993. Biodiversity prospecting: Using genetic resources for sustainable development. World Resources Institute, USA, Instituto Nacional de Biodiversidad, Costa Rica, Rainforest Alliance, USA, and African Centre for Technology Studies, Kenya.

Robbers JE, Tyler VE. 1999. Tyler's herbs of choice: The therapeutic use of phytomedicinals, 2nd ed. Haworth Herbal Press, New York, NY.

Rogers ES. 1967. Subsistence areas of the Cree-Ojibwa of the eastern subarctic: A preliminary study. National Museum of Canada Bulletin 204, Contributions to Ethnology 5:59-90.

Rogers ES, Rogers JH. 1959. The yearly cycle of the Mistassini Indians. Arctic 12(3):131-138.

Rogers R. 1997. Aromatics and their use as medicine. *In* Proceedings of the Prairie Medicinal and Aromatic Plants Conference '97, Brandon, MB. pp. 53-54.

Ross BR. 1862. An account of the botanical and mineral products useful to the Chipewyan tribes of Indians inhabiting the Mackenzie River District. Can. Nat. Geol. 7:133-137.

Royal Botanic Gardens. 1999. Royal Botanical Gardens, Kew: Online Databases. World Wide Web address: http://www.rbgkew.org.uk/web.dbs/

Savishinsky JS. 1974. The trail of the hare: Life and stress in an Arctic community. Gordon and Breach Science Publishers, New York, NY.

Savoie D (ed.). 1970. The Amerindians of the Canadian Northwest in the 19th Century, as seen by Emile Petitot, Vol. 2: The Loucheux Indians. Northern Science Research Group. Department of Indian Affairs and Northern Development, Ottawa, ON.

Schulz V, Hänsel R, Tyler VE. 1998. Rational phytotherapy. A physicians' guide to herbal medicine. Springer-Verlag, Berlin, Germany.

Science Council of Canada. 1992. Sustainable agriculture: The research challenge. Report No. 43, Science Council of Canada, Ottawa, ON.

Scoggan HJ. 1957. Flora of Manitoba. Bulletin No. 140, Biological Series No. 47, National Museum of Canada, Ottawa, ON.

Scoggan HJ. 1978-1979. The flora of Canada. National Museum of Natural Sciences, National Museums of Canada, Ottawa, ON.

Scott GAJ. 1995. Canada's vegetation: A world perspective. McGill-Queen's University Press, Montreal, QC.

Sharp HS. 1973. The kinship system of the Black Lake Chipewyan. PhD dissertation, Department of Anthropology, Duke University, Durham, NC.

Shay CT. 1980. Food plants of Manitoba. In Petipas L (ed.). Directions in Manitoba prehistory. Association of Manitoba Archaeologists, Winnipeg, MB. pp. 233-290.

Siegfried EV. 1994. Ethnobotany of the Northern Cree of Wabasca/Desmarais. MA thesis, Department of Archaeology, University of Calgary, Calgary, AB.

Simpson BB, Ogorzaly MC. 1995. Economic botany: Plants in our world, 2nd ed. McGraw-Hill, New York, NY.

Simpson G. 1821. Report on Athabasca District to the Governor, Deputy Governor, and Committee of the Honourable Hudson's Bay Company. In Rich EE (ed.). (1938) Journal of occurrences in the Athabasca Department by George Simpson, 1820 and 1821, and report. Champlain Society for the Hudson's Bay Record Society, London, UK.

Smith DM. 1973. Inkonze: Magico-religious beliefs of contact: Traditional Chipewyan trading at Fort Resolution, NWT, Canada. Ethnology Division Paper No. 6, National Museum of Man, Mercury Series, Ottawa, ON.

Smith DM. 1976. Cultural and ecological change: the Chipewyan of Fort Resolution. Arctic Anth. 13(1):35-42.

Smith GW. 1973. Arctic pharmacognosia. Arctic 26(4):324-333.

Smith HI. 1920-1923a. The material culture of the Carrier Indians of British Columbia, Part I, 1-11, Introduction to food starvation. Microfiche VI-B-32M (B88 F1). Canadian Museum of Civilization, Hull, QC.

Smith HI. 1920-1923b. The material culture of the Carrier Indians of British Columbia, Part II, 12-58, Securing food to dwellings. Microfiche VI-B-32M (B88 F2). Canadian Museum of Civilization, Hull, QC.

Smith HI. 1920-1923c. The material culture of the Carrier Indians of British Columbia, Part III, 59-87, Clothing, ornaments, and toilet to tools. Microfiche VI-B-32M (B88 F3). Canadian Museum of Civilization, Hull, QC.

Smith HI. 1920-1923d. The material culture of the Carrier Indians of British Columbia, Part IV, 88-183, Axes to Christianity. Microfiche VI-B-32M (B88 F4). Canadian Museum of Civilization, Hull, QC.

Smith HI. 1920-1923e. The material culture of the Carrier Indians of British Columbia, Part V, 184, Art to end. Microfiche VI-B-32M (B88 F5). Canadian Museum of Civilization, Hull, QC.

Smith HI. 1920-1923f. The uses of plants by the Carrier Indians of British Columbia, Vol I. Microfiche VI-B-21M (B86 F3). Canadian Museum of Civilization, Hull, QC.

Smith HI. 1920-1923g. The uses of plants by the Carrier Indians of British Columbia, Vol II. Microfiche VI-B-21M (B86 F4). Canadian Museum of Civilization, Hull, QC.

Smith HI. 1928. Materia medica of the Bella Coola and neighboring tribes of British Columbia. Nat. Mus. Can. Bull. 56:47-68.

Speck FG. 1935. Naskapi: The savage hunters of the Labrador peninsula. Reprinted 1977. University of Oklahoma Press, Norma, OK.

Strath R. 1903. Materia medica, pharmacy, and therapeutics of the Cree Indians of the Hudson Bay Territory. St. Paul Med. J. 1903:735-746.

Sun IC, Wang HK, Kashiwada Y, Shen JK, Cosentino LM, Chen CH, Yang LM, Lee KH. 1998. Anti-AIDS agents. 34. Synthesis and structure-activity relationships of betulin derivatives as anti-HIV agents. J. Med. Chem. 41(23):4648-4657.

Szczawinski AF, Turner NJ. 1978. Edible garden weeds of Canada. Edible Wild Plants of Canada No. 1. National Museum of Natural Sciences, National Museums of Canada, Ottawa, ON.

Szczawinski AF, Turner NJ. 1980. Wild green vegetables of Canada. Edible Wild Plants of Canada No. 4. National Museum of Natural Sciences, National Museums of Canada, Ottawa, ON.

Tanner HH. 1976. The Ojibwas: A critical bibliography. The Newberry Library Center for the History of the American Indian Bibliographic Series, F. Jennings (general ed.). Indiana University Press, Bloomington, IN.

Turner NJ. 1978. Food plants of British Columbia Indians. Part II: Interior peoples. Handbook No. 36, British Columbia Provincial Museum, Victoria, BC.

Turner NJ. 1979. Plants in British Columbia Indian technology. Handbook No. 38. British Columbia Provincial Museum, Victoria, BC.

Turner NJ. 1981. A gift for the taking: The untapped potential of some food plants of North American Native peoples. Can. J. Bot. 59:2331-2357.

Turner NJ, Johnson-Gottesfeld LM, Kuhnlein HV, Ceska A. 1992. Edible wood fern rootstocks of western North America: Solving an ethnobotanical puzzle. J. Ethnobiol. 12(1):1-34.

Turner NJ, Szczawinski AF. 1978. Wild coffee and tea substitutes of Canada. Edible Wild Plants of Canada No. 2. National Museum of Natural Sciences, National Museums of Canada, Ottawa, ON.

Turner NJ, Szczawinski AF. 1979. Edible wild fruits and nuts of Canada. Edible Wild Plants of Canada No. 3. National Museum of Natural Sciences, National Museums of Canada, Ottawa, ON.

Turner NJ, Szczawinski AF. 1991. Common poisonous plants and mushrooms of North America. Timber Press, Portland, OR.

Underhill JE. 1974. Wild berries of the Pacific Northwest. Superior Publishing Company, Seattle, WA.

United States Agricultural Research Service. 1999. Dr. Duke's phytochemical and ethnobotanical databases. World Wide Web address: http://www.ars-grin.gov/duke/index.html.

United States Department of Agriculture. 1999. PLANTS National Database. USDA Natural Resources Conservation Service. World Wide Web address: http://plants.usda.gov/plantproj/plants/cgi_bin/topics.cgi?earl=checklist.html

VanStone JW. 1974. Athapaskan adaptations: Hunters and fishermen of the subarctic forests. AHM Publishing Corporation, Arlington Heights, IL.

Veninga L, Zaricor BR. 1976. Goldenseal/Etc.: A pharmacognosy of wild herbs. Ruka Publications, Santa Cruz, CA.

Viereck EG. 1987. Alaska's wilderness medicines: Healthful plants of the far north. Alaska Northwest Books, Anchorage, AK.

Vitt DH, Marsh JE, Bovey RB. 1988. Mosses, lichens and ferns of northwest North America. Lone Pine, Edmonton, AB.

Vogel VJ. 1970. American Indian medicine. Ballantine Books, New York, NY.

Wahab J. 1997. Saskatchewan herb and spice industry ... What's new? In Proceedings of the Prairie Medicinal and Aromatic Plants Conference '97, Brandon, MB. pp. 11-16.

Wallis WD. 1959. Historical background of the Micmac Indians of Canada. Nat. Mus. Can. Bull. 173:42-63.

Waugh FW. 1919. Canadian Aboriginal canoes. Can. Field-Nat. 33(2):23-33.

Wein EE, Sabry JH, Evers FT. 1991. Food consumption patterns and use of country foods by native Canadians near Wood Buffalo National Park, Canada. Arctic 44(3):196-205.

Weiner MA. 1972. Earth medicine–Earth foods: Plant remedies, drugs, and natural foods of the North American Indians. Collier Books, New York, NY.

Wijesekera ROB (ed.). 1991. The medicinal plant industry. CRC Press, Boca Raton, FL.

Willard T. 1992. Edible and medicinal plants of the Rocky Mountains and neighboring territories. Wild Rose College of Natural Healing, Calgary, AB.

Williamson EM, Okpako DT, Evans FJ. 1996. Selection, preparation and pharmacological evaluation of plant material. Pharmacological Methods in Phytotherapy Research, Vol. I. J Wiley, Chichester, UK.

Wilson MR. 1978. Notes on ethnobotany in Inuktitut. W. Can. J. Anth. 8(4):180-196.

Winterhalder B, Smith EA (eds.). 1981. Hunter-gatherer foraging strategies: Ethnographic and archaeological analyses. Prehistoric Archeology and Ecology Series. University of Chicago Press, Chicago, IL.

Wood Sheldon J, Balick MJ, Laird SA. 1997. Medicinal plants: Can utilization and conservation coexist? Adv. Econ. Bot.:1-104.

World Health Organization. 1991. Guidelines for the assessment of herbal medicines. Publication WHO/TRM/91.4, Programme on Traditional Medicines, World Health Organization, Geneva, Switzerland.

World Health Organization, World Conservation Union, and World Wide Fund for Nature. 1993. Guidelines on the conservation of medicinal plants. The International Union for Conservation of Nature and Natural Resources, Gland, Switzerland.

Young D, Ingram G, Swartz L. 1989. Cry of the eagle: Encounters with a Cree healer. University of Toronto Press, Toronto, ON.

Young SB, Hall ES Jr. 1969. Contributions to the ethnobotany of the St. Lawrence Island Eskimo. Anth. Pap. Univ. Alaska 14(2):43-53.

Zoladeski CA, Wickware GM, Delorme RJ, Sims RA, Corns IGW. 1995. Forest ecosystem classification for Manitoba: Field guide. Special Report 2, Canada-Manitoba Partnership Agreement in Forestry, Natural Resources Canada, Canadian Forest Service, and Manitoba Natural Resources, Forestry. University of British Columbia Press, Vancouver, BC.

Index

𝔊ᕲ

colic, 105, 203
conception, 145-6
congestion, 267, 270
constipation, 136, 154, 170, 215, 227, 253, 272
coughing up blood, 170, 203, 225, 226, 250, 270
coughs, 50, 84, 105, 109, 135, 159, 166, 171, 172, 175, 195, 200, 202, 210, 228, 238, 244, 251, 258, 269, 277
cramps, 272
cuts, 70, 91, 92, 116, 170, 284
depression, 90
diabetes, 115, 195, 203, 247, 248, 251, 270
diaper rash, 70, 181
diarrhea, 83, 95, 166, 180, 197, 202, 229, 230, 232, 237, 238, 242, 251, 253, 270, 278
digestive aid, 202
diuretic, 83, 115, 122, 125, 154, 156-7, 160, 226
dizziness, 166
"Doctrine of Signatures," 41, 112
douche, 237
dysentery, 242
ear infection, 95
ear irrigation, 90
earache, 51, 261, 268, 270
eczema, 84
emetic, 120, 125, 142, 166, 237
endurance, while running, 95
expectorant, 270
eye problems, 117, 133, 189
eyedrops, 47, 64, 95, 238, 242
eyewash, 65, 90, 122, 153, 156, 166, 180, 235, 260
facial paralysis, 125, 270
fainting, 215
fatigue, 202, 254, 270
fever, 84, 111, 122, 124, 125, 156, 166, 170, 171, 177, 186, 202, 204, 225, 229, 234, 235, 237, 242, 251, 258, 265, 271, 277
food poisoning, 251
frostbite, 90, 99
gonorrhea, 146
hair growth, 154, 295
hair lice, 224
hair loss, 180
headache, 49, 51, 106, 109, 111, 116, 122, 125, 130, 132, 180, 202, 204, 209, 244, 258, 262, 263, 268, 269, 270, 271
heart ailments, 52, 80, 90, 95, 111, 113, 125, 131, 146, 151, 152, 154, 170, 180, 210, 215, 217, 221, 225, 230, 237, 239, 244, 248, 250-1, 267-8, 269, 271, 272

heartburn, 272, 273, 288
hemorrhoids, 90
hiccups, 201
high blood pressure, 20, 52, 95, 177, 221, 237, 247, 270
hyperactivity soother, 127, 201
indigestion, 90
infection, 90, 92, 95, 114, 135, 180, 203, 209, 212, 215, 217, 232, 248, 271
influenza, 152, 237
"insanity," 79, 125
insect repellent, 121
insect stings, 116, 117, 145, 239, 250
insomnia, 133, 160
intestinal ailments, 275
jaundice, 139
kidney ailments, 74, 79, 83, 84, 122, 125, 126, 133, 136, 157, 175, 180, 226, 244
lactation, 112, 114, 146, 153
laxative, 167, 170, 237
leg sores, 274
liniment (external use), 106
liver ailments, 120, 139
love potion, 51, 157, 267
lung ailments, 84, 146, 152, 228
menstrual problems, 55, 84, 125, 142, 146, 175, 183, 194, 195, 199, 202, 204, 238, 242, 258, 270, 275
migraine headaches, 117, 129, 180
miscarriage, 170, 175
miscarriage prevention, 183, 197
mosquito deterrent, 48, 95
mouth wash, 95
muscle pain, 269, 271
muscle spasm, 228, 270
nerve relaxant, 127, 133, 139, 180, 201, 262
nipples, cracked, 181
nosebleed, 65, 116, 203, 227, 248
ointment, 146, 230, 267
painkiller, 87, 203, 209, 217
paralysis, 254
pinched nerves, 228
pink-eye (conjunctivitis), 123
pneumonia, 86, 114, 180, 237, 268, 270
poultice, 83, 87, 90, 99, 109, 114, 117, 121, 128, 134, 146, 209, 215, 217, 254, 258, 260, 270, 271, 273, 284, 297
pregnancy diagnostic, 212
pregnancy prevention, 183
psoriasis, 84
purgative, 227
rashes, 92, 95, 181
rheumatism, 122, 245, 269, 271, 296
scabies, 215
scalding, 142

Set in Palatino and Franklin Gothic by Artegraphica Design Co.

Printed and bound in Canada by DeJong Printing Ltd.

Copy editor: Fran Aitkens

Proofreader: Peggy Robinson

Cartographer: Eric Leinberger

Indexer: Annette Lorek